AF574389

Intimate Seasons

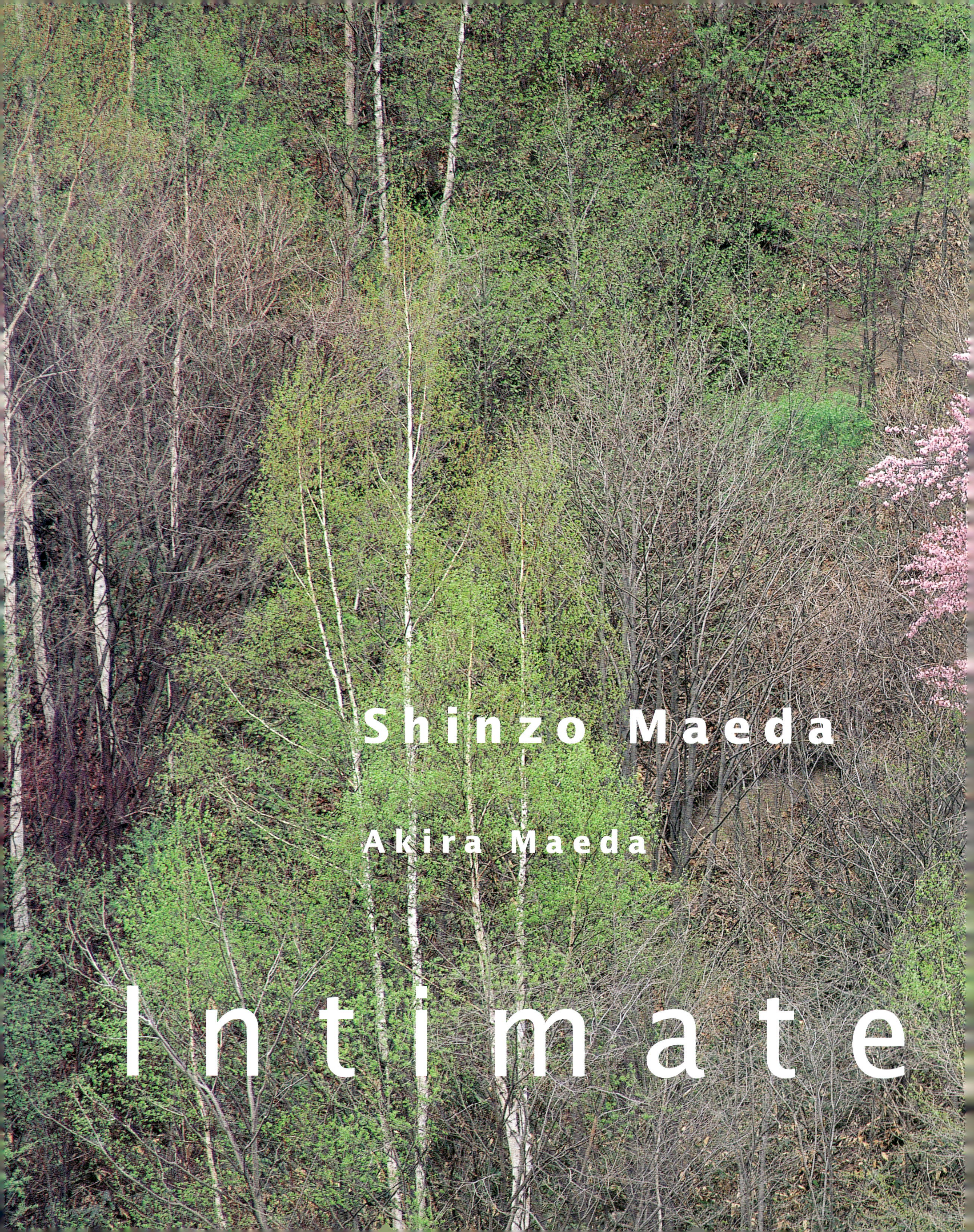

Shinzo Maeda

Akira Maeda

Intimate

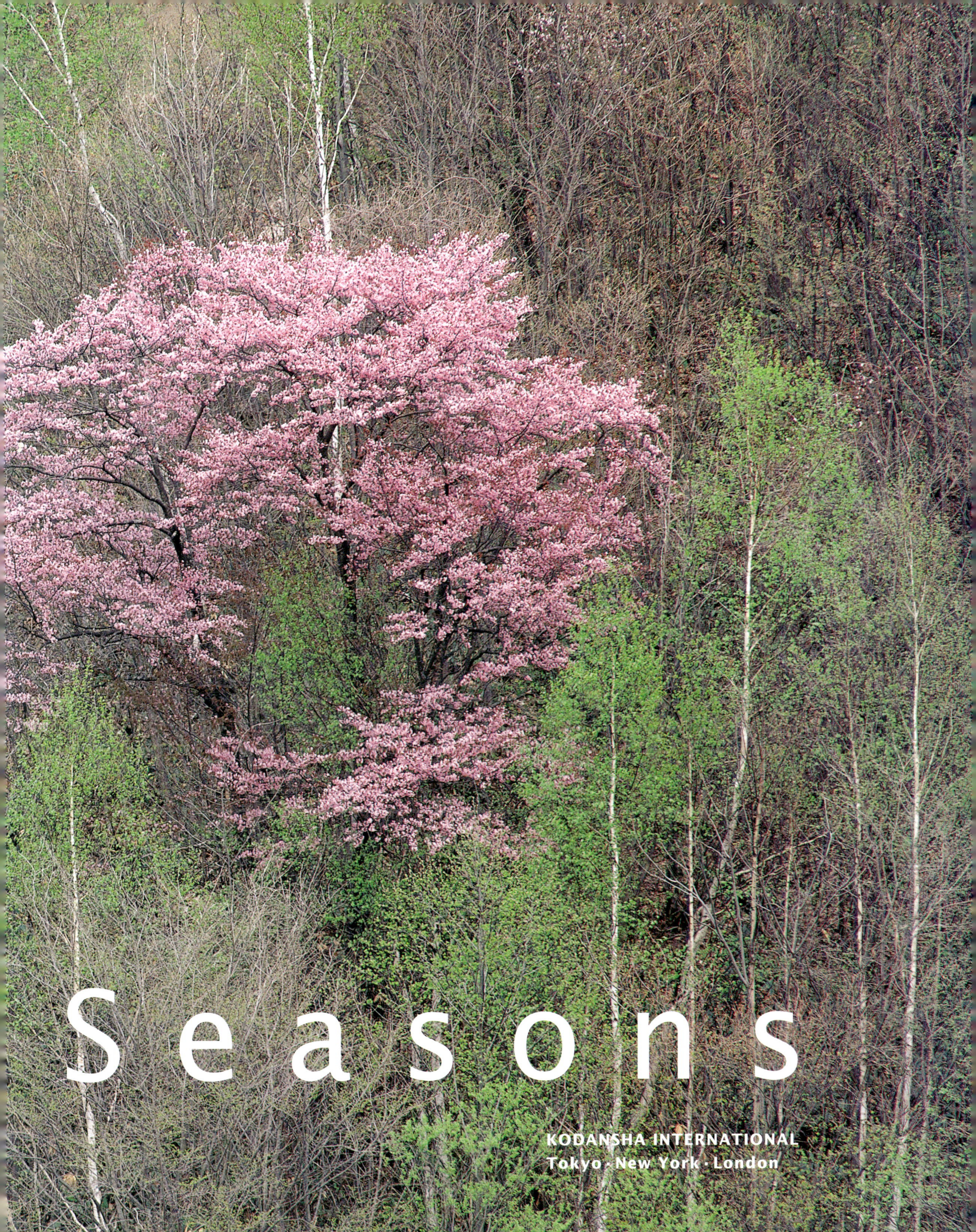

Seasons

KODANSHA INTERNATIONAL
Tokyo · New York · London

Photographs by Shinzo and Akira Maeda
Poems translated by Timothy Harris (from *Classical Cats*, a CD-ROM published by IBM Corporation, 1995)
Designed by Toshio Shiratani

Distributed in the United States by Kodansha America, Inc., and in the United Kingdom and continental Europe by Kodansha Europe Ltd.

Published by Kodansha International Ltd., 17-14, Otowa 1-chome, Bunkyo-ku, Tokyo 112-8652, and Kodansha America, Inc.

First edition, 2001
ISBN 4-7700-2687-0
10 09 08 07 06 05 04   10 9 8 7 6 5 4 3

www.thejapanpage.com

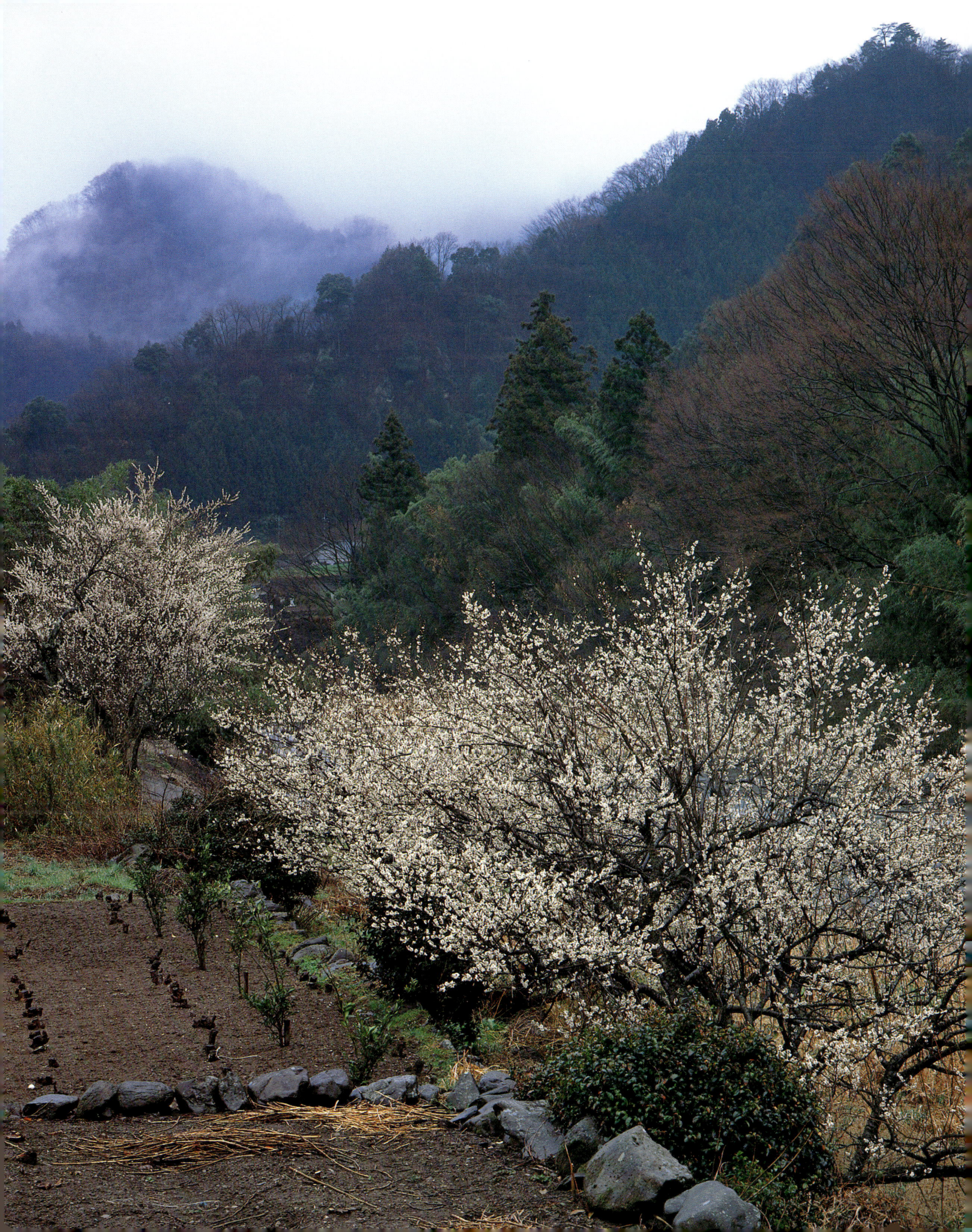

INTRODUCTION

About the hills of Biei on the northernmost island of Japan, which we visited and photographed countless times together, my late father said: "When I first stood there, I was so moved I started trembling from head to foot. And, ever since, every time I see them, the hills have shown me a different aspect of themselves. Instead of growing tired of them, I seem to appreciate them more and more. My feelings for the place just keep on growing."

The reason my father and I carried on taking photographs of those hills and other similar sites can only be explained by the fact that we were fascinated by the way the scenery of this country shifts with the passing of each month.

The Japanese can be said to have a more acute awareness of seasonal change than perhaps most people. This finds its fullest expression in a wealth of seasonal expressions, from references we make in everyday conversation and letters, to the more specific allusions in haiku poetry. With all manner of associations accumulating over the centuries, a particular aesthetic has developed—one that I would call an *intimate* sense of seasonal change.

The Japanese archipelago arches from northeast to southwest across the temperate regions of the east coast of the Eurasian continental landmass. Although there are great variations due to differences in elevation and complex topography, it generally enjoys temperate conditions throughout the year.

There are all kinds of ways of dividing the seasons here. The conventional four in their allotted order can be subdivided into early and late, doubling the number. Some would add the month-long summer rains, and perhaps the rainy periods in spring and autumn too. The dry winter of the Pacific coast and the spell of heavy snowfall on the Japan Sea side might also be included as seasonal variations.

Just as varied are the poignant words associated with certain phases of the year. *Hakuro*, for example, written with the characters for "white dew," means the beginning of September, when the dew begins to stay on the ground long enough to make a white veil.

It is with this awareness of subtle changes—sometimes consciously appreciated, sometimes just felt in the heart—that my father (and I hope myself) worked for more than thirty years: in intimacy with his surroundings.

Akira Maeda

Summer, 2001

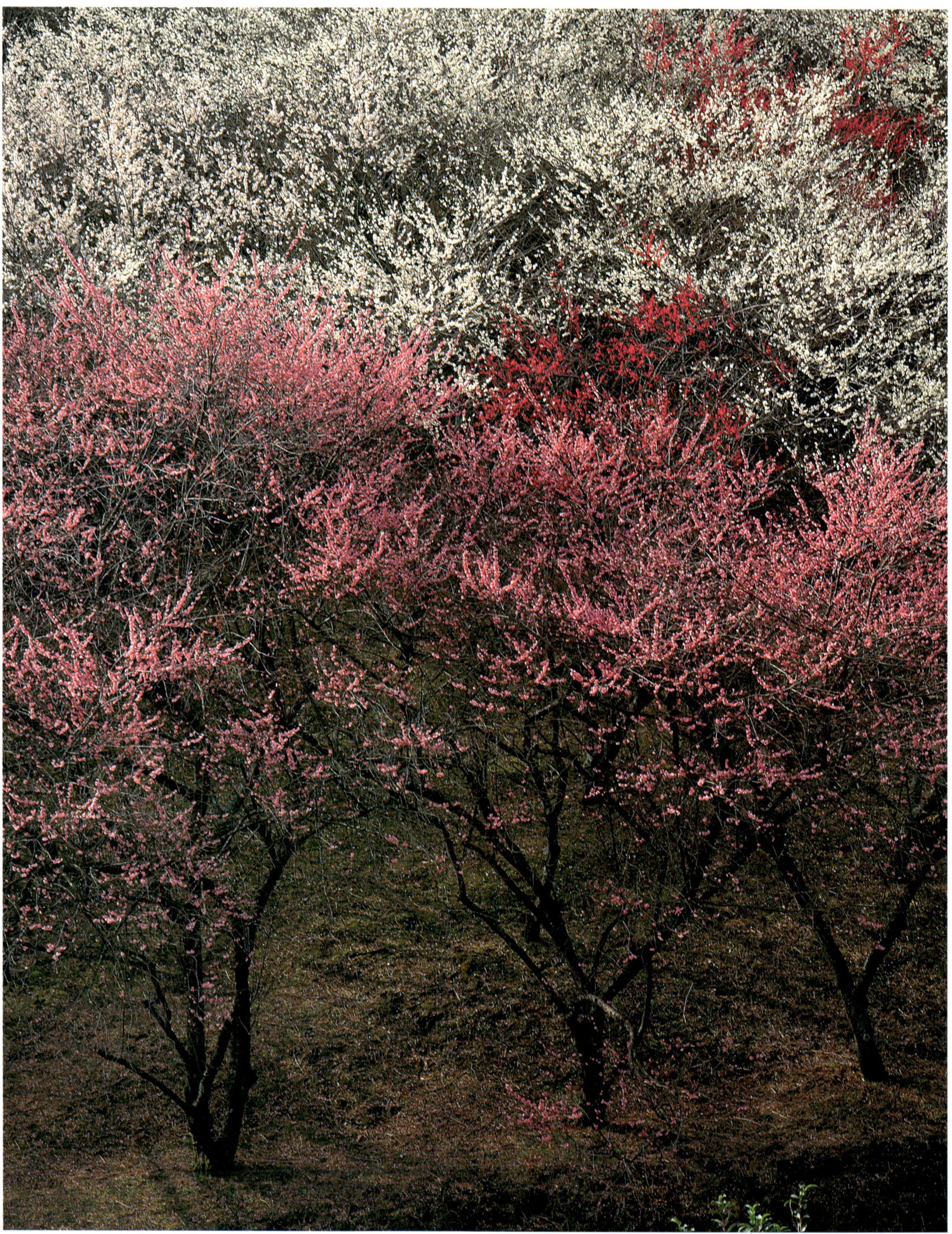

東風吹かば
にほひおこせよ
梅の花
あるじなしとて
春を忘るな

菅原道真

SPRING 春

When warm winds blow
send me your subtle perfume,
plum-tree flowers.
Your lord will be in exile,
but do not forget the spring.

SUGAWARA NO MICHIZANE

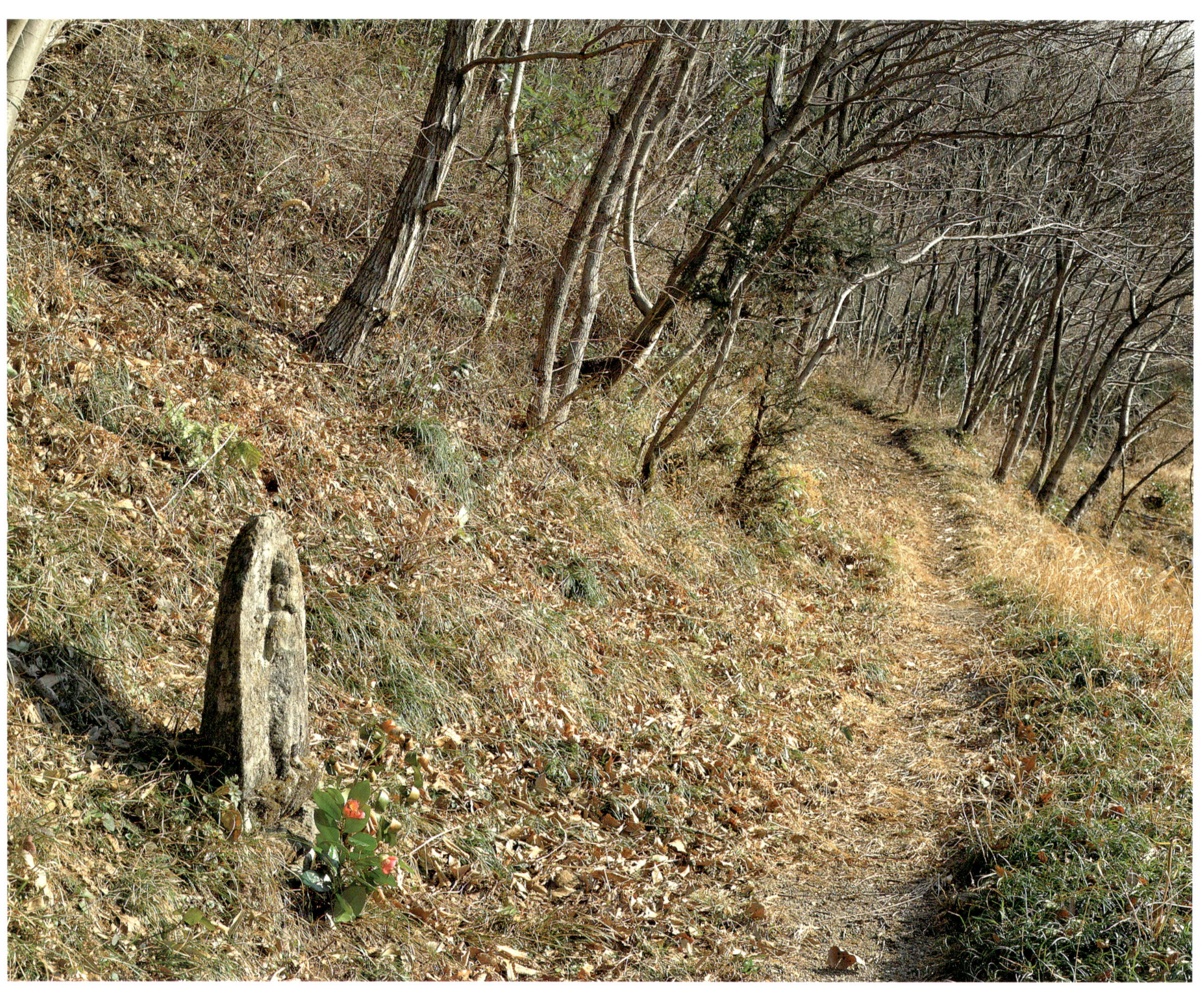

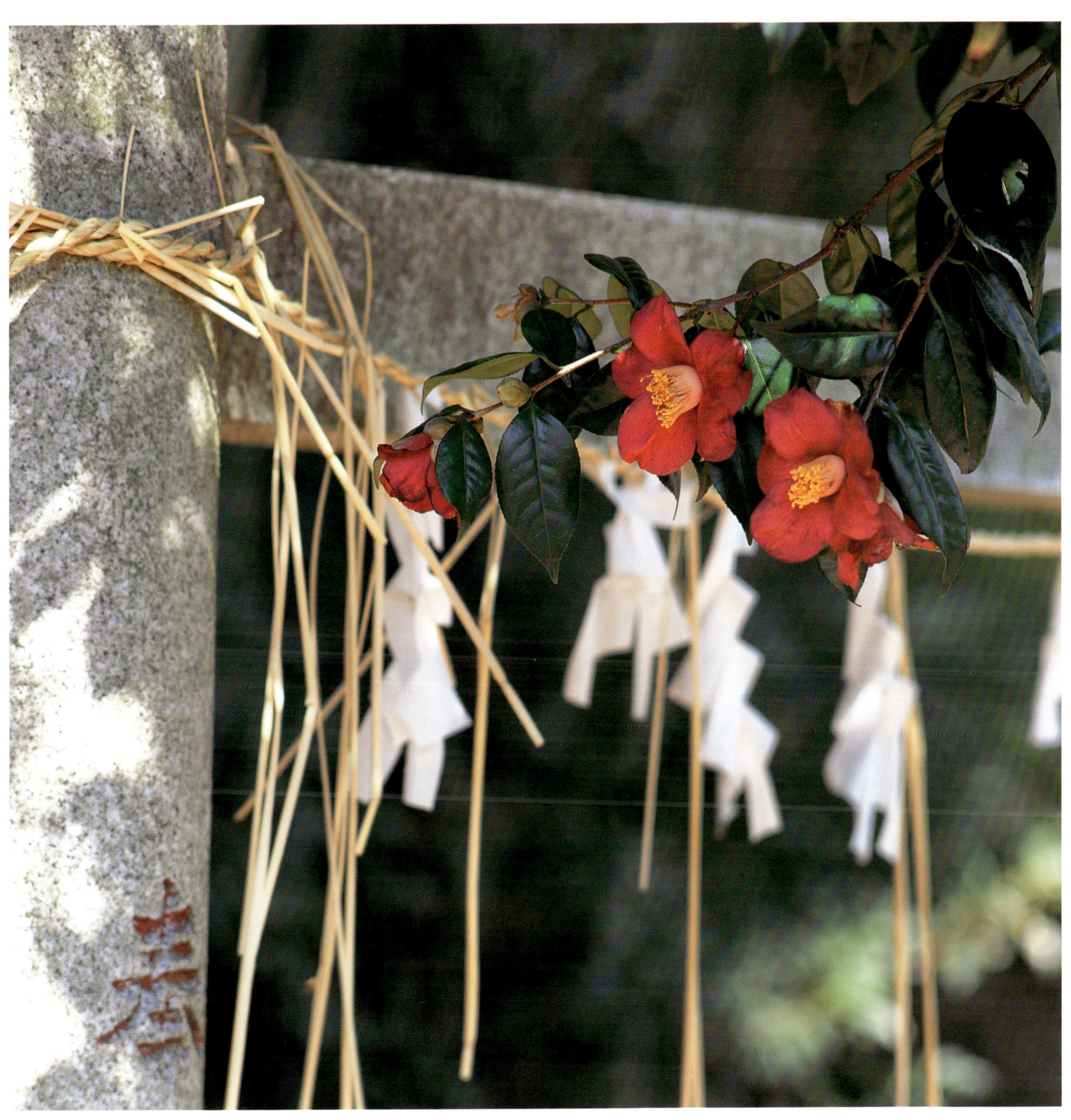

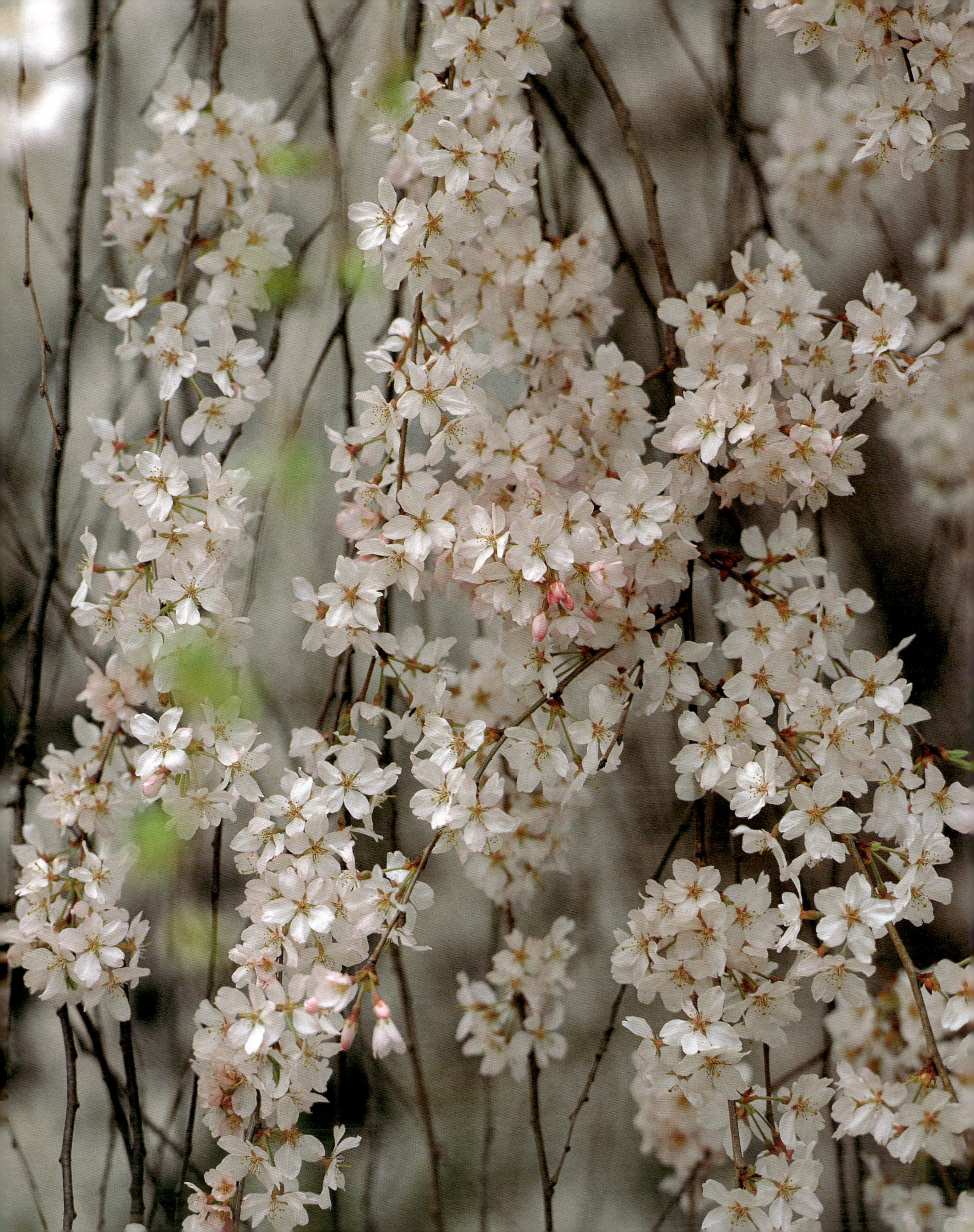

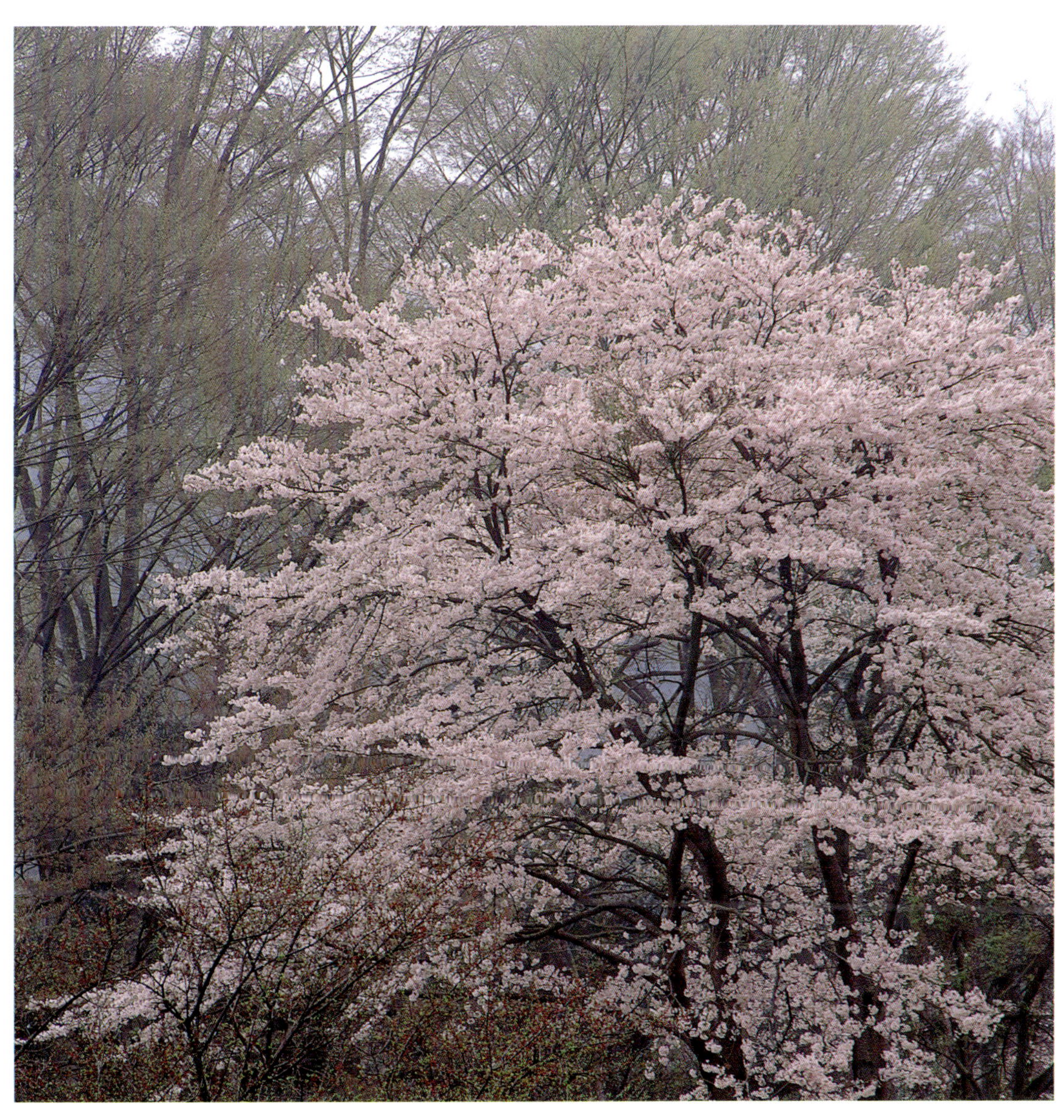

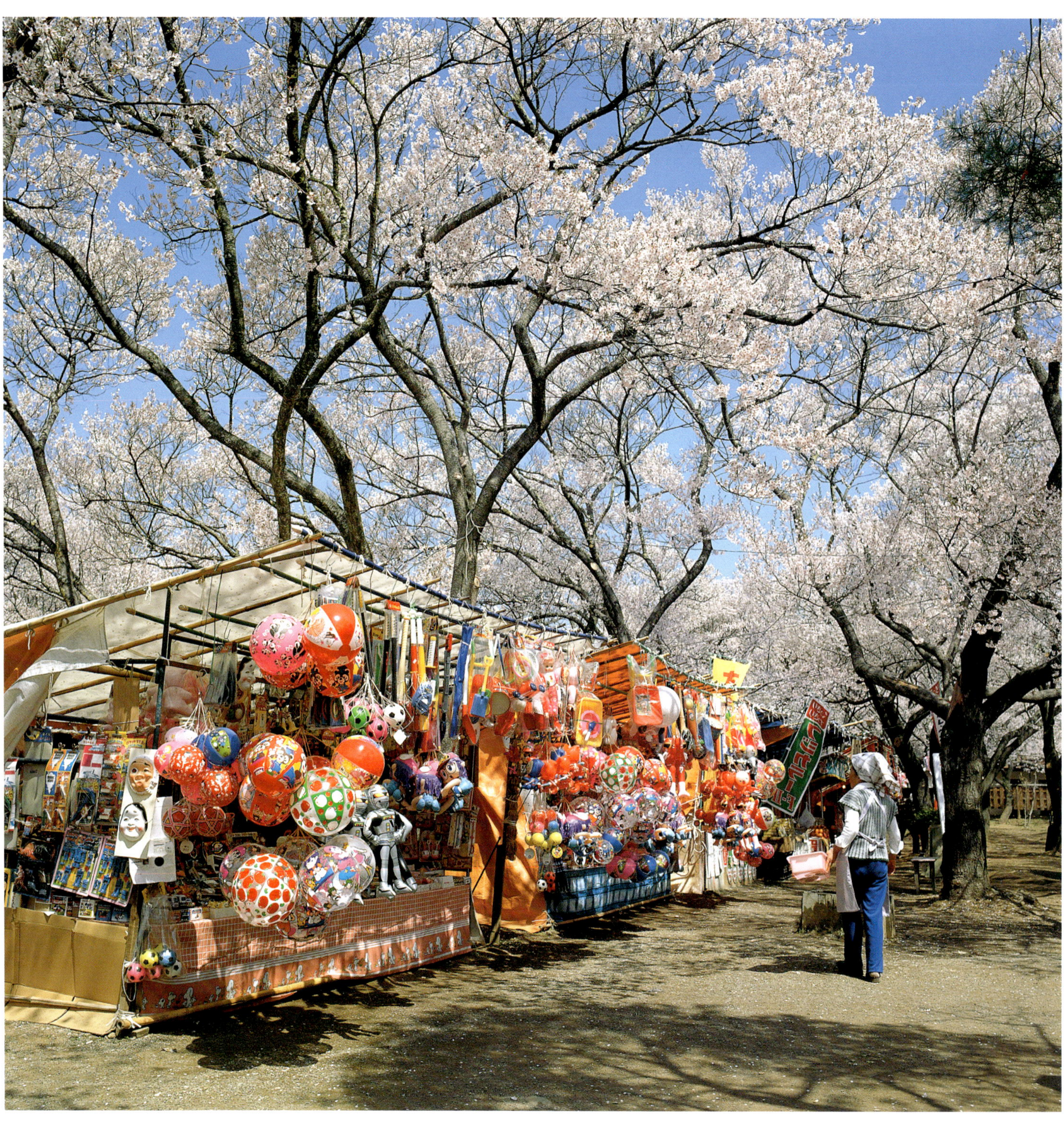

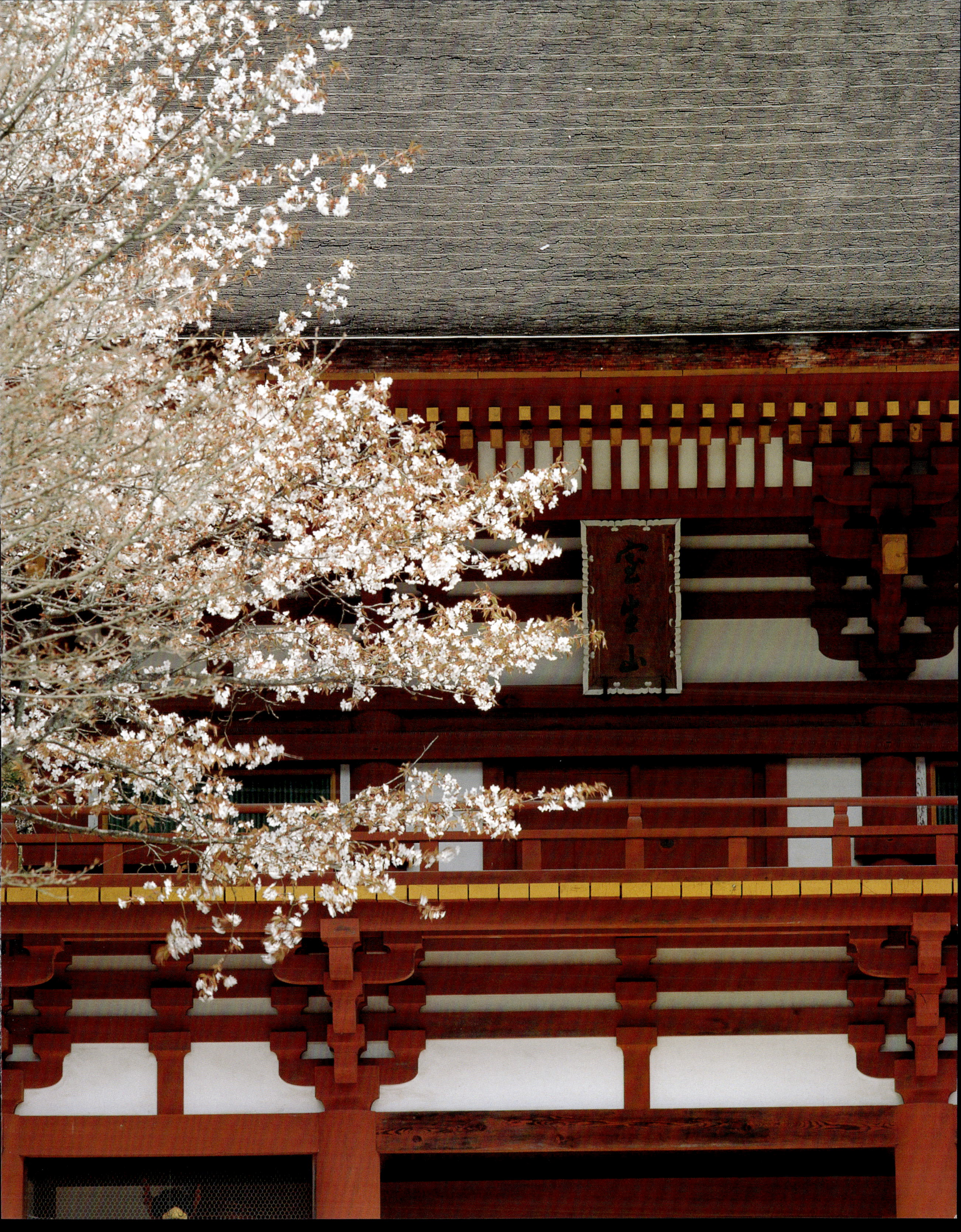
室生山

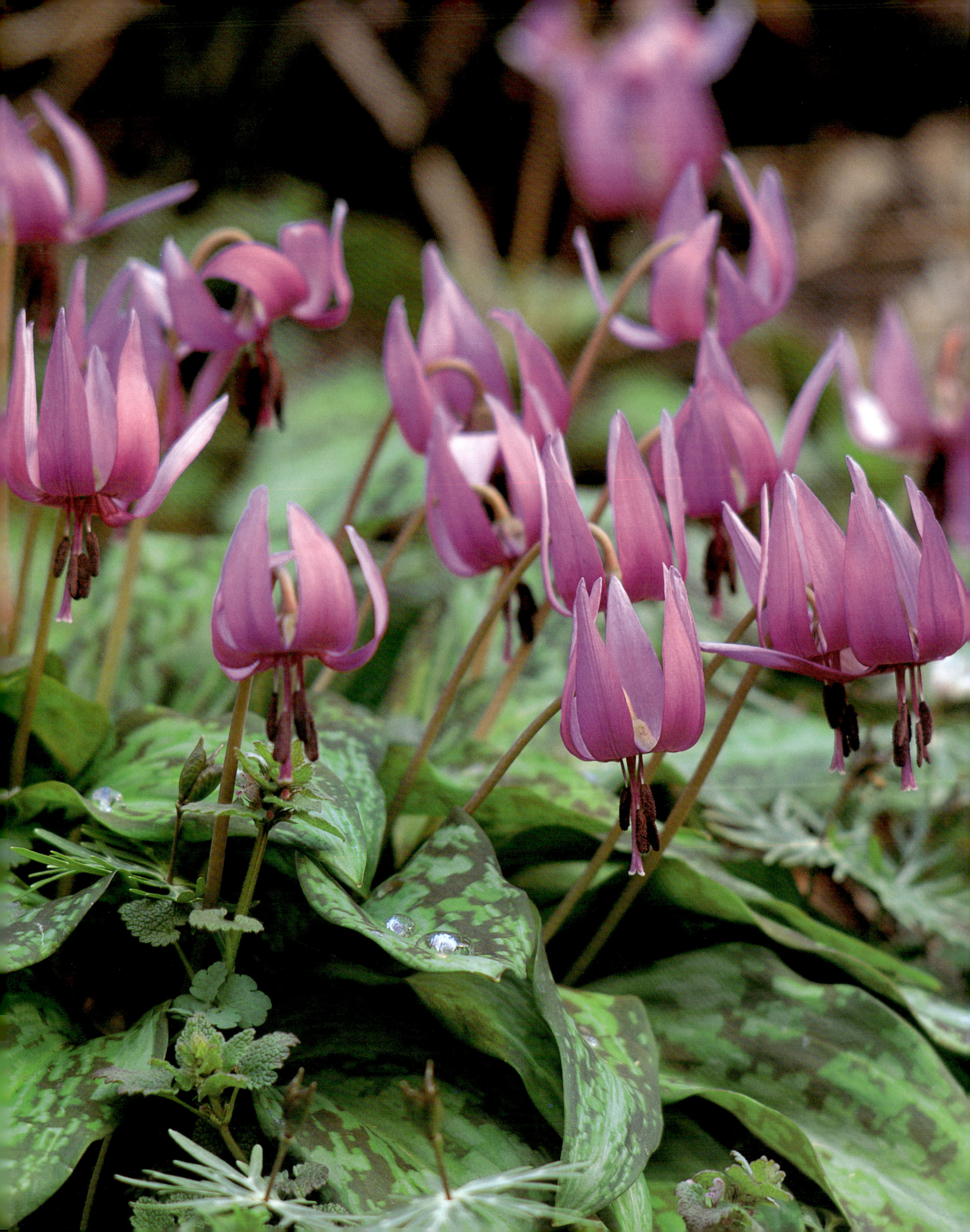

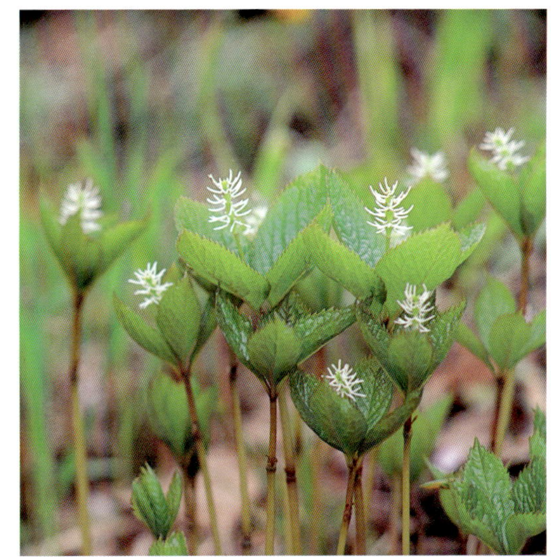

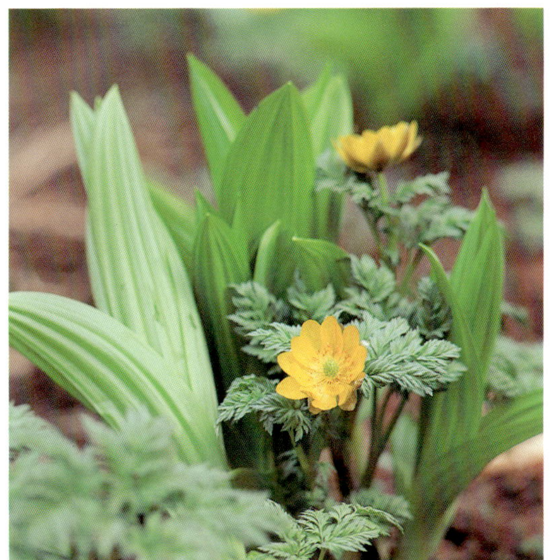

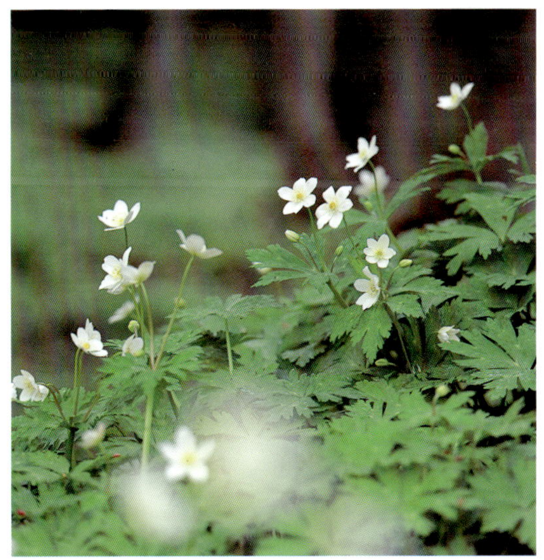

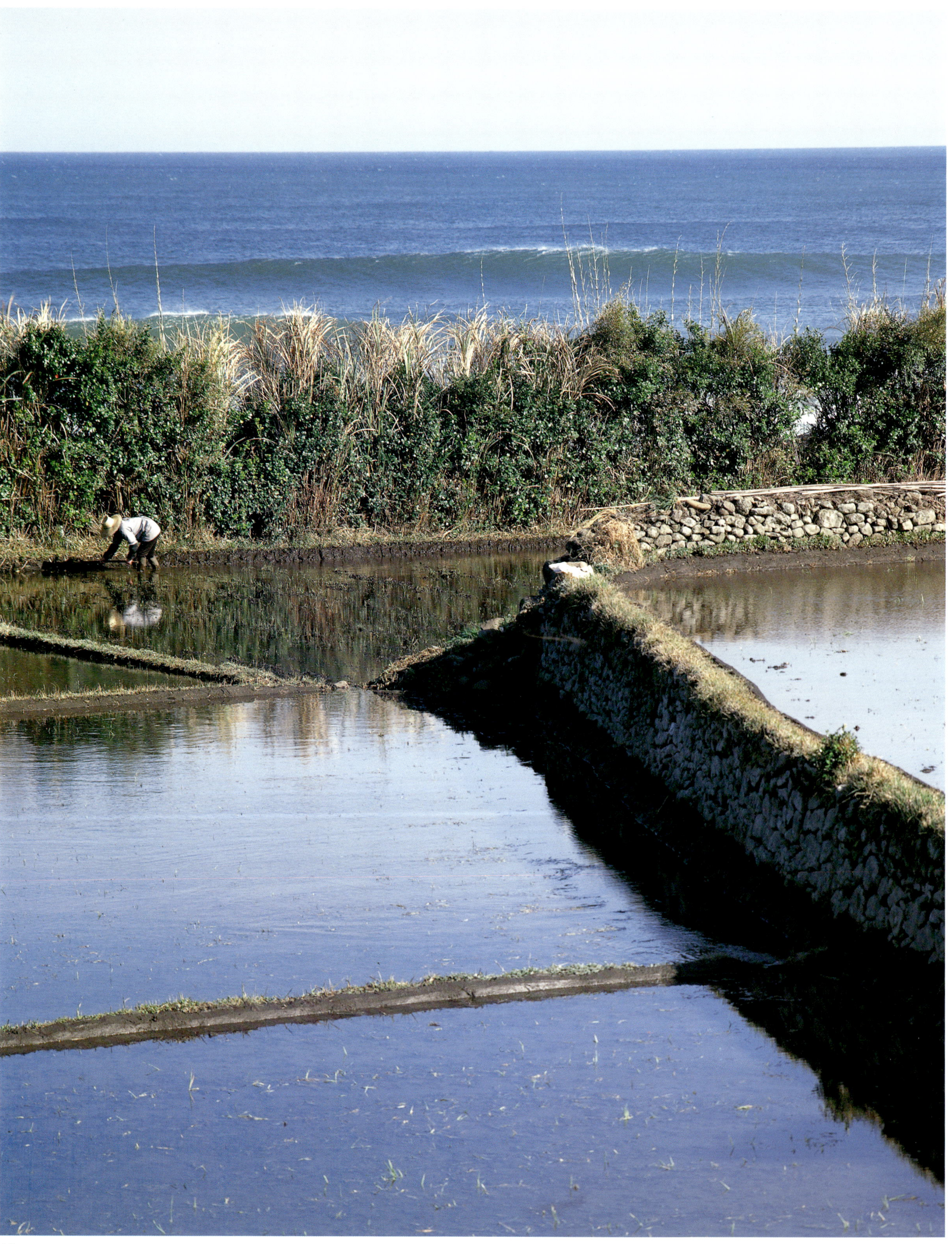

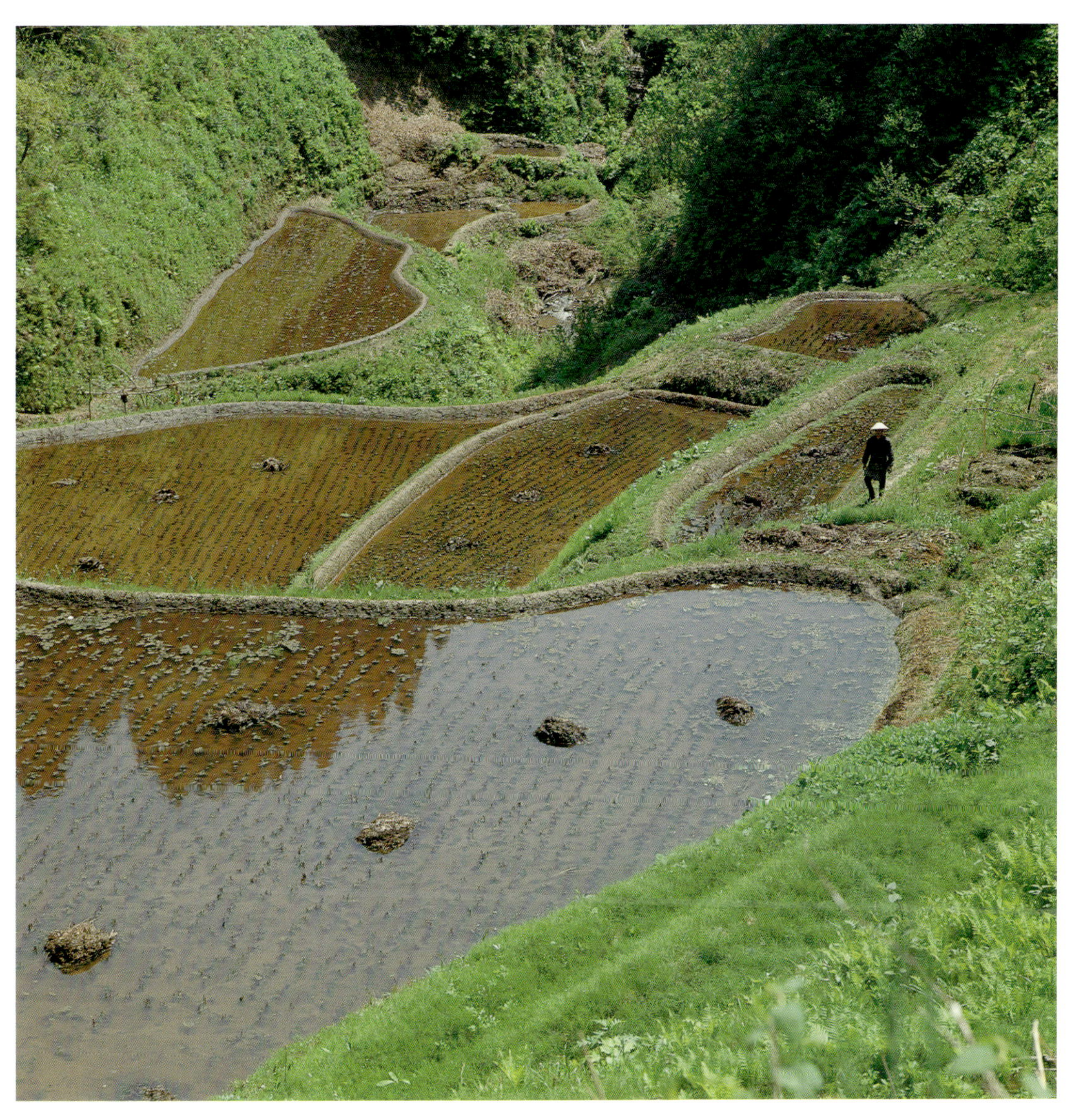

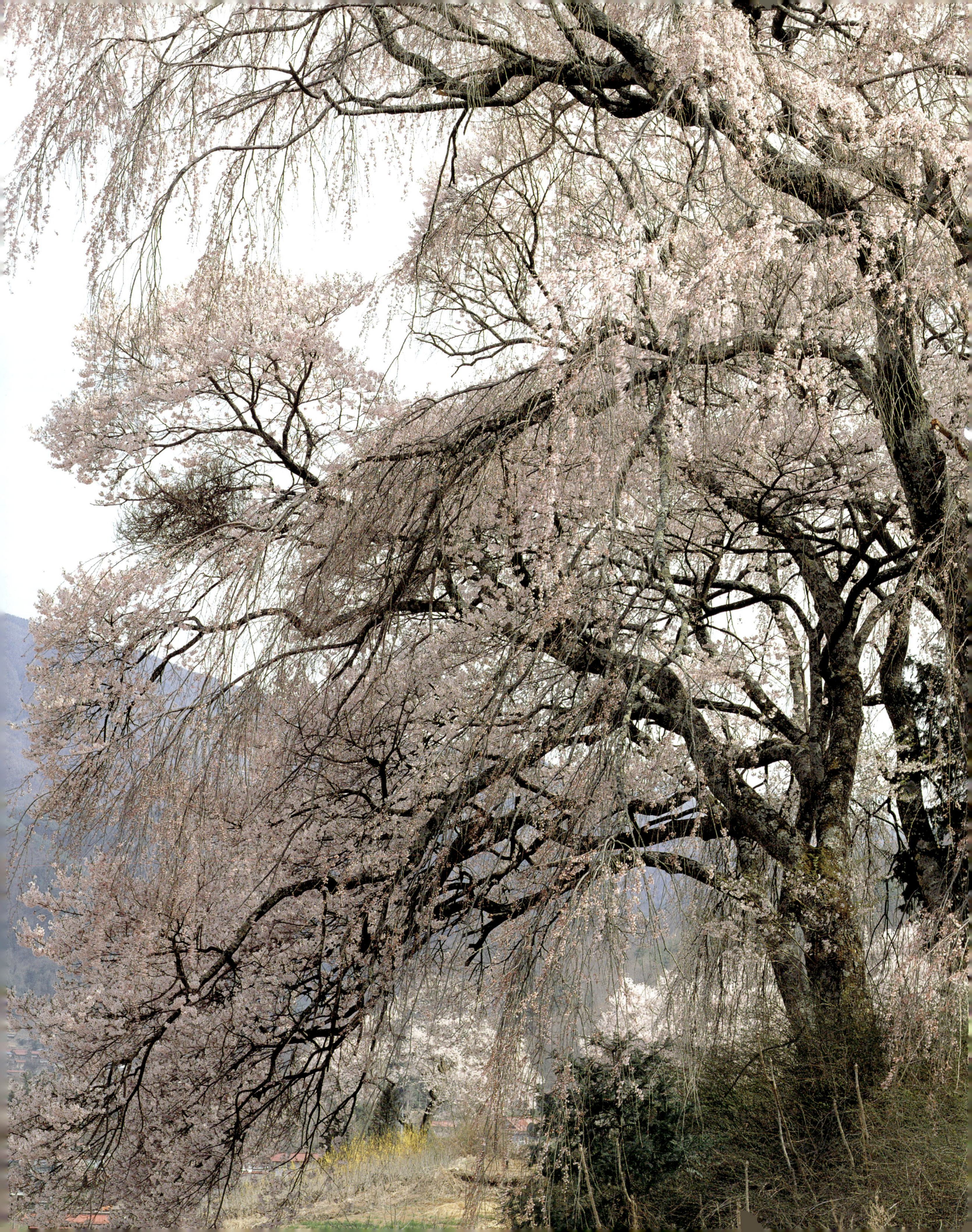

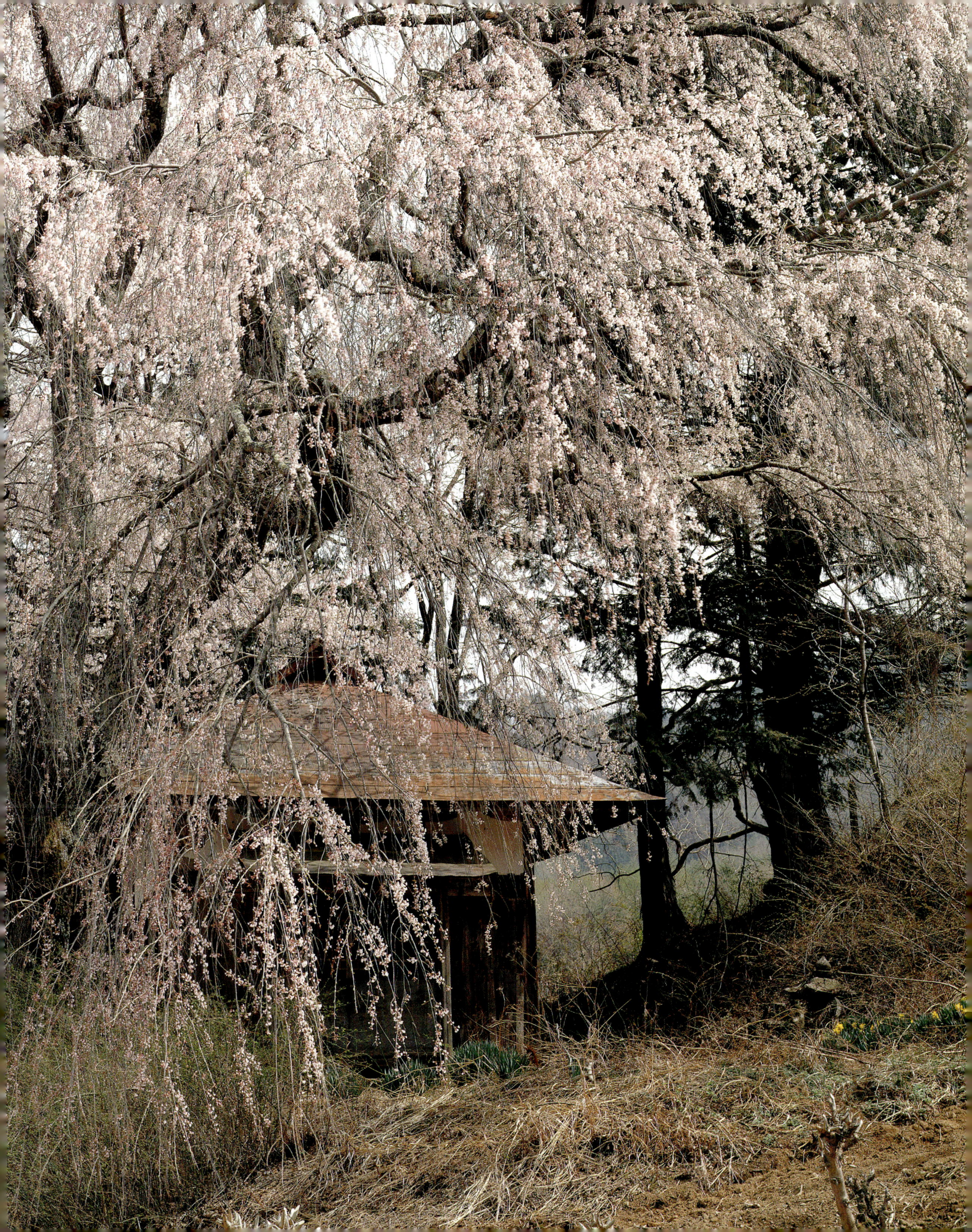

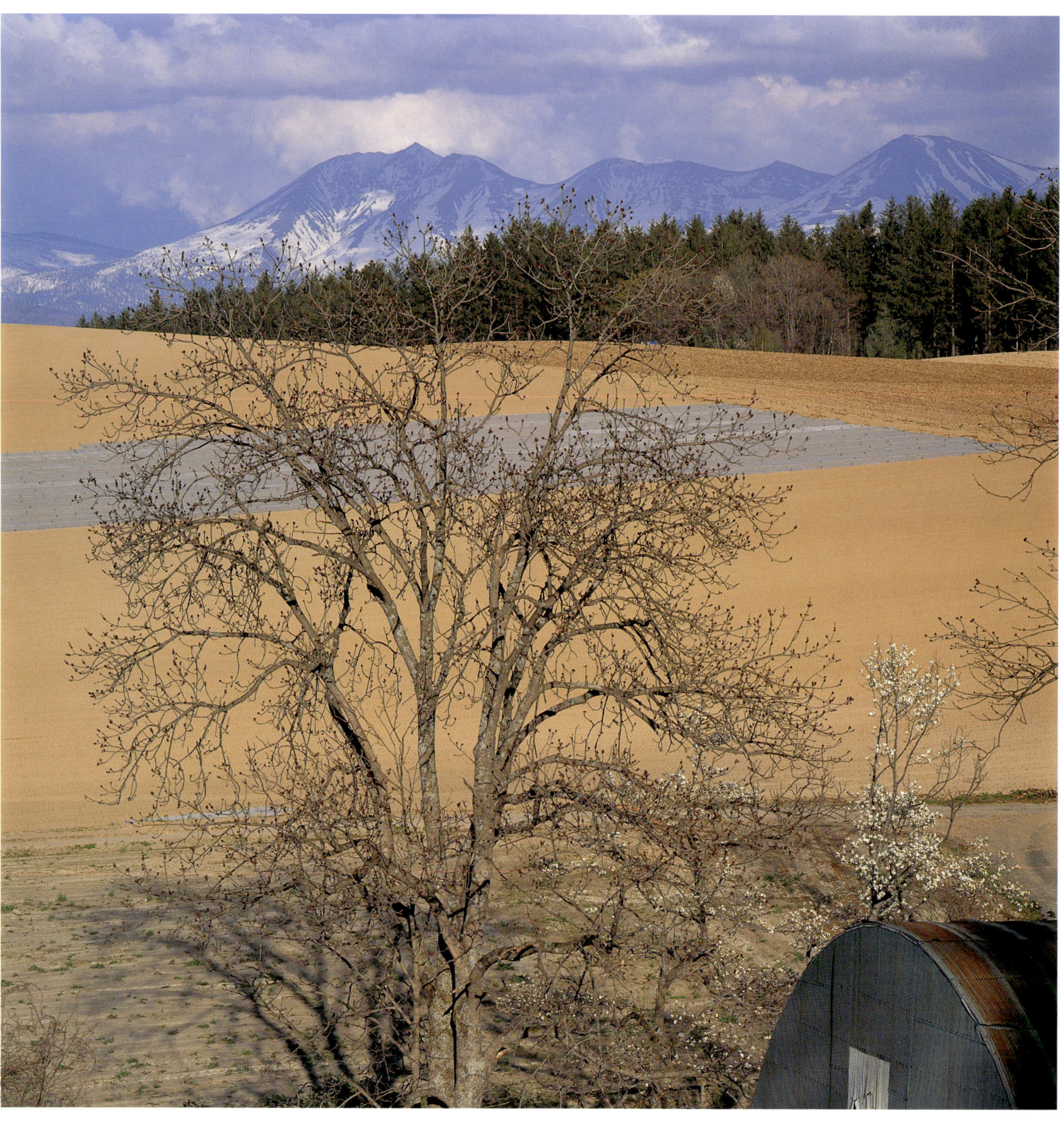

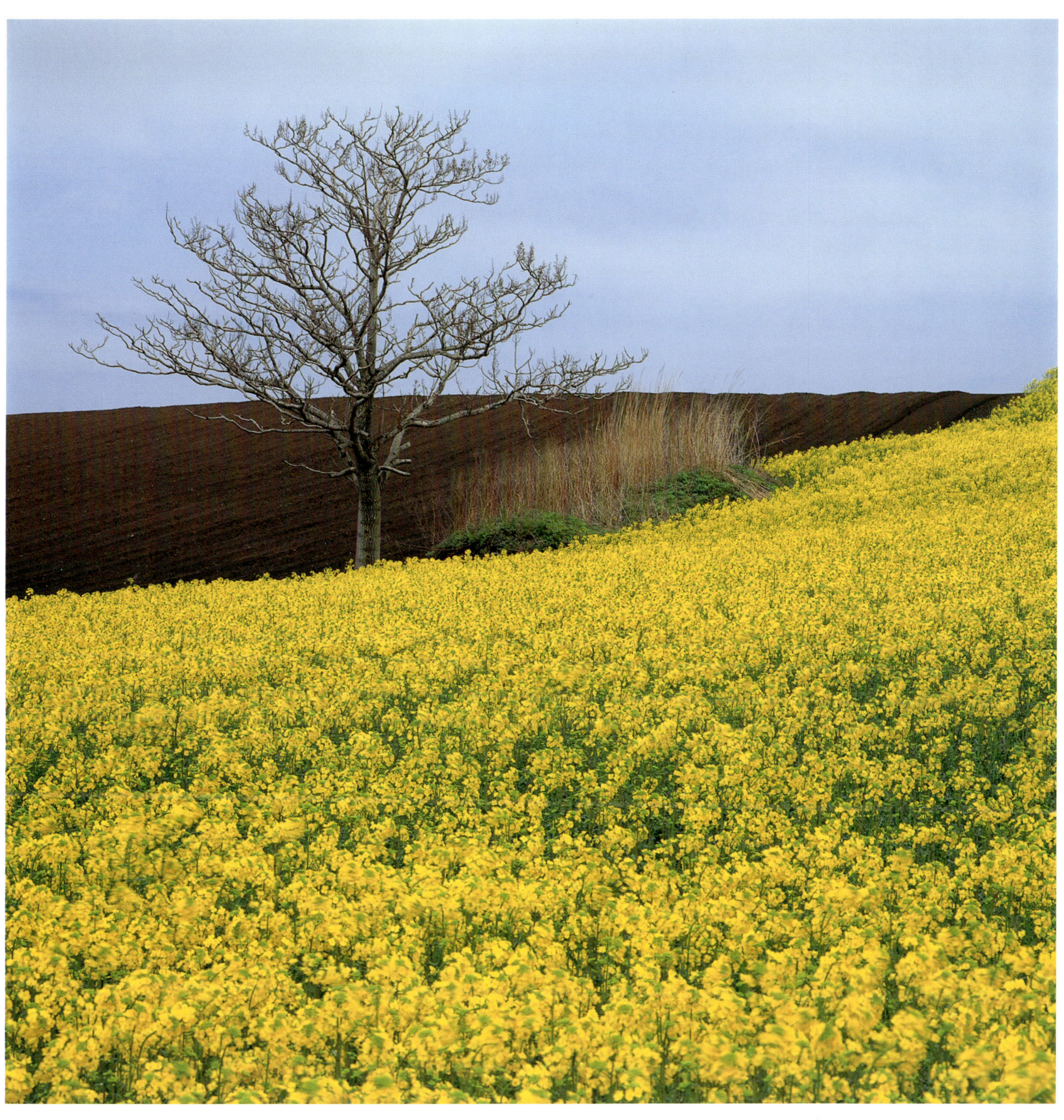

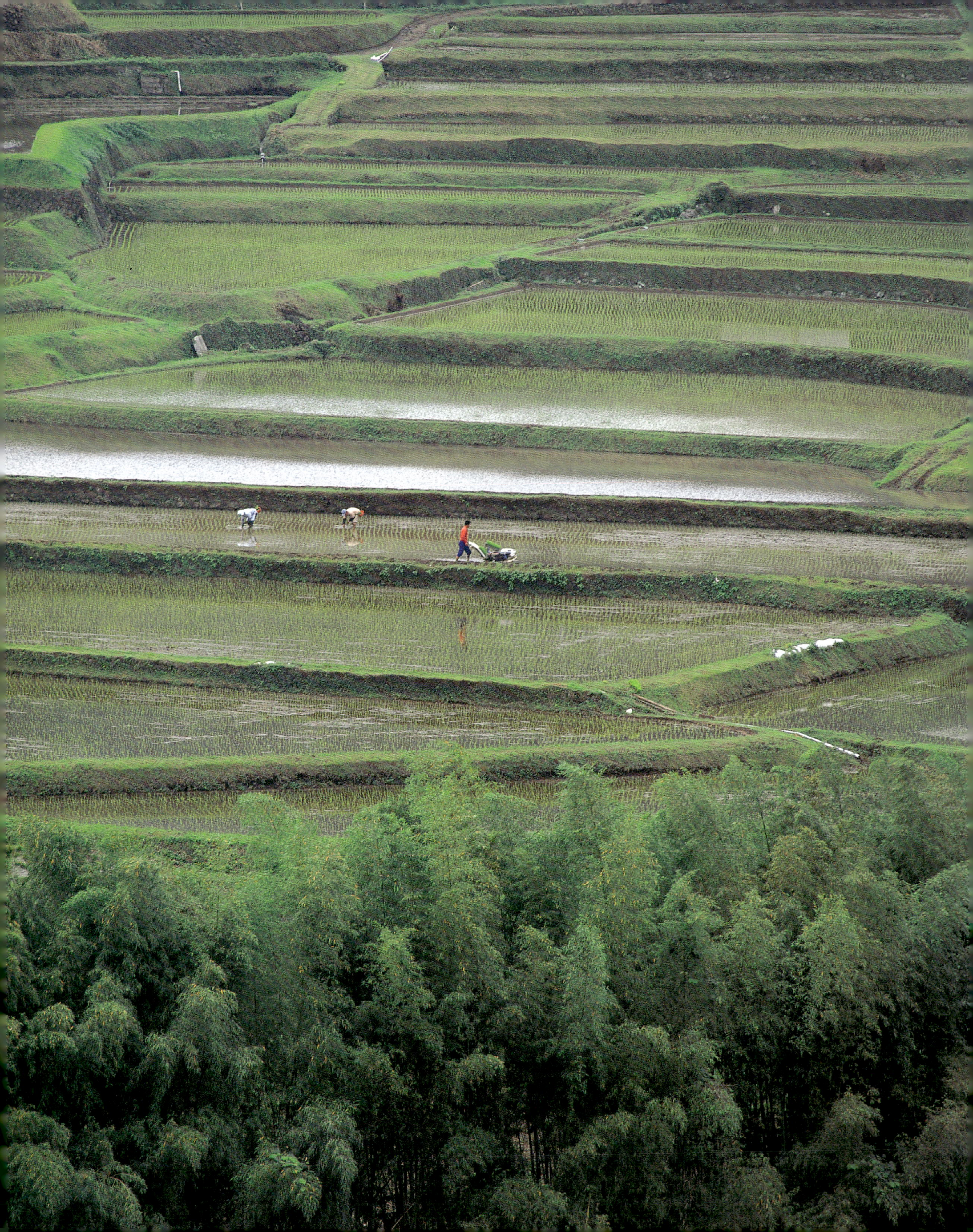

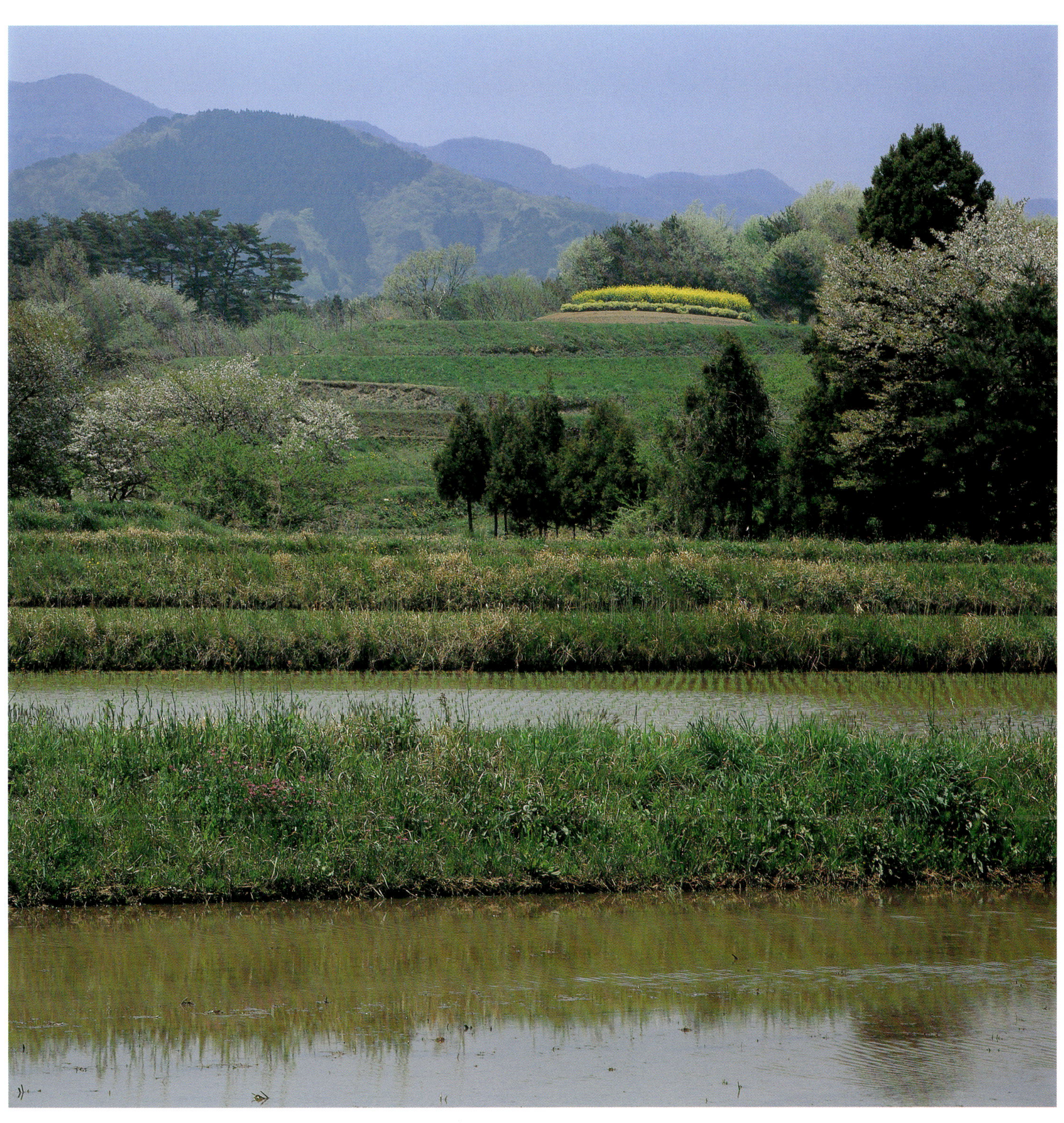

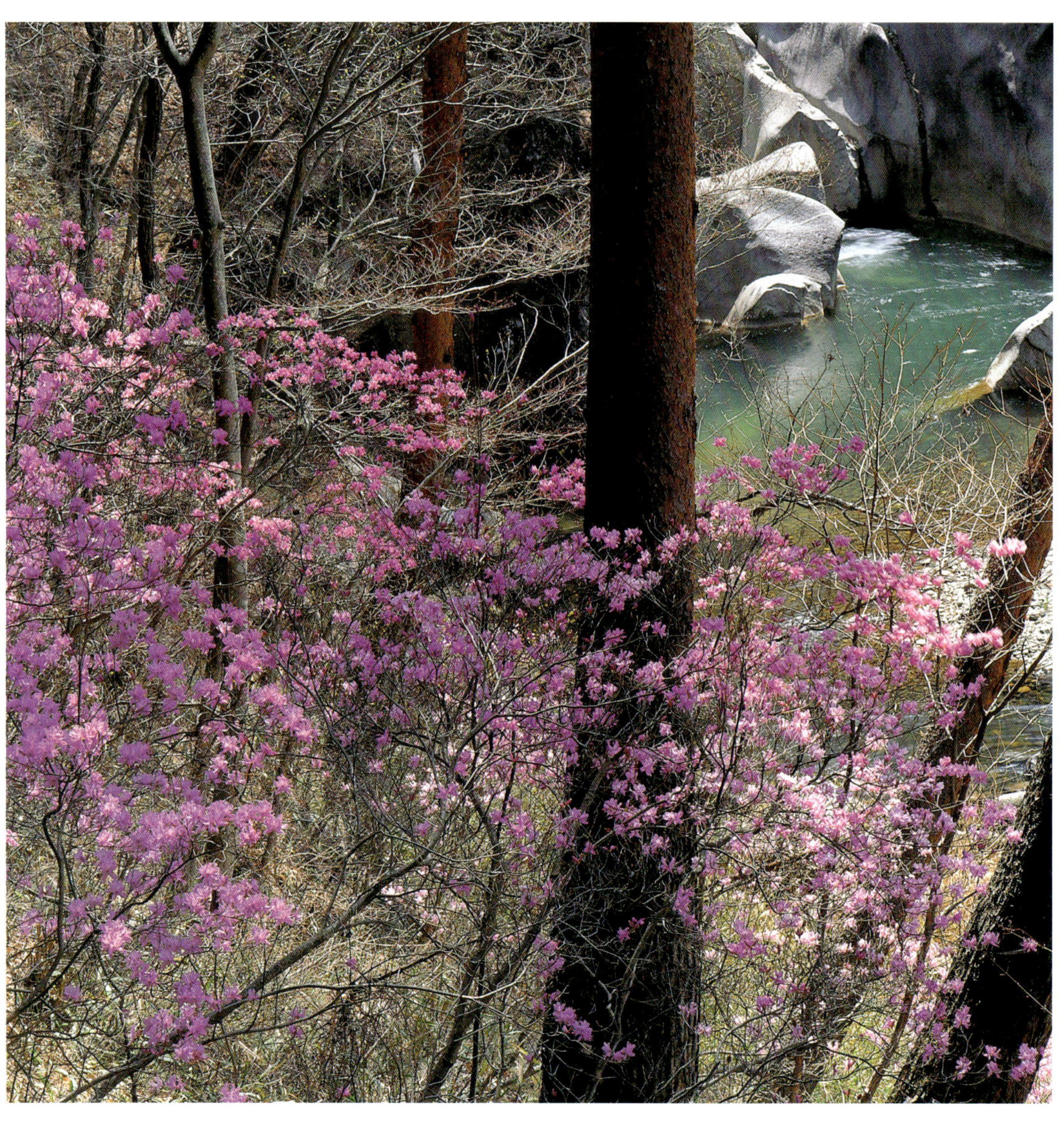

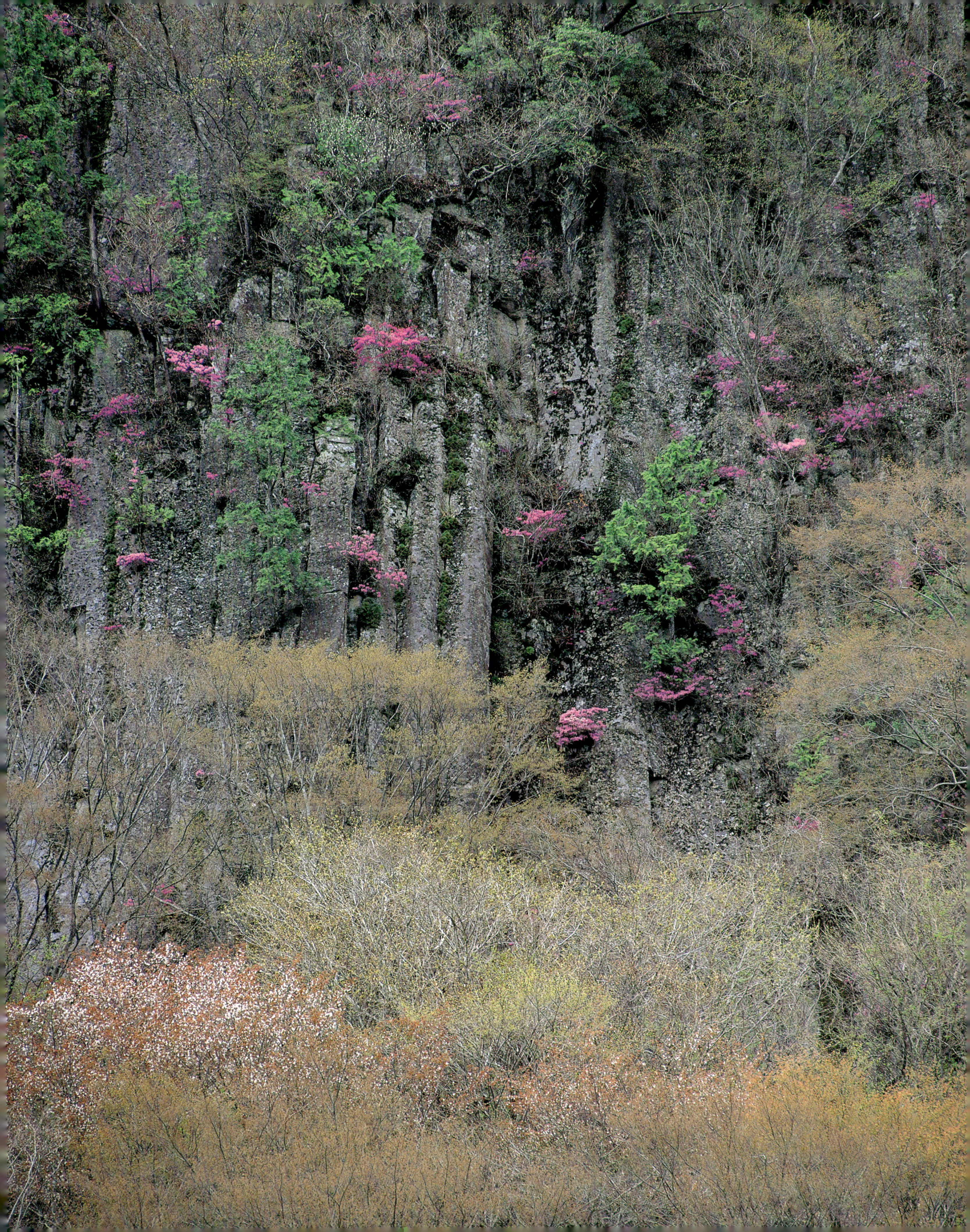

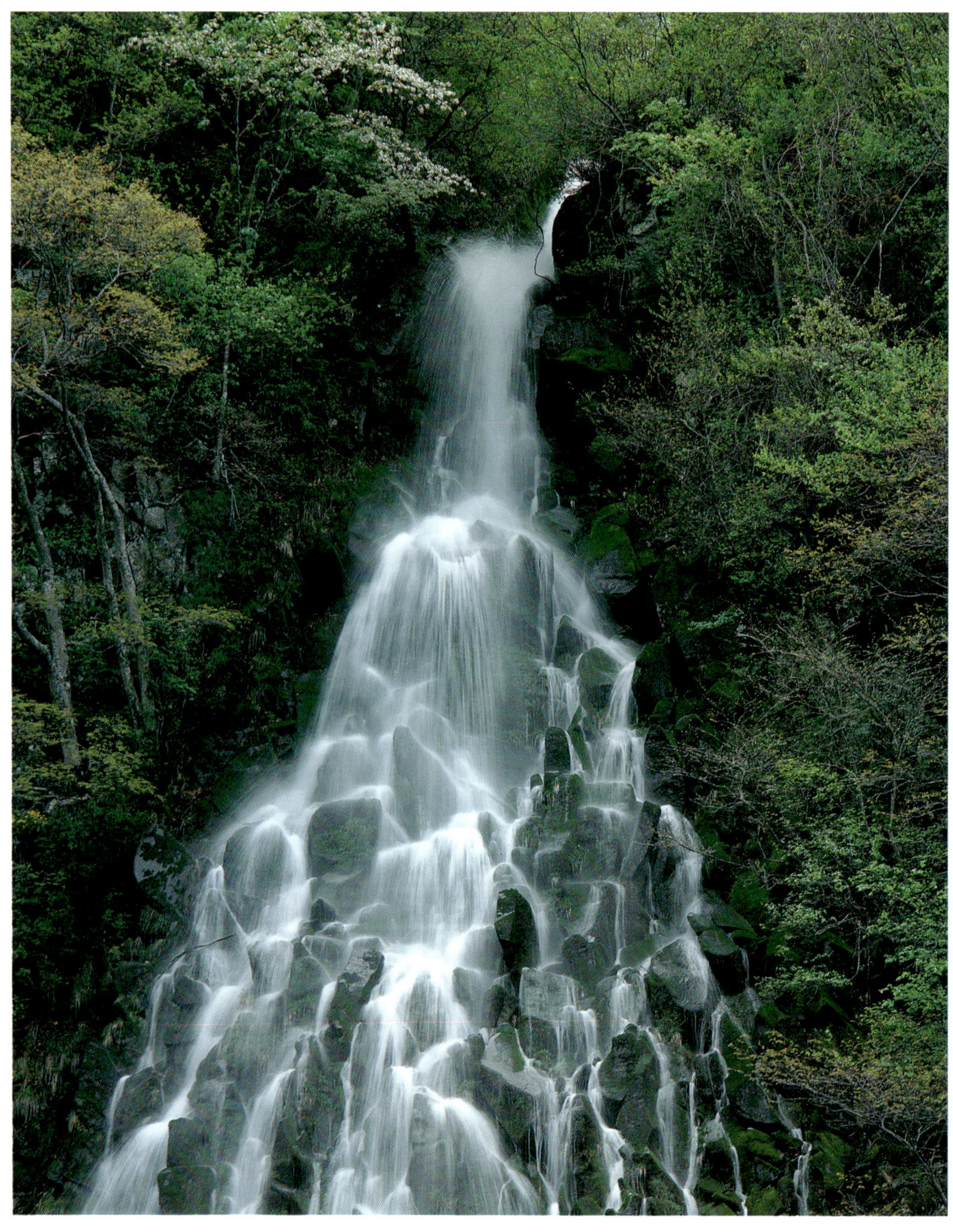

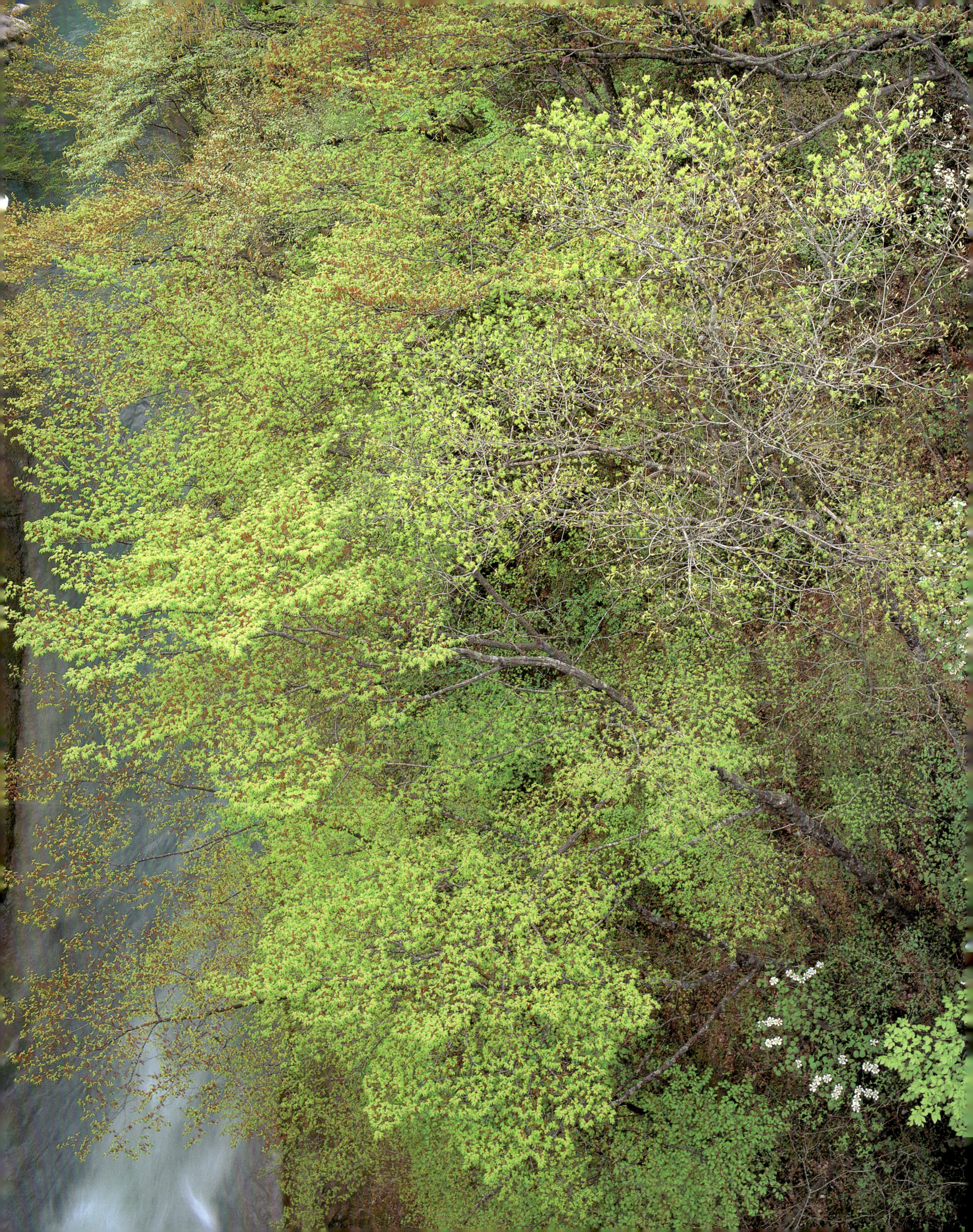

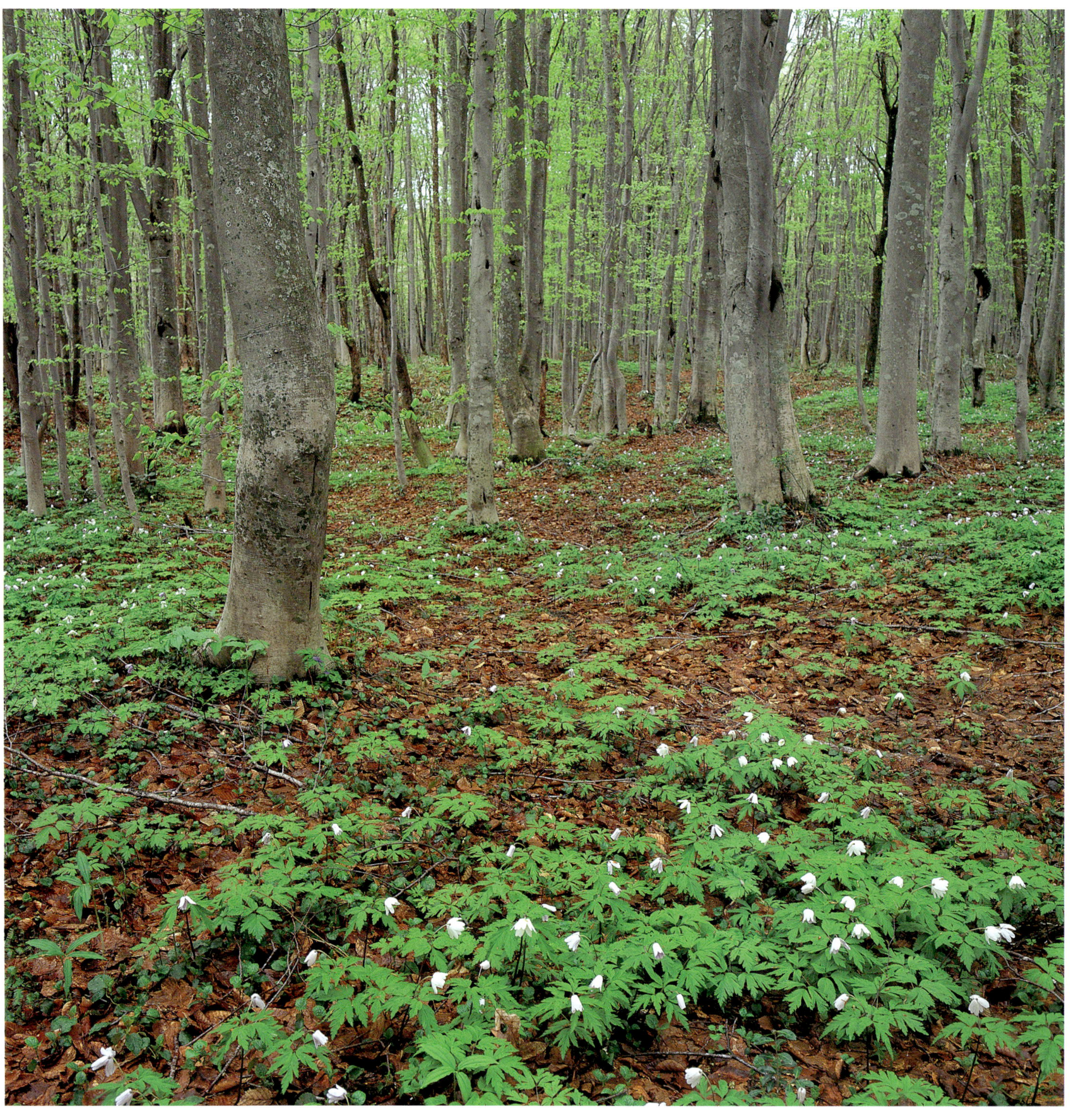

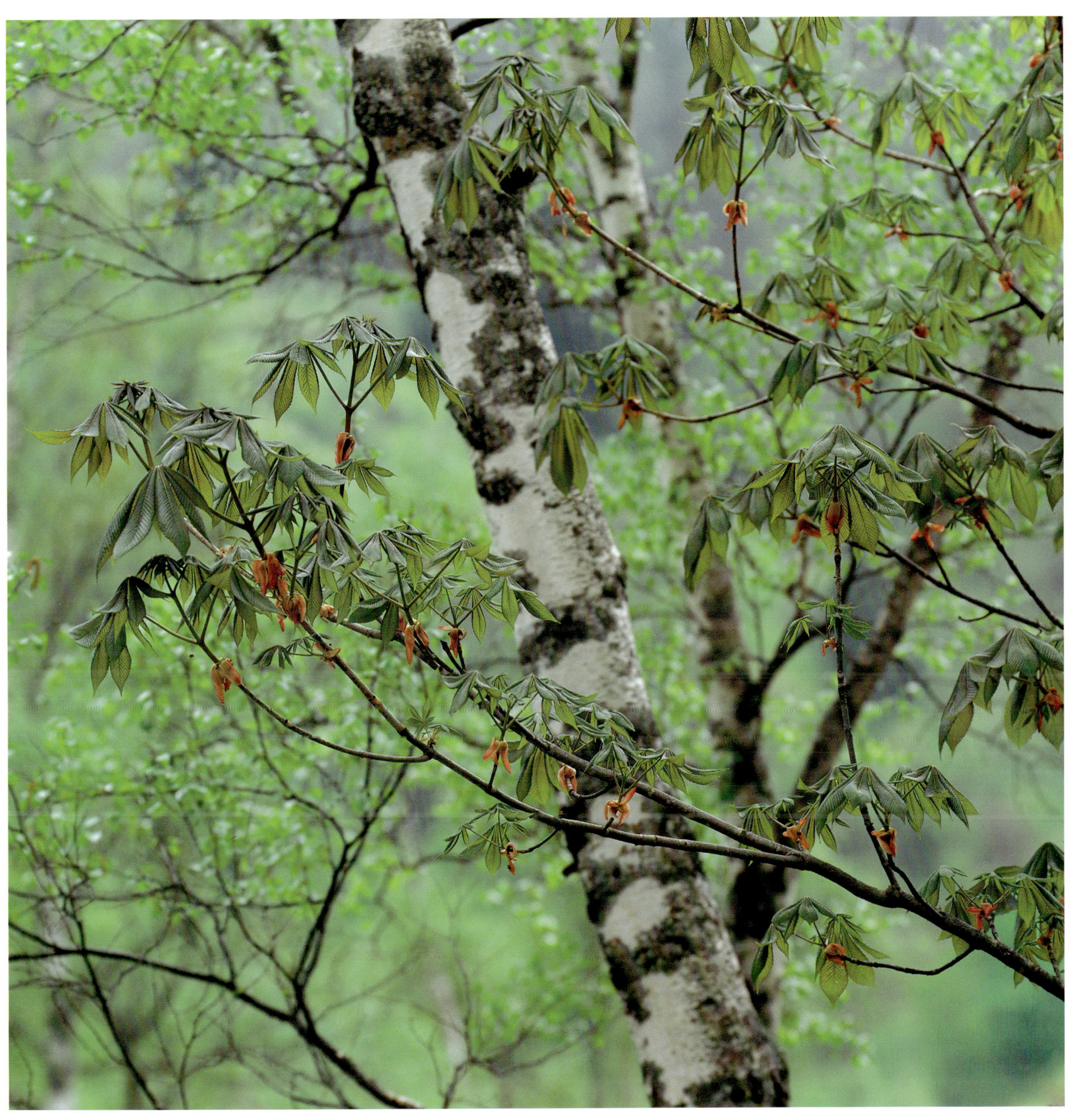

松尾芭蕉

夏草や
兵どもが
夢の跡

S U M M E R 夏

Summer grasses!
Of noble warriors' dreams
the aftermath.

MATSUO BASHO

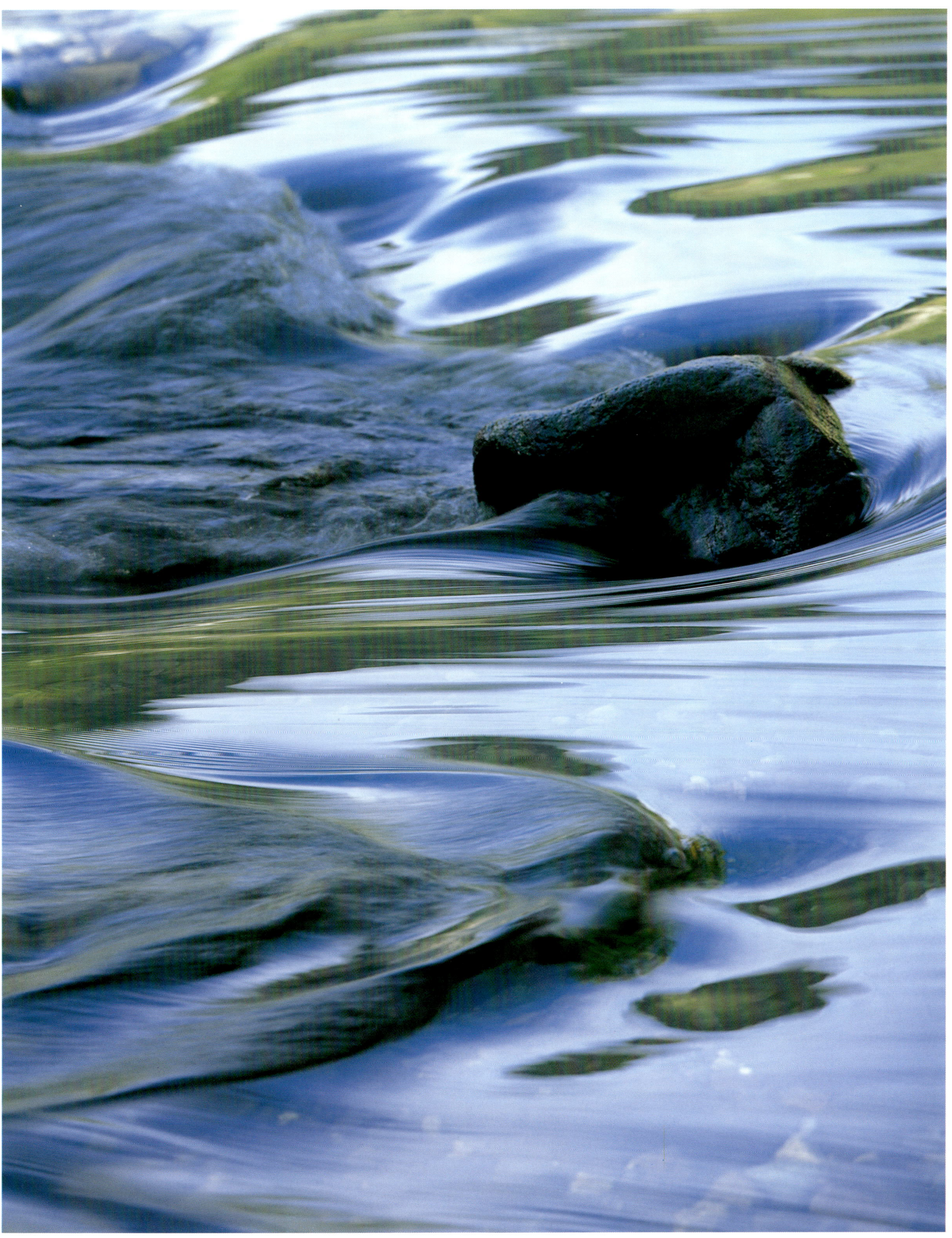

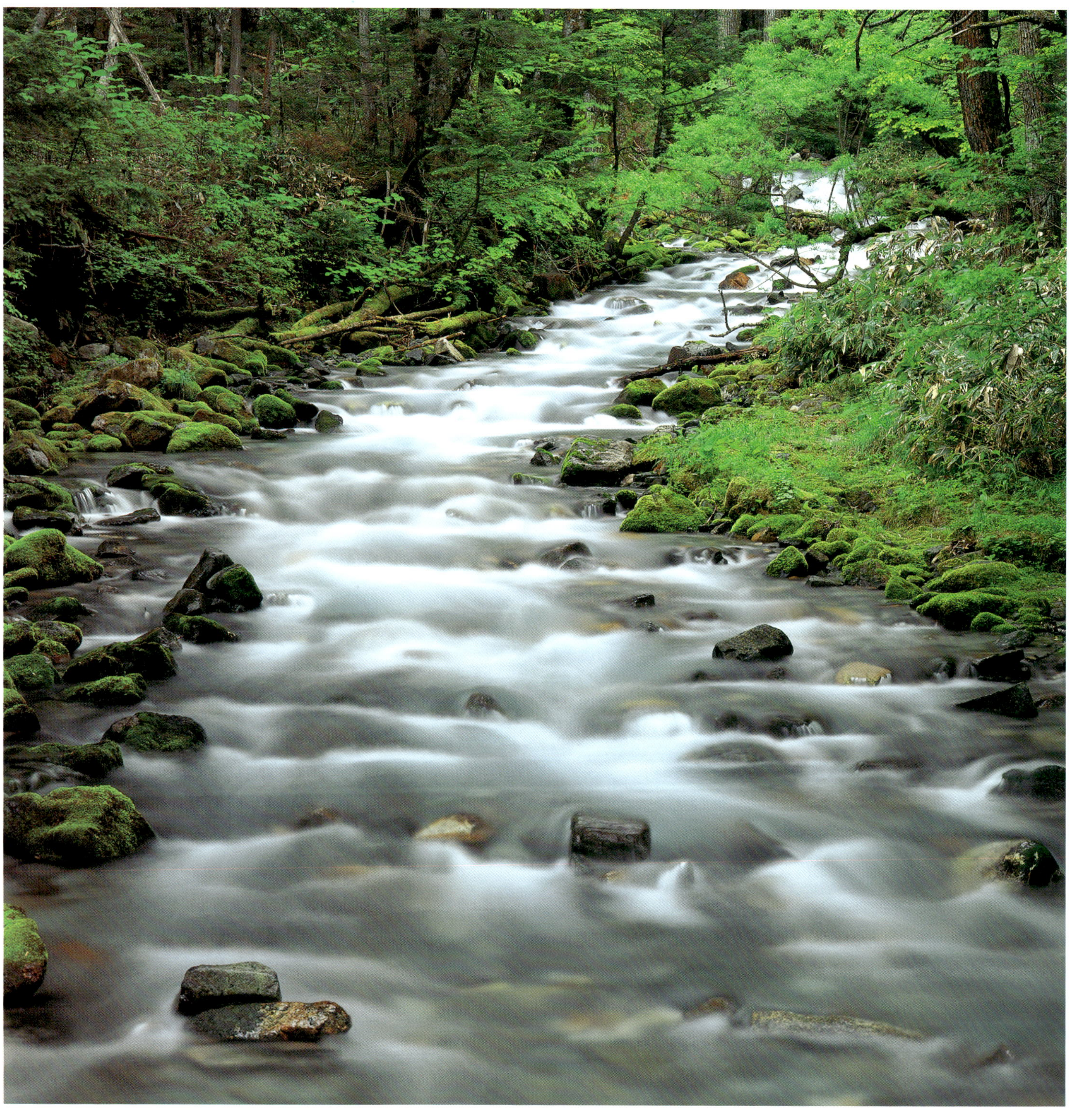

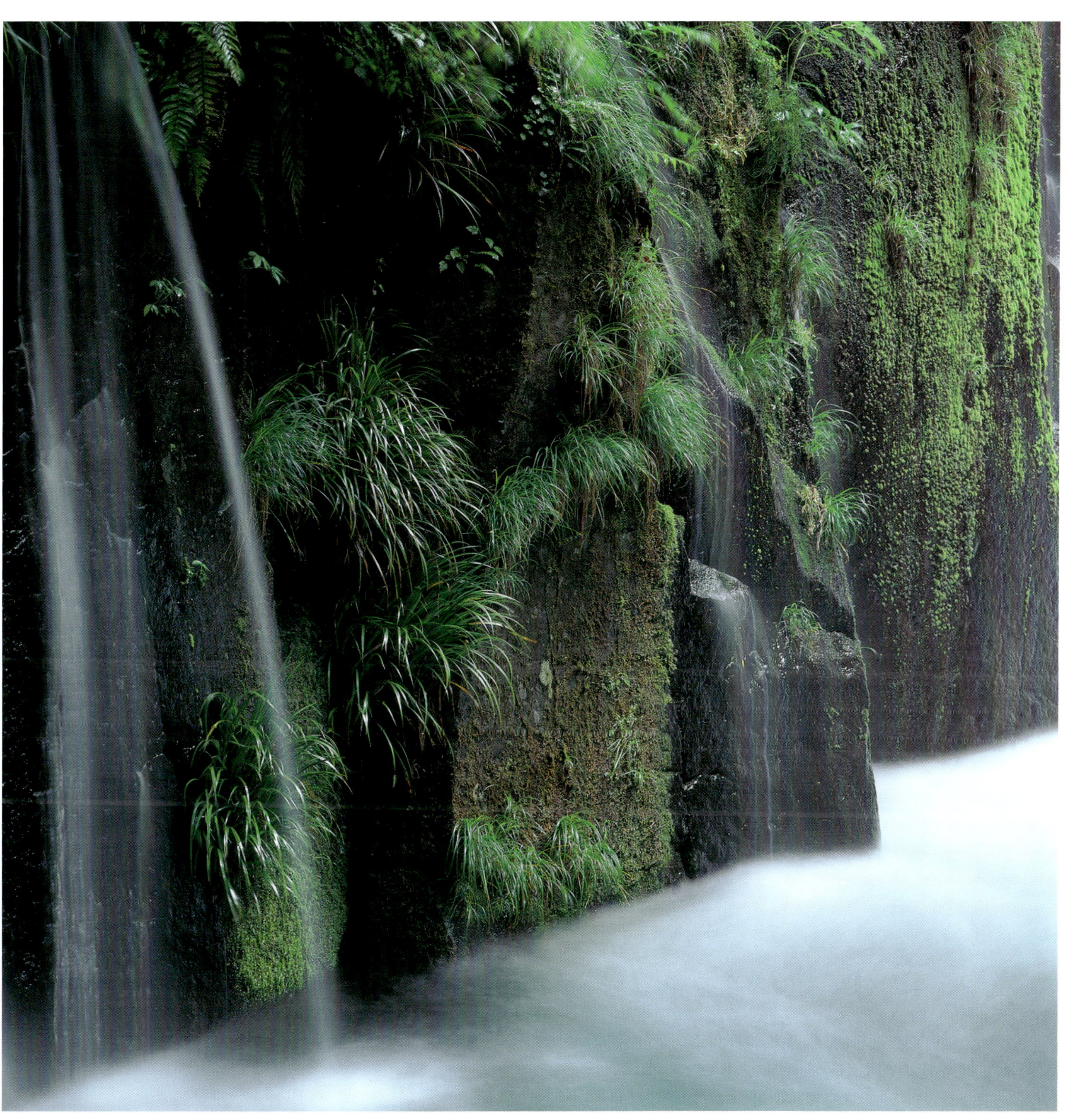

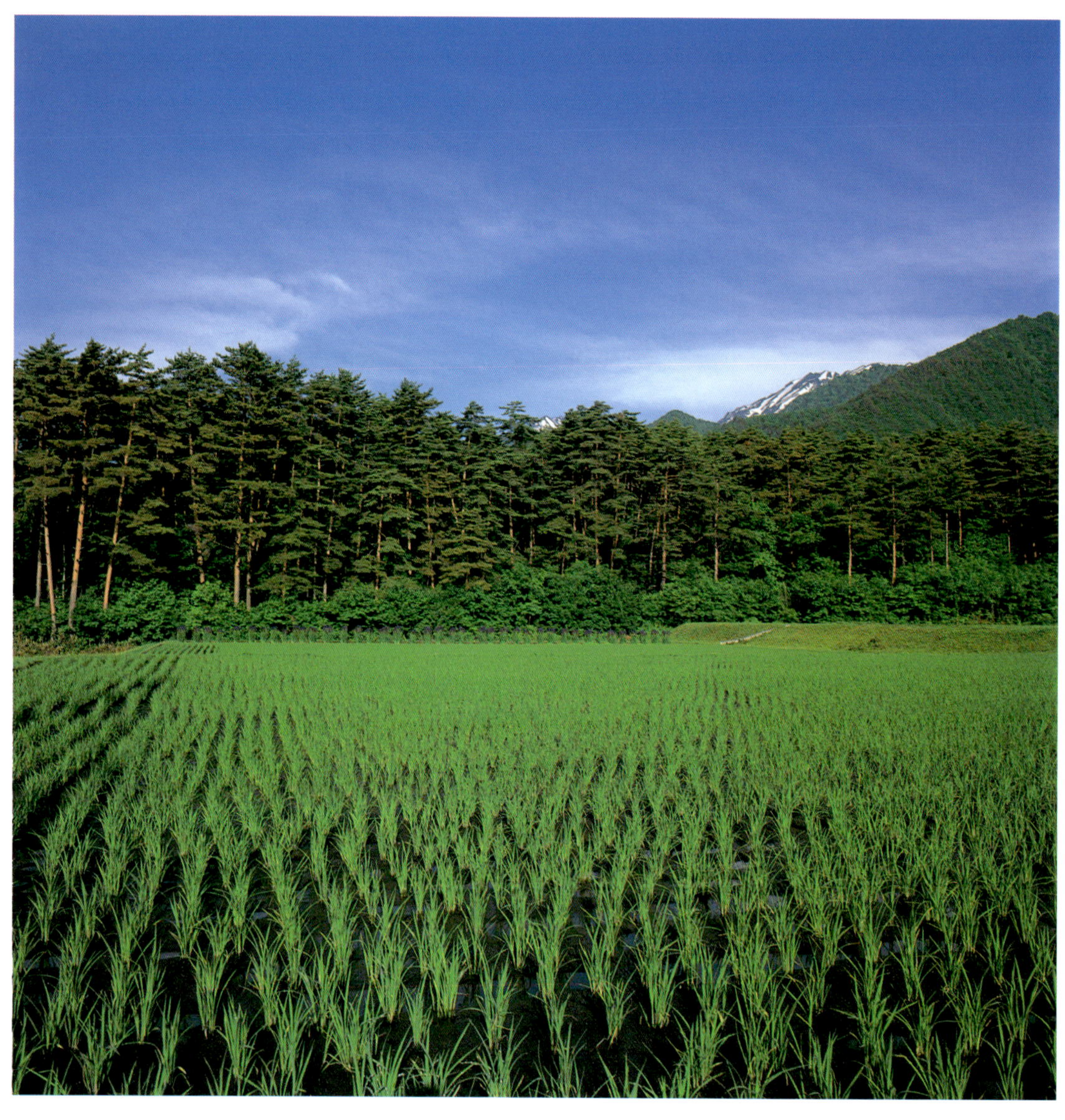

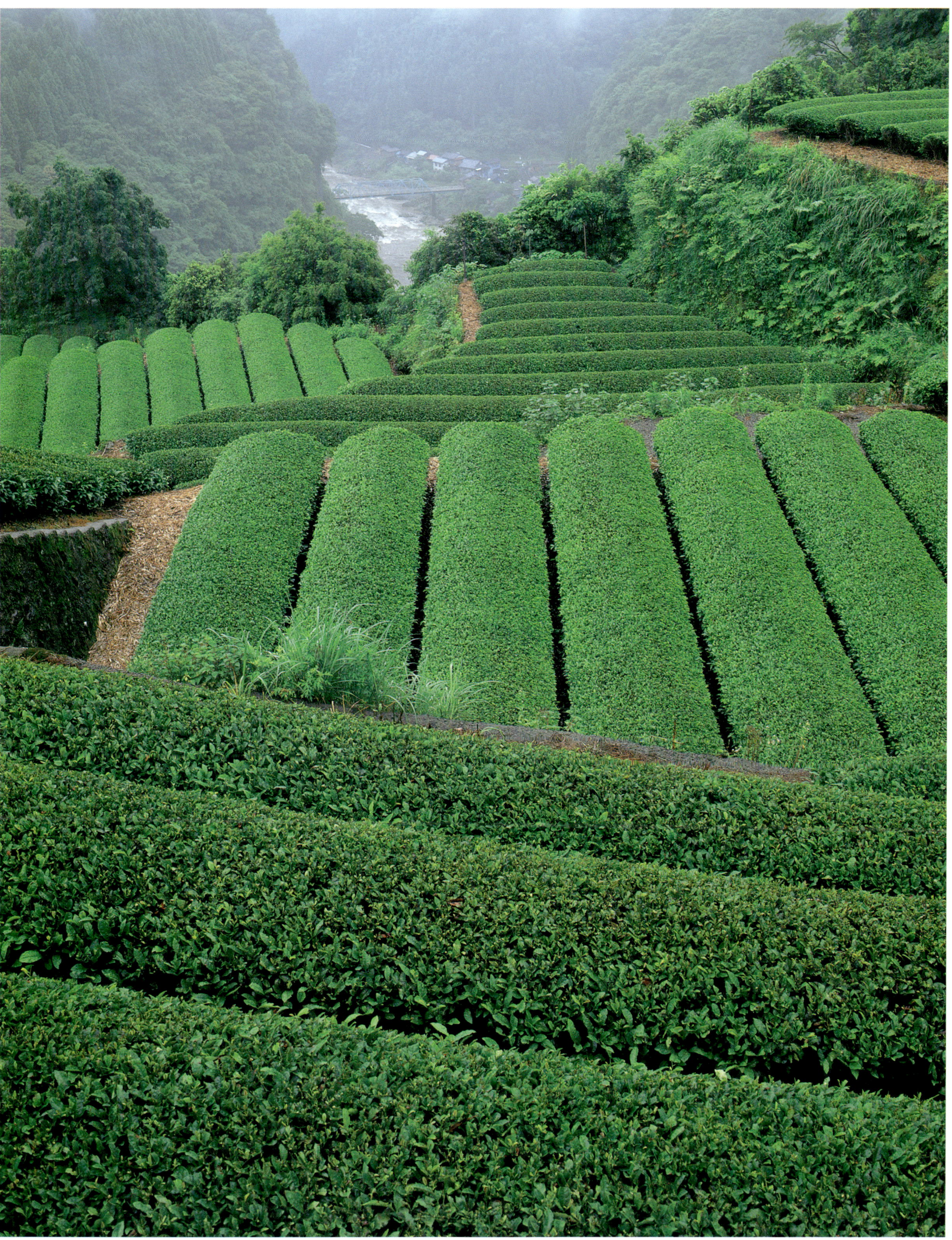

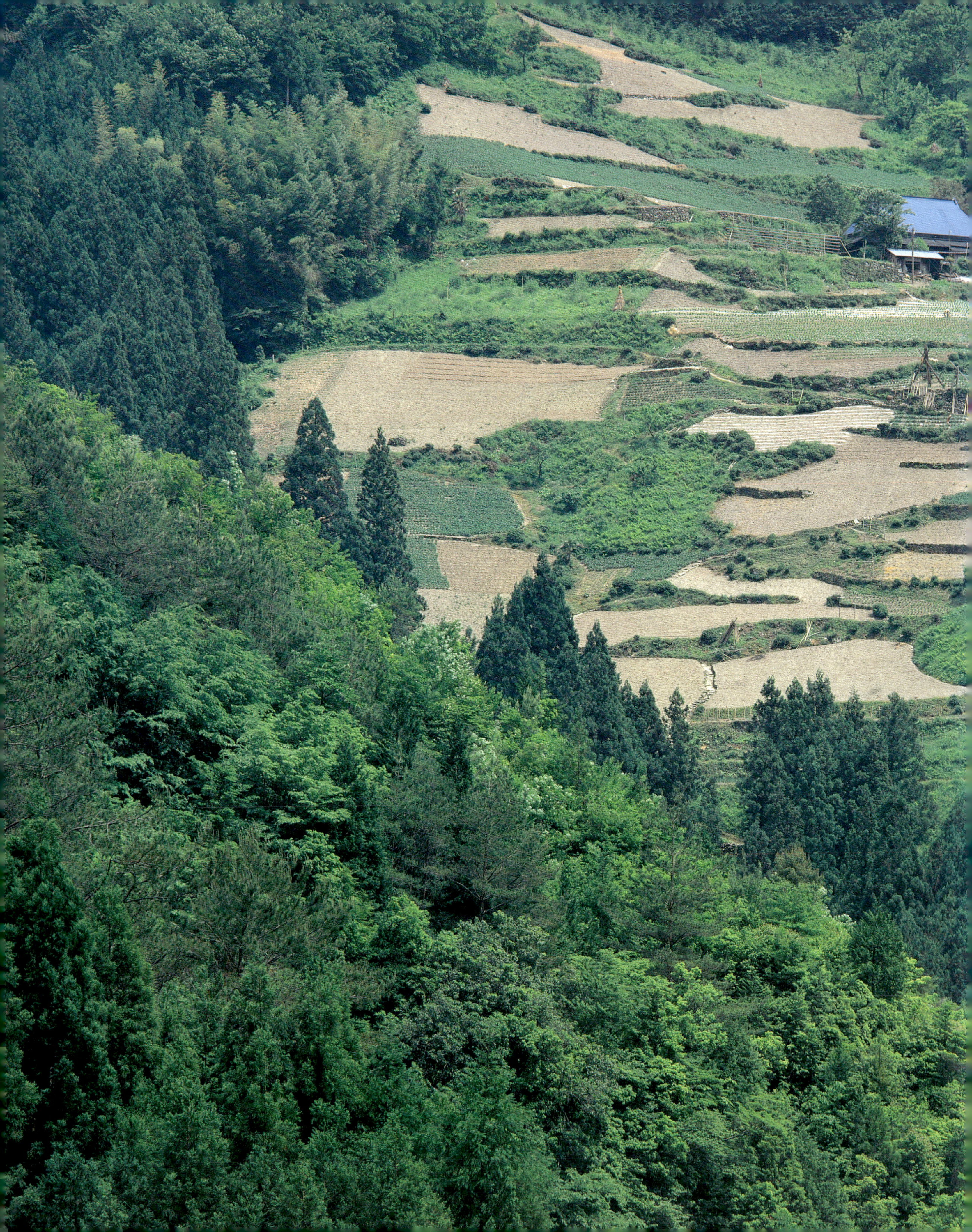

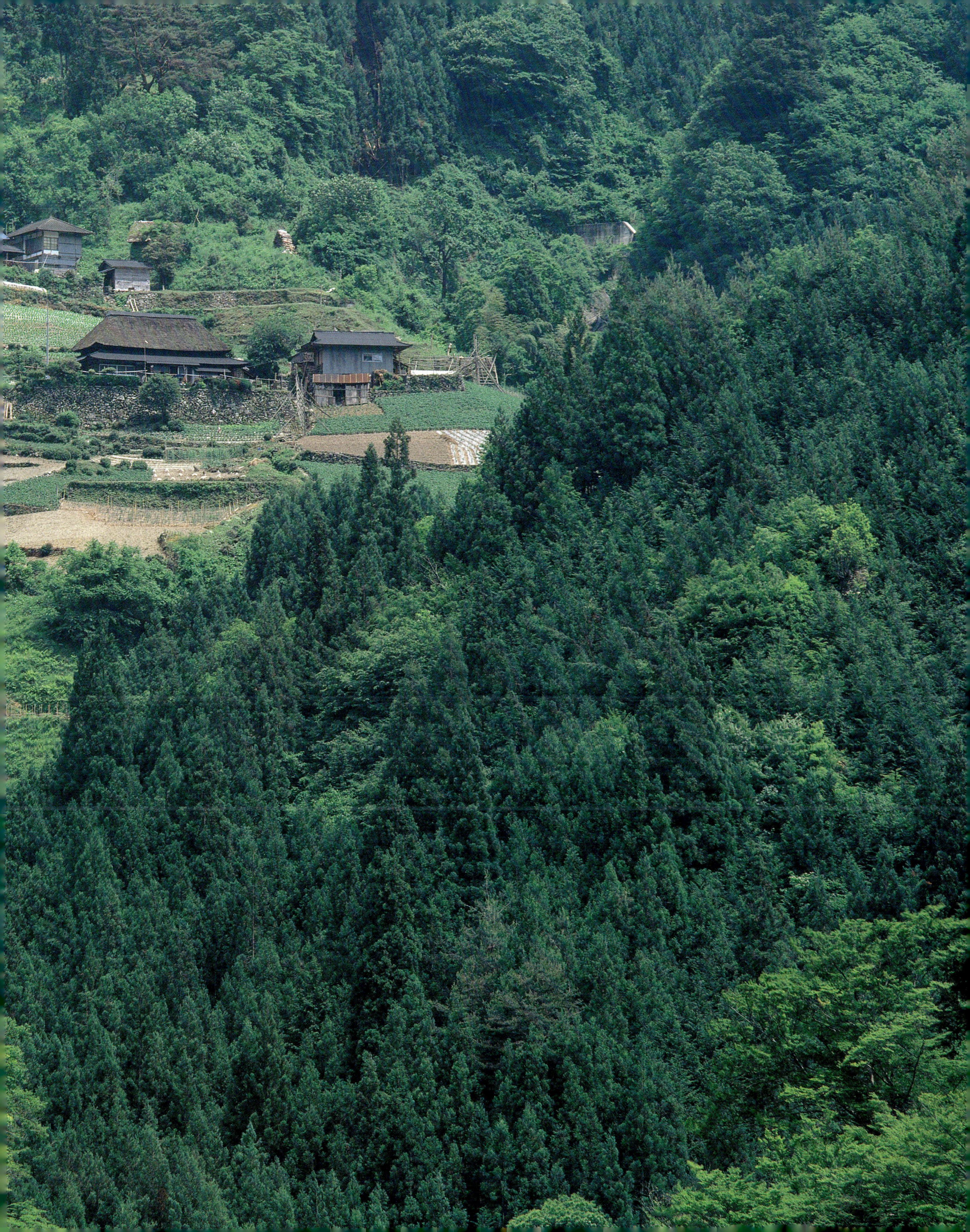

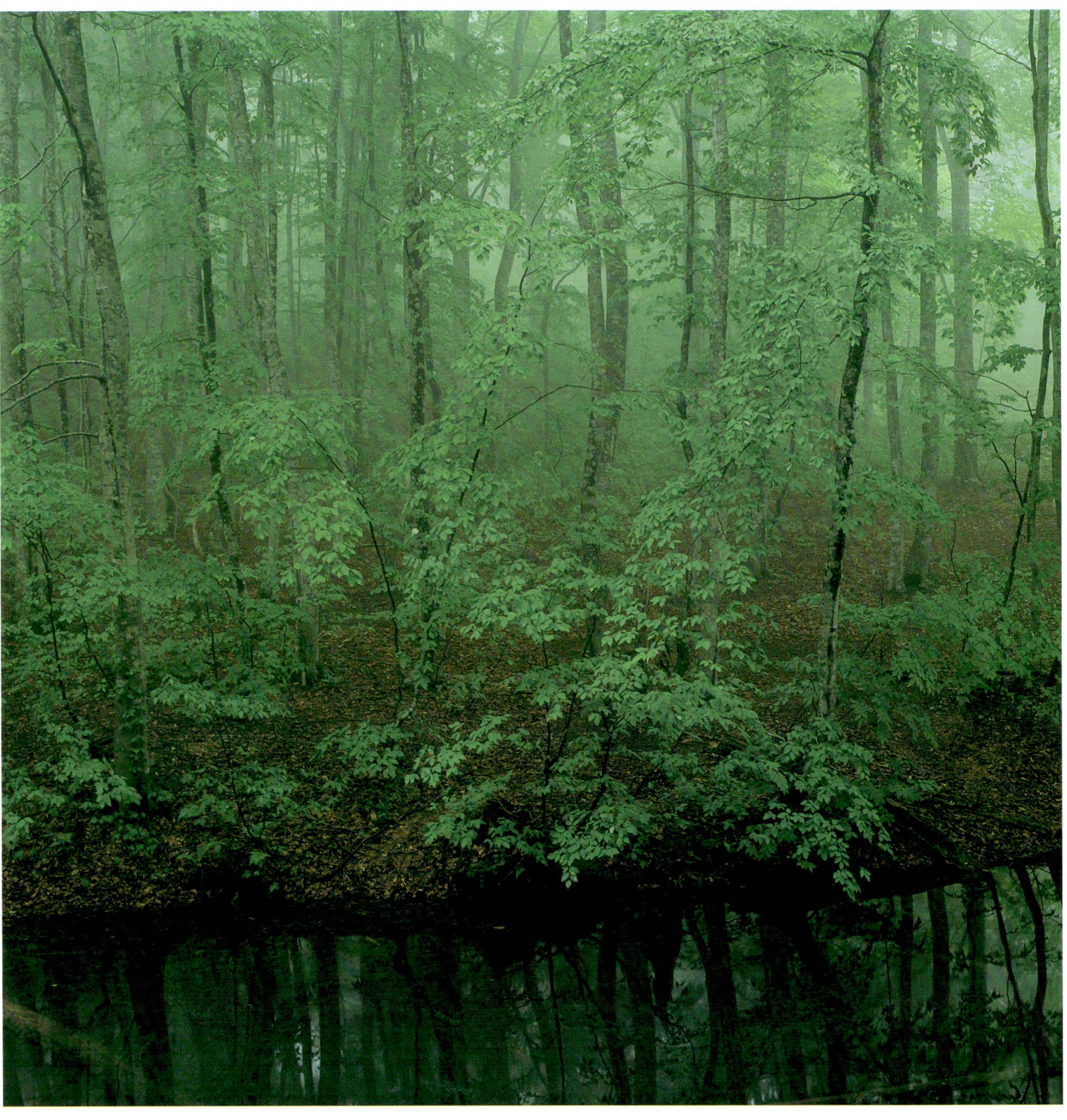

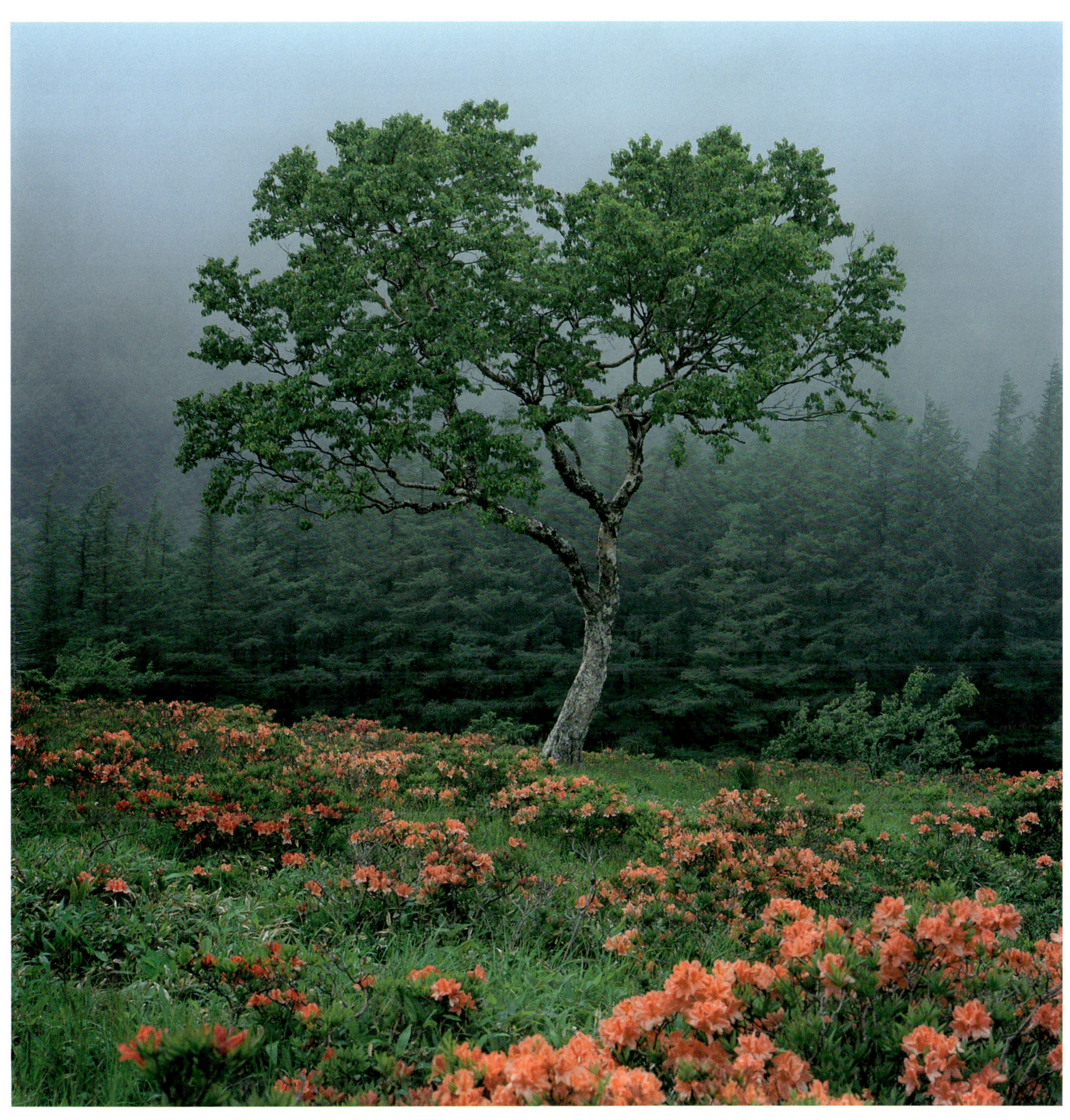

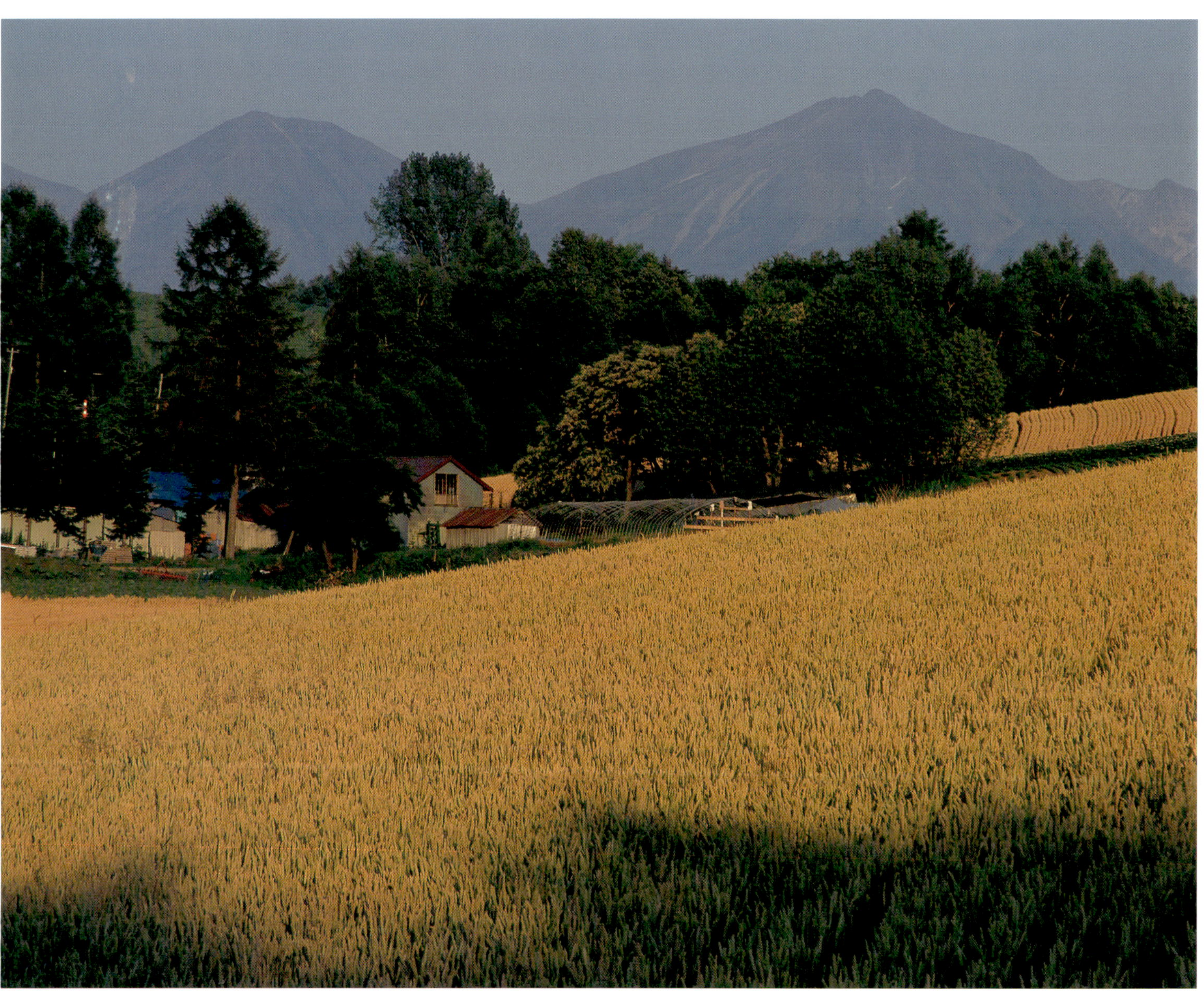

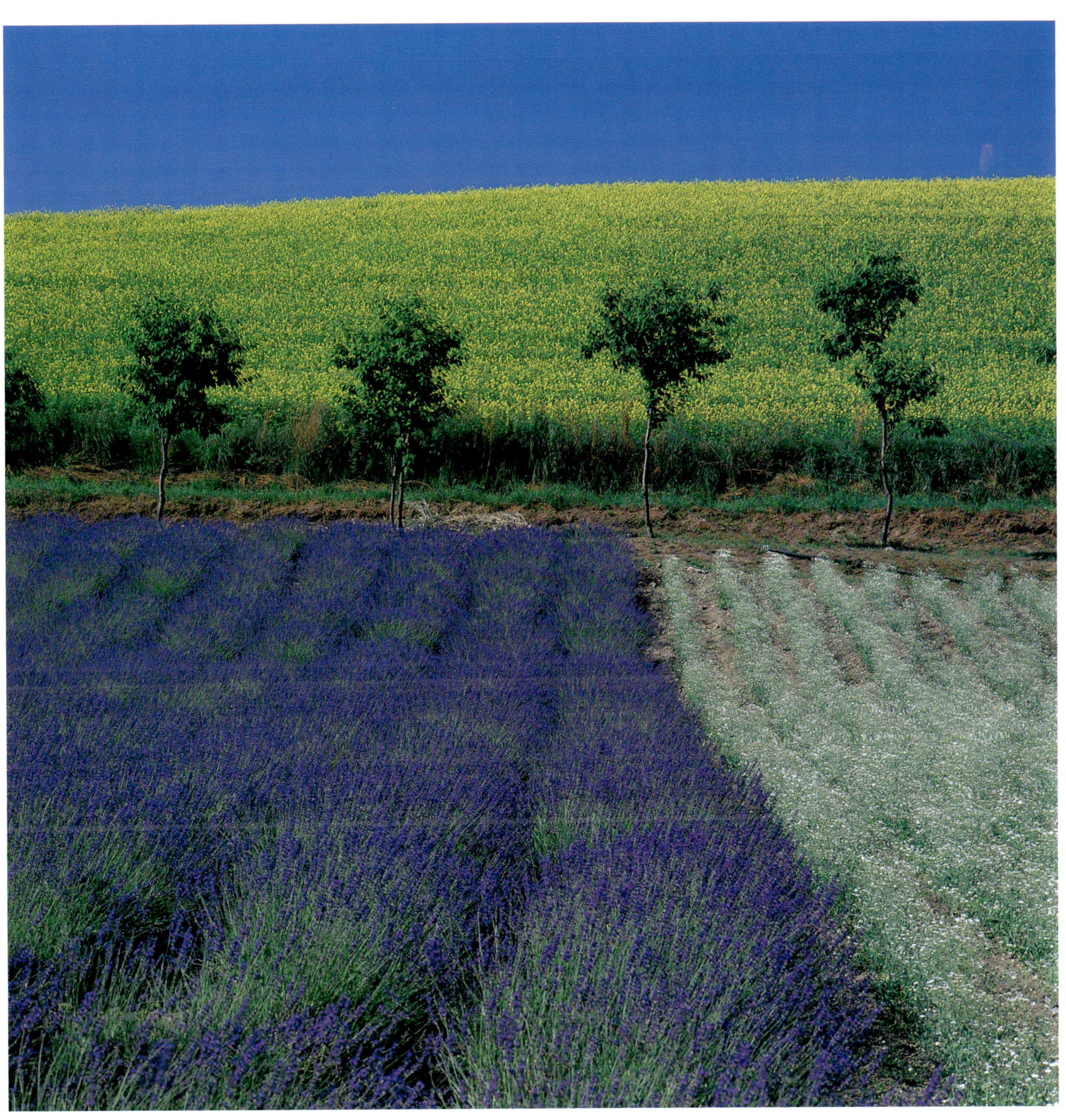

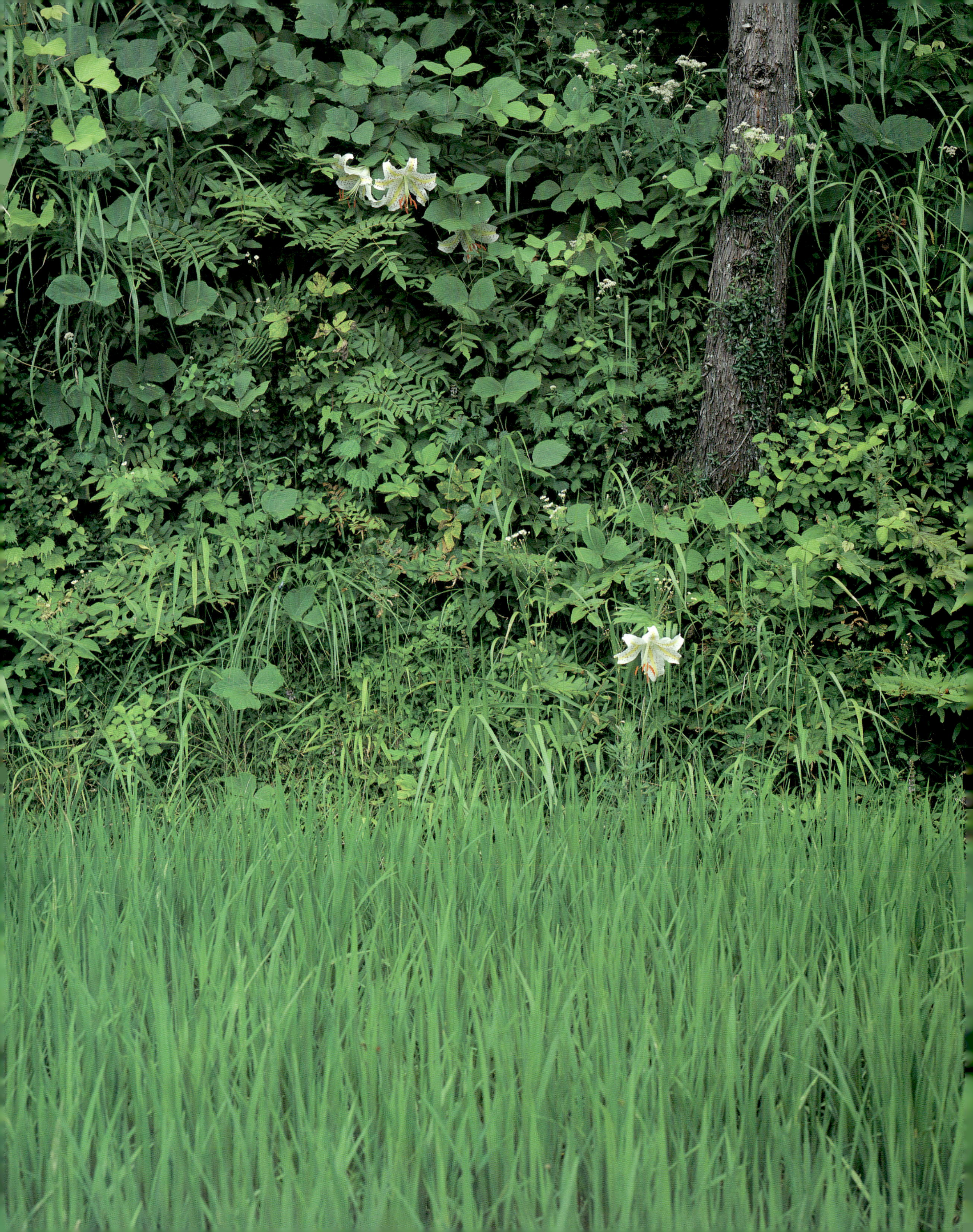

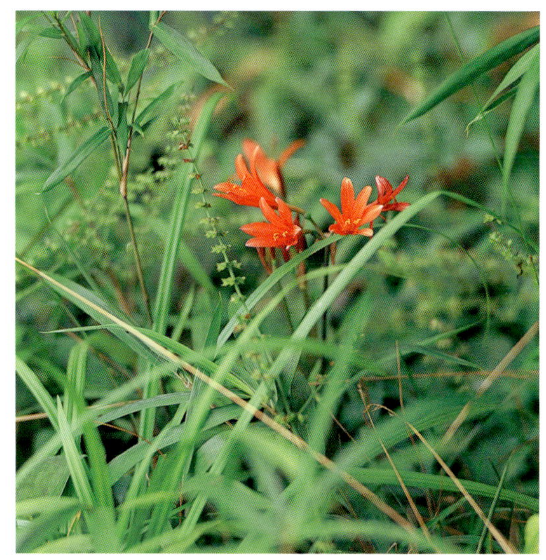

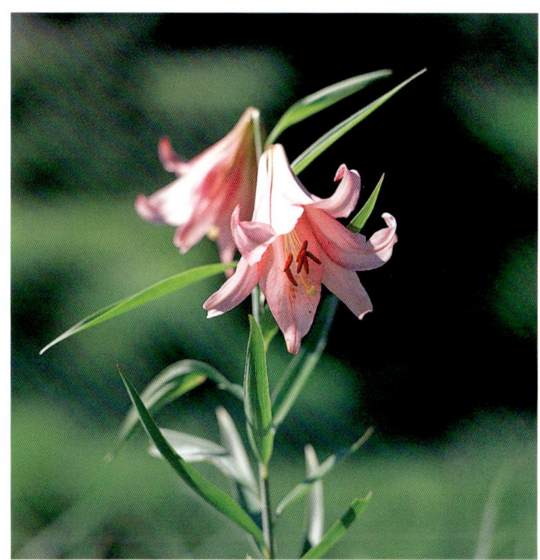

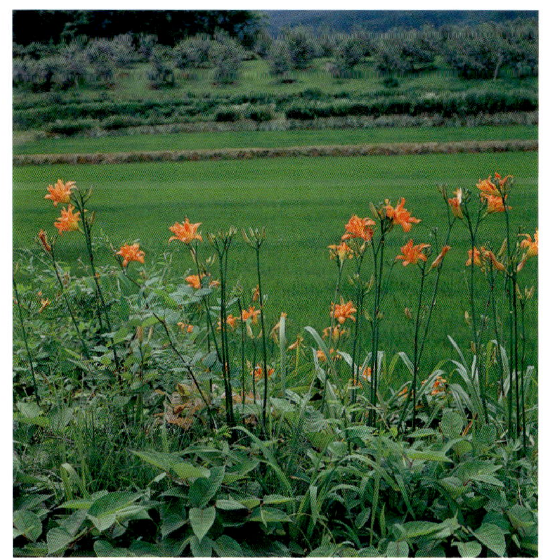

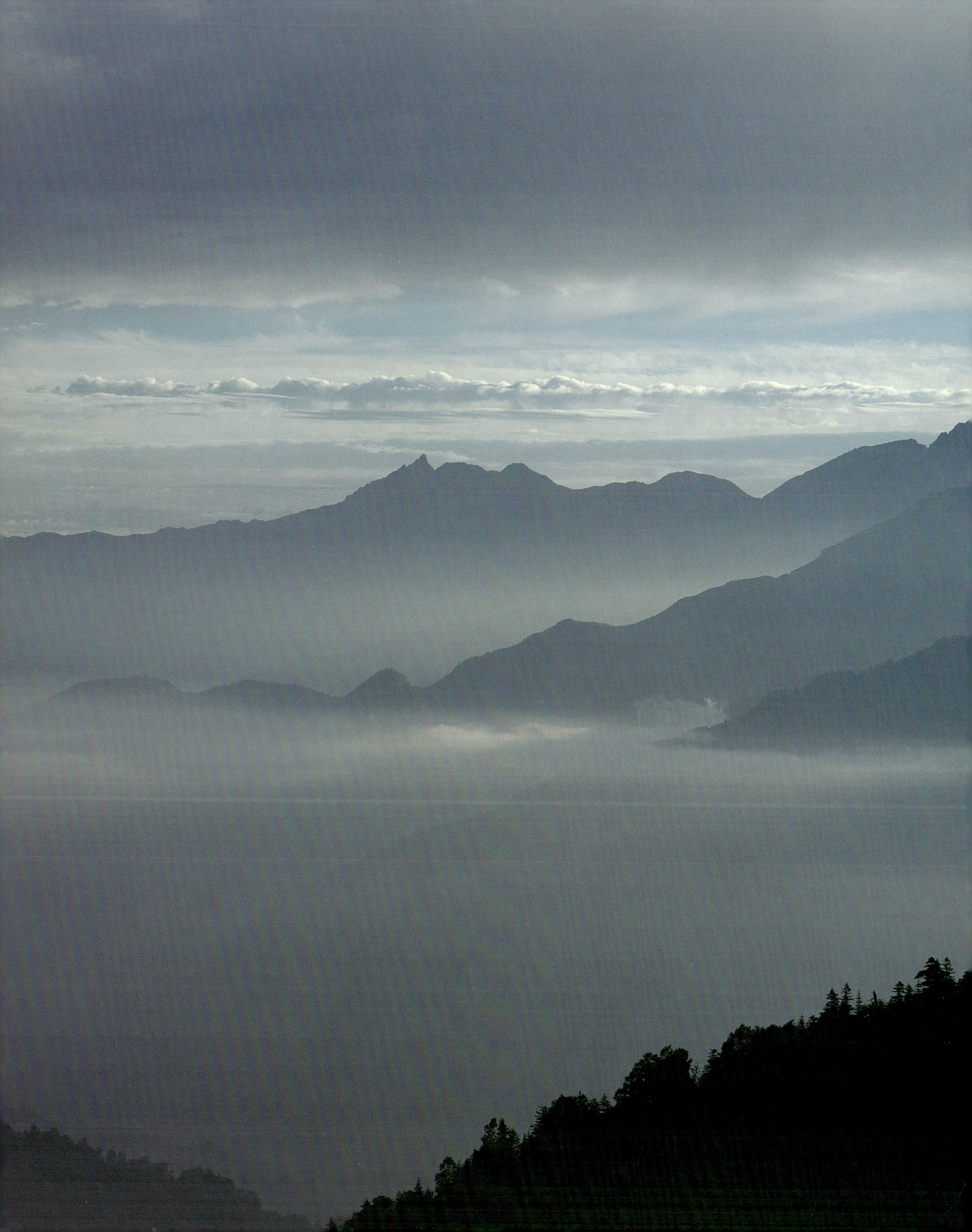

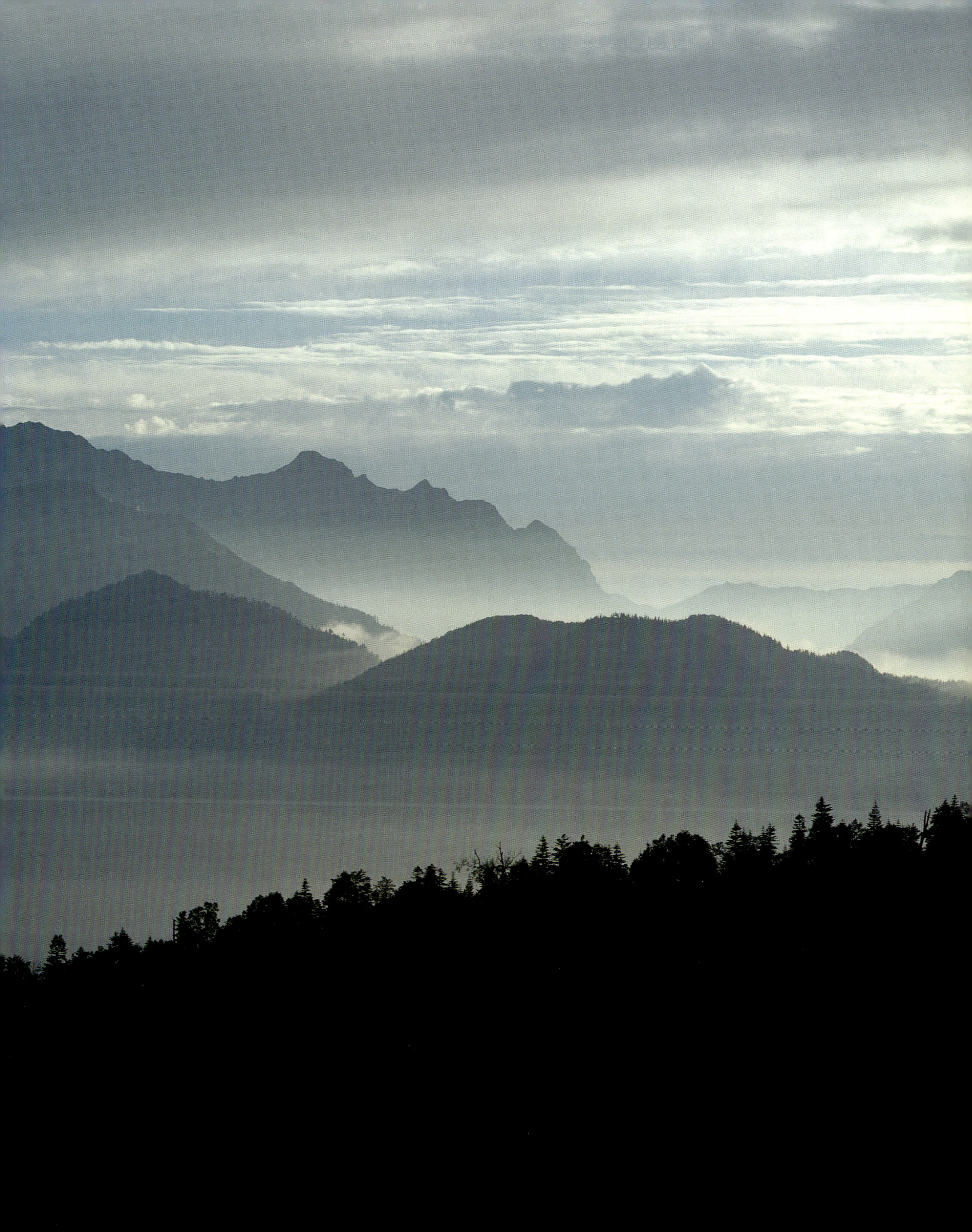

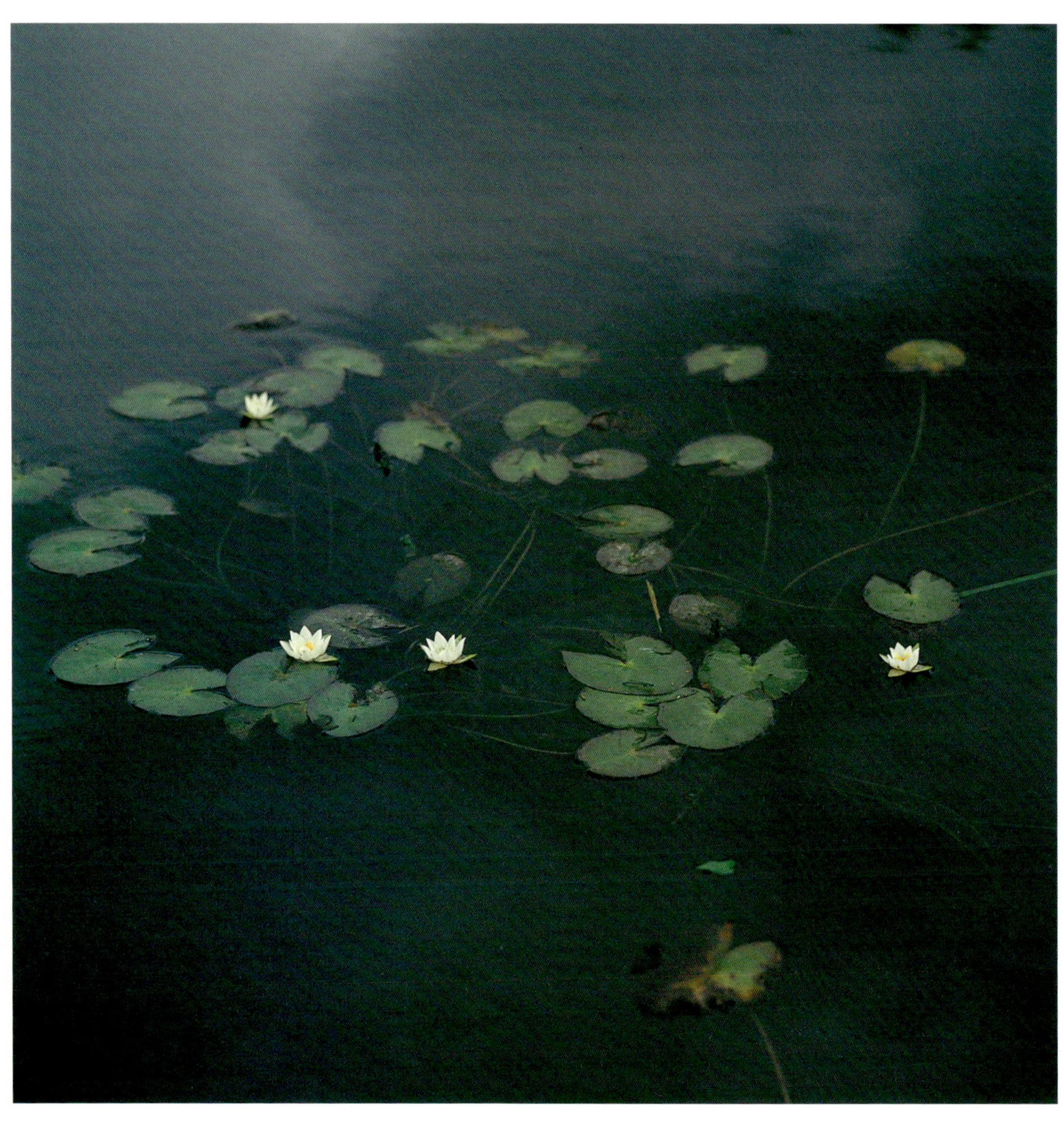

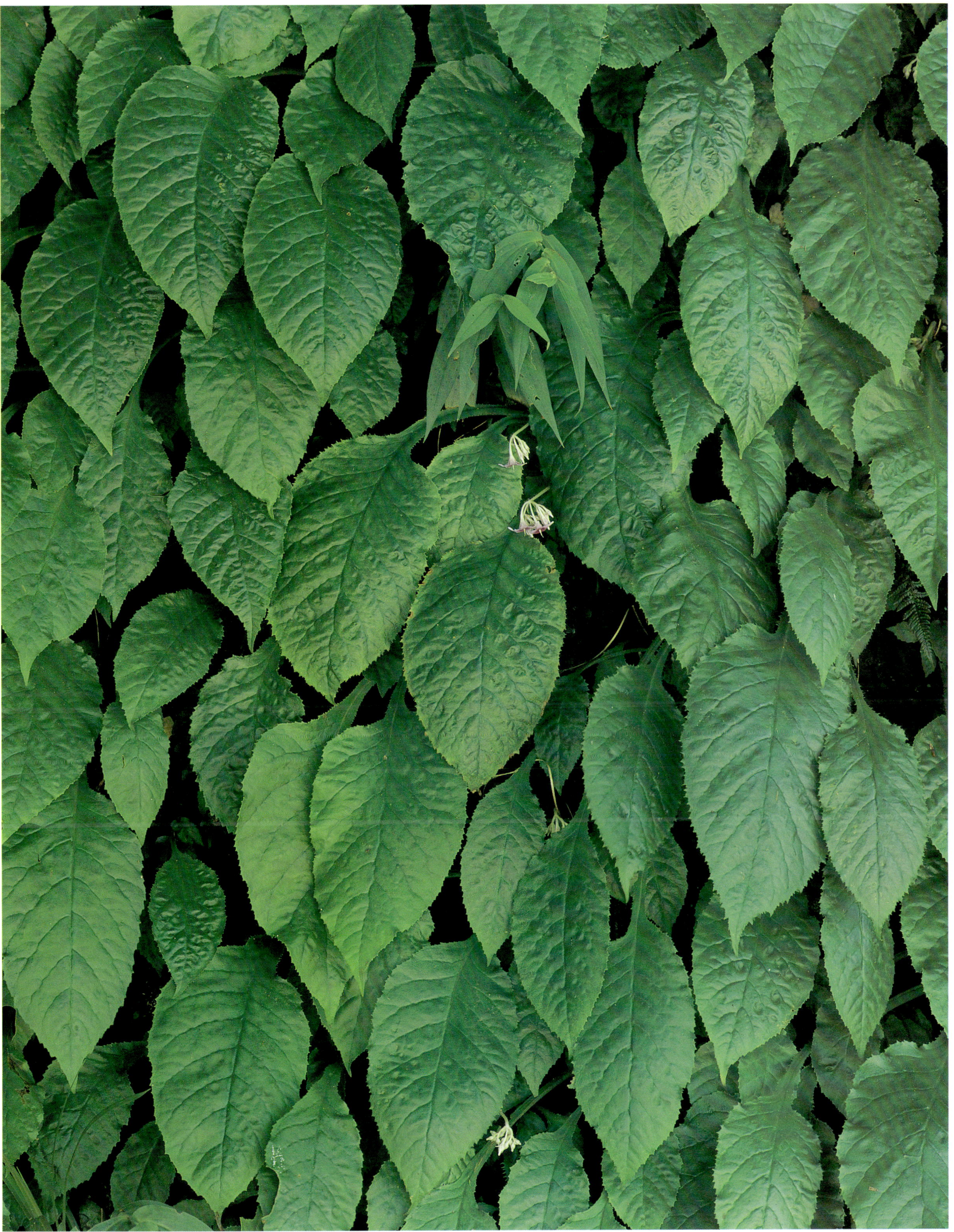

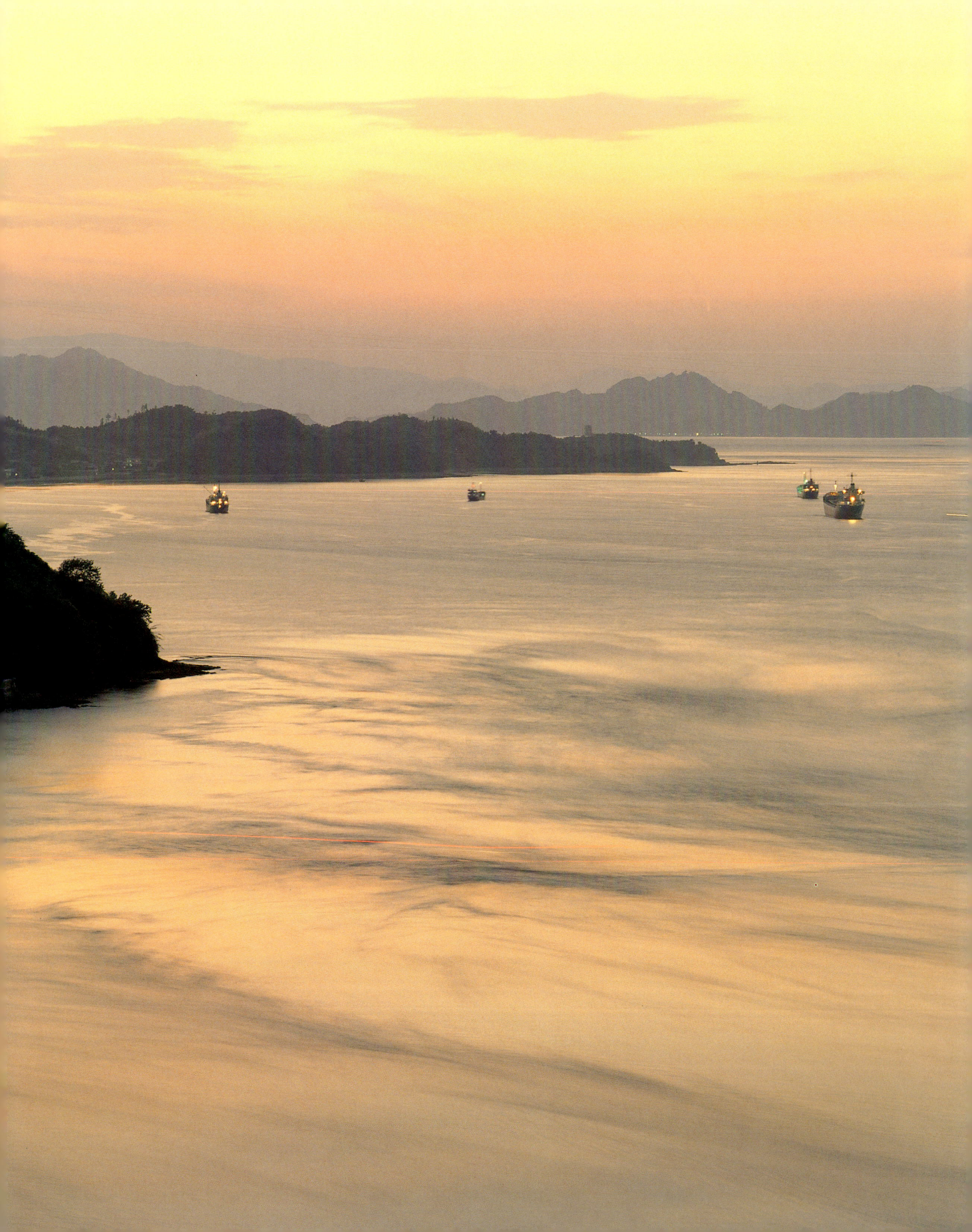

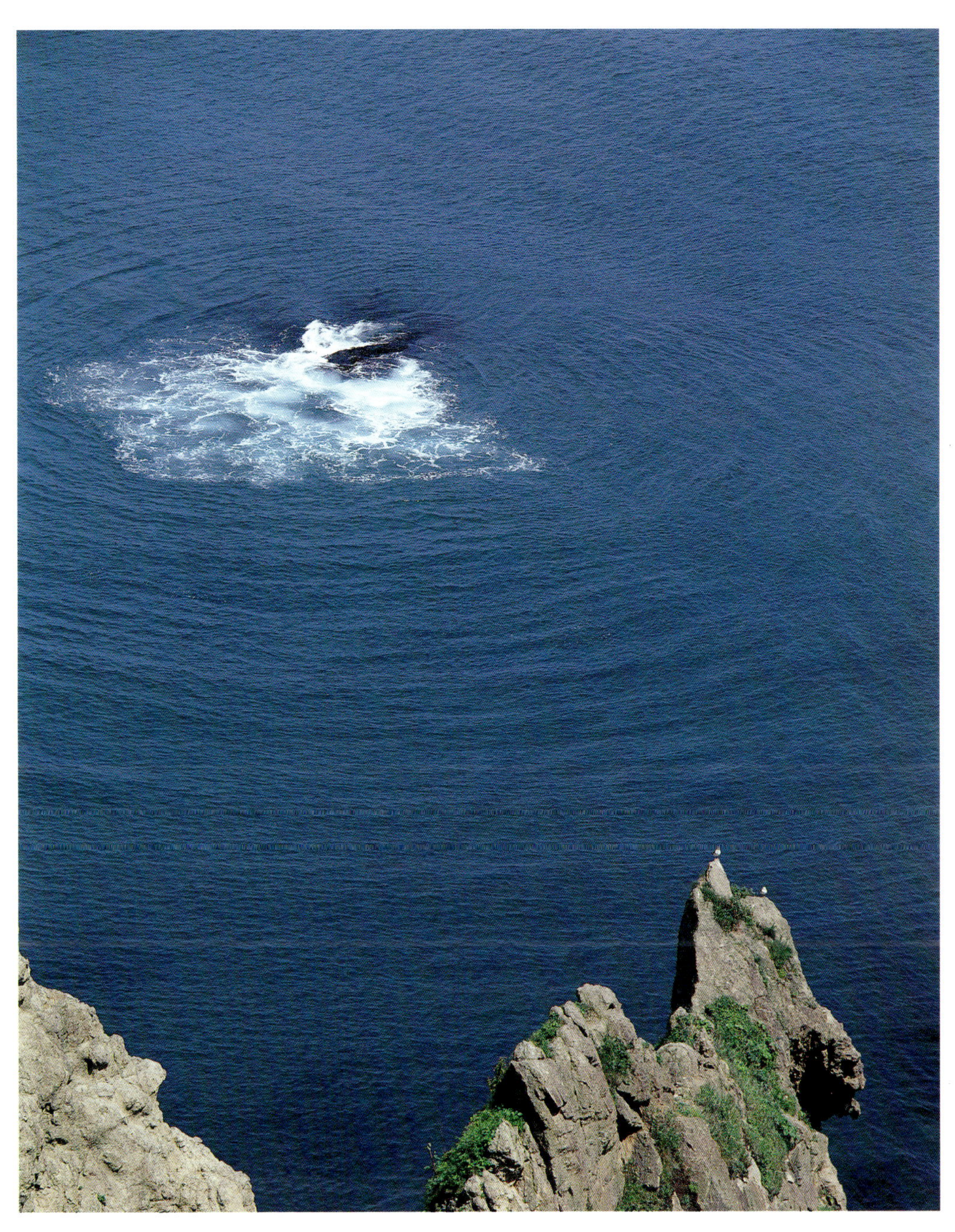

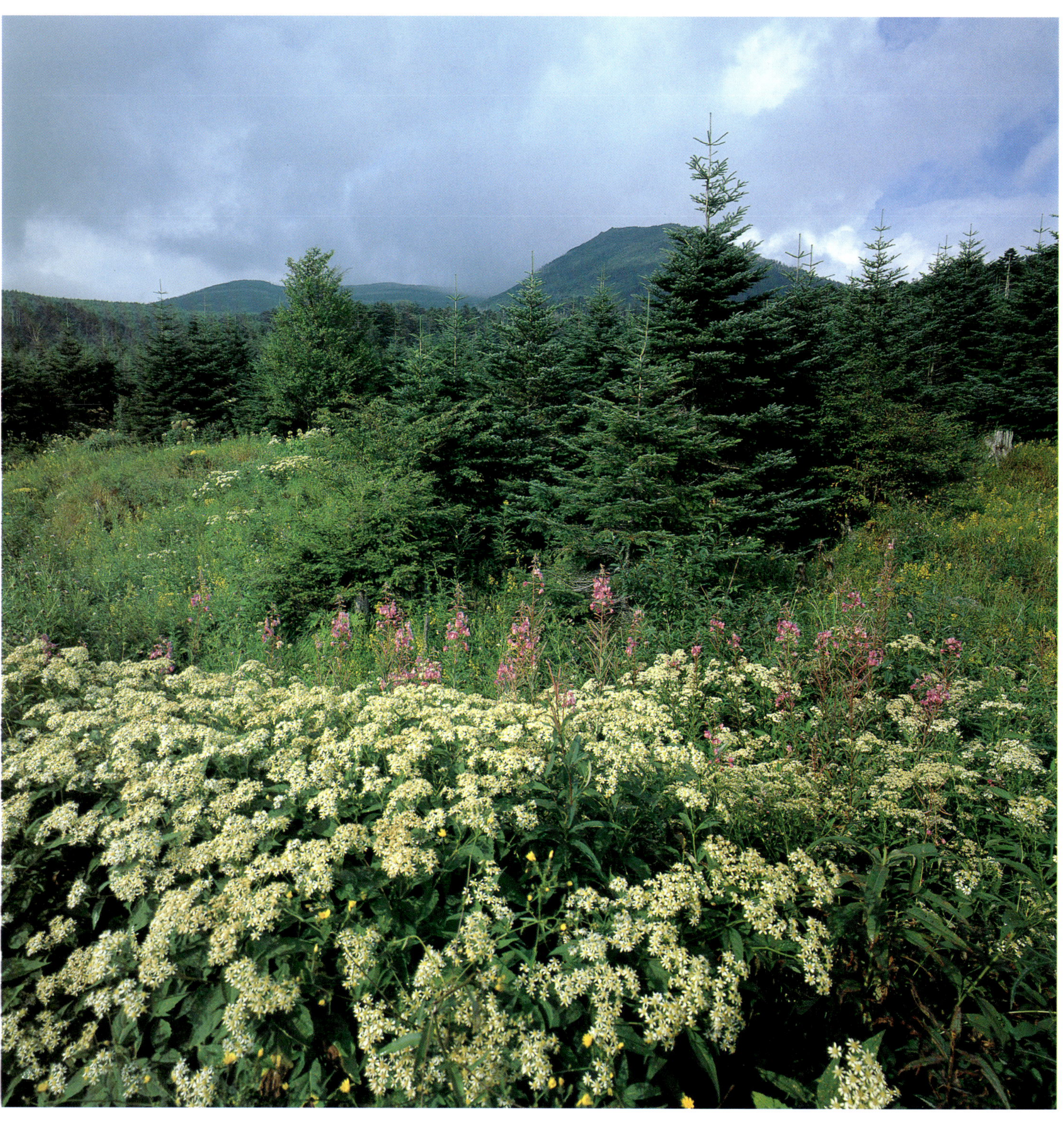

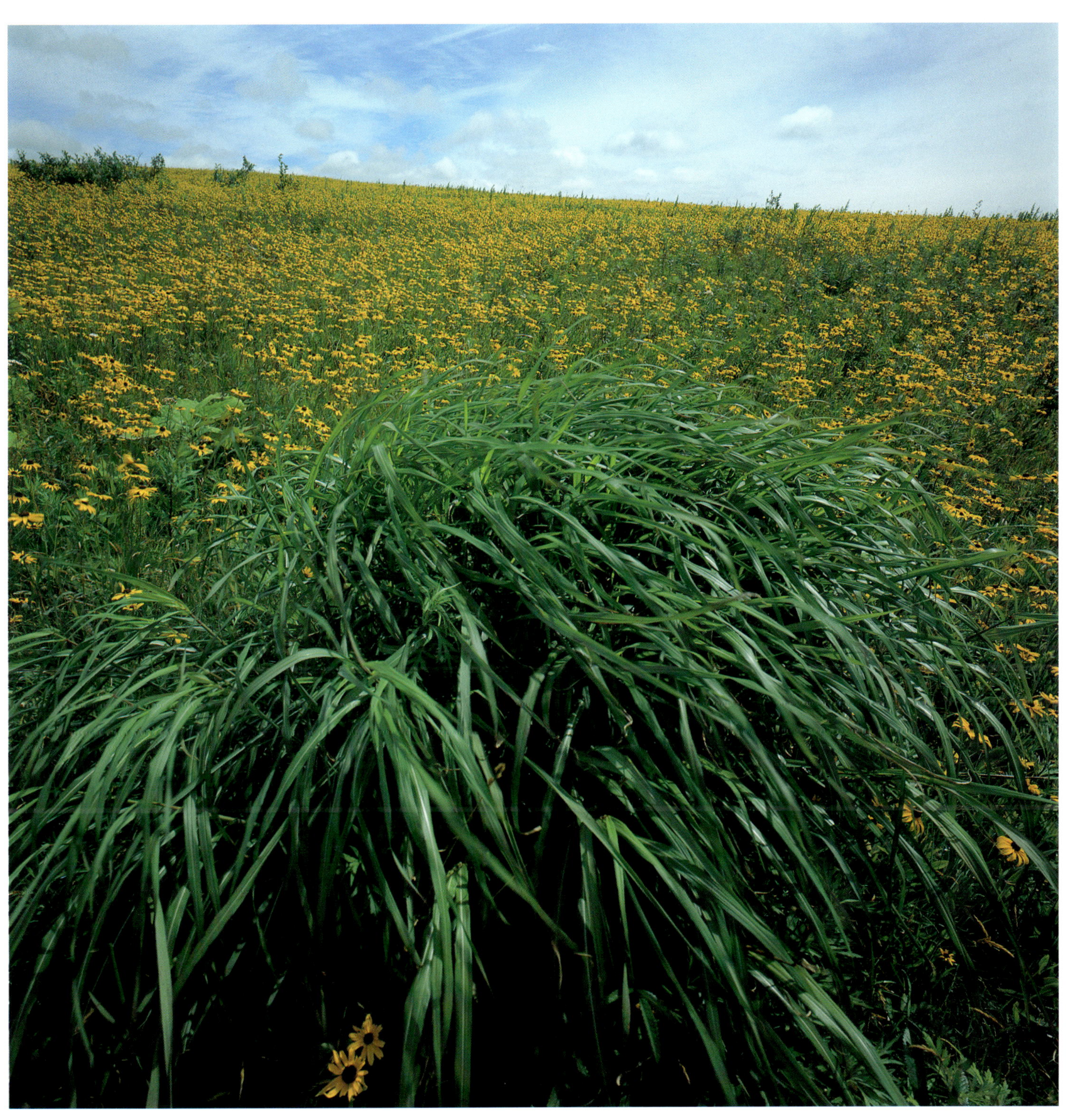

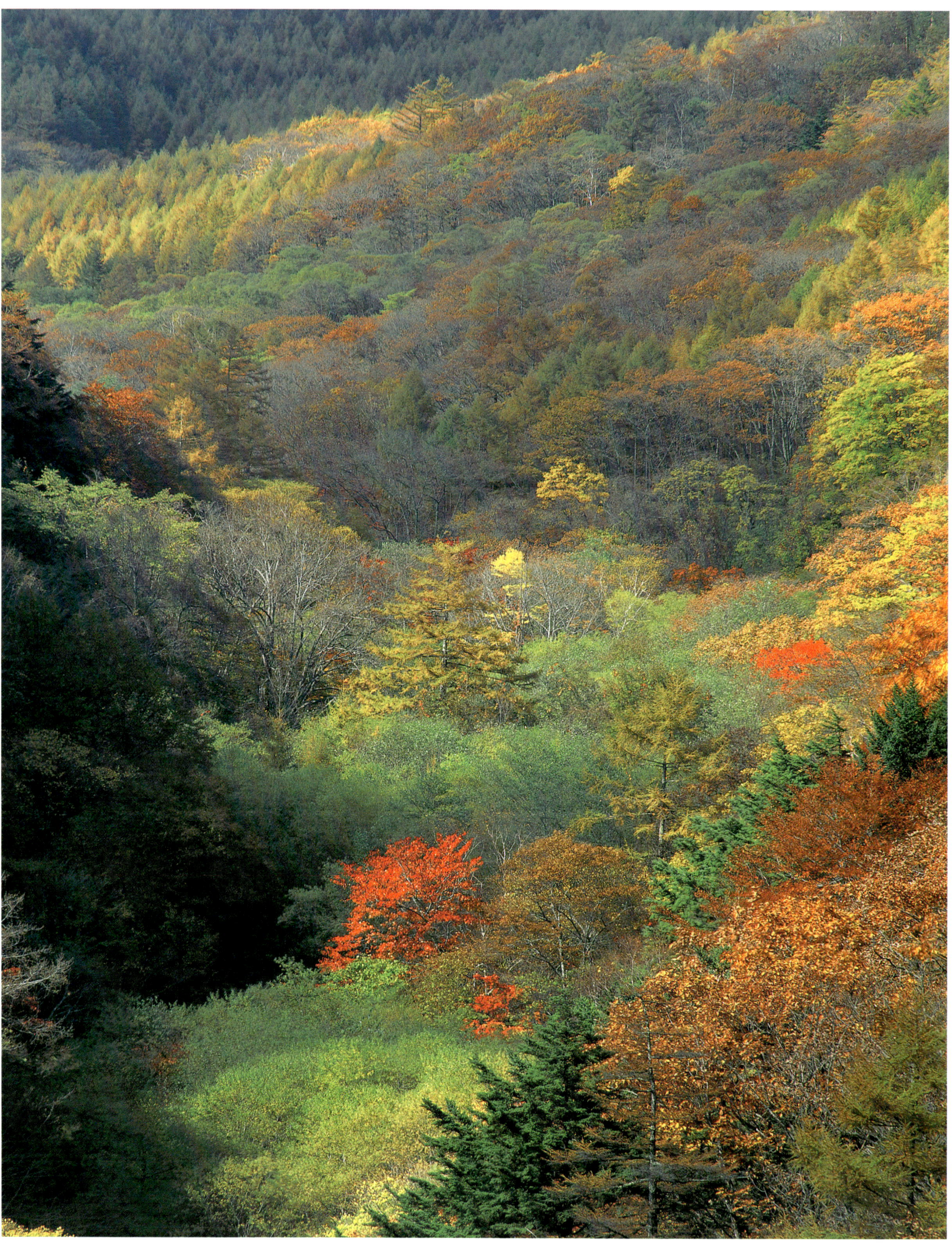

Now that the chill
of autumn evenings grows,
the cricket—does it
weaken? The little voice
is more and more remote.

SAIGYO

AUTUMN 秋

西行

きりぎりす　夜寒に秋の　成ままに
よはるか声の　遠ざかりゆく

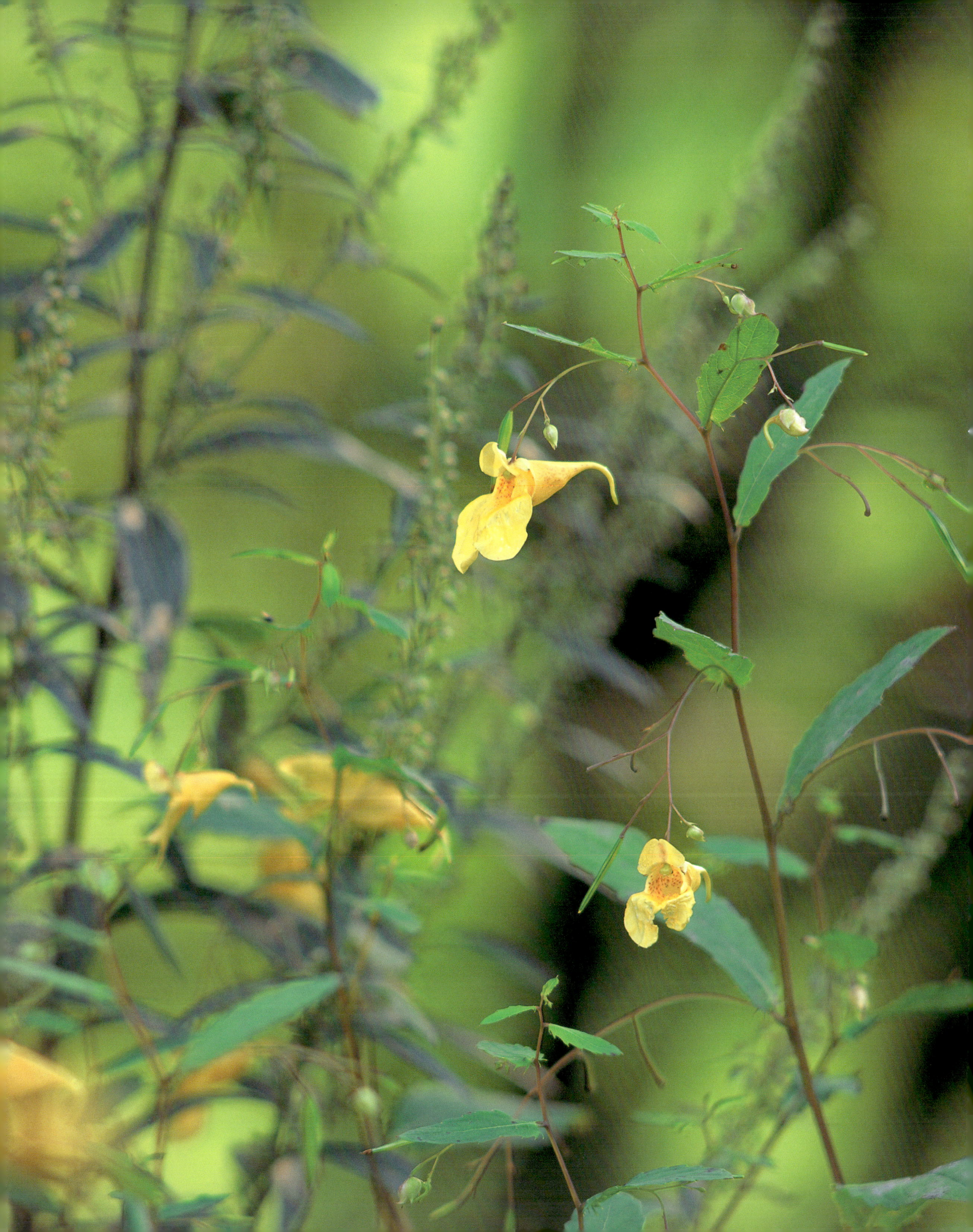

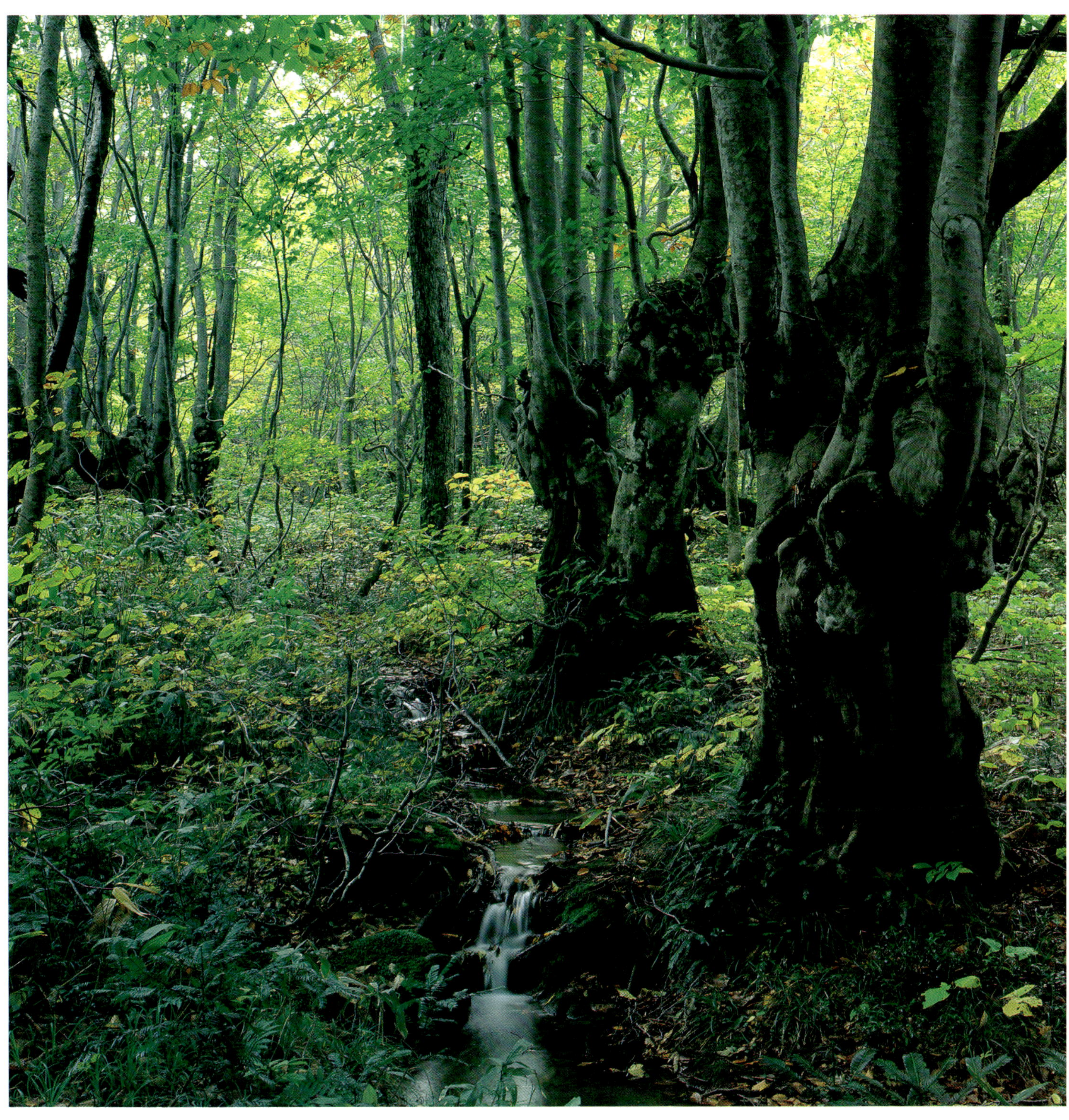

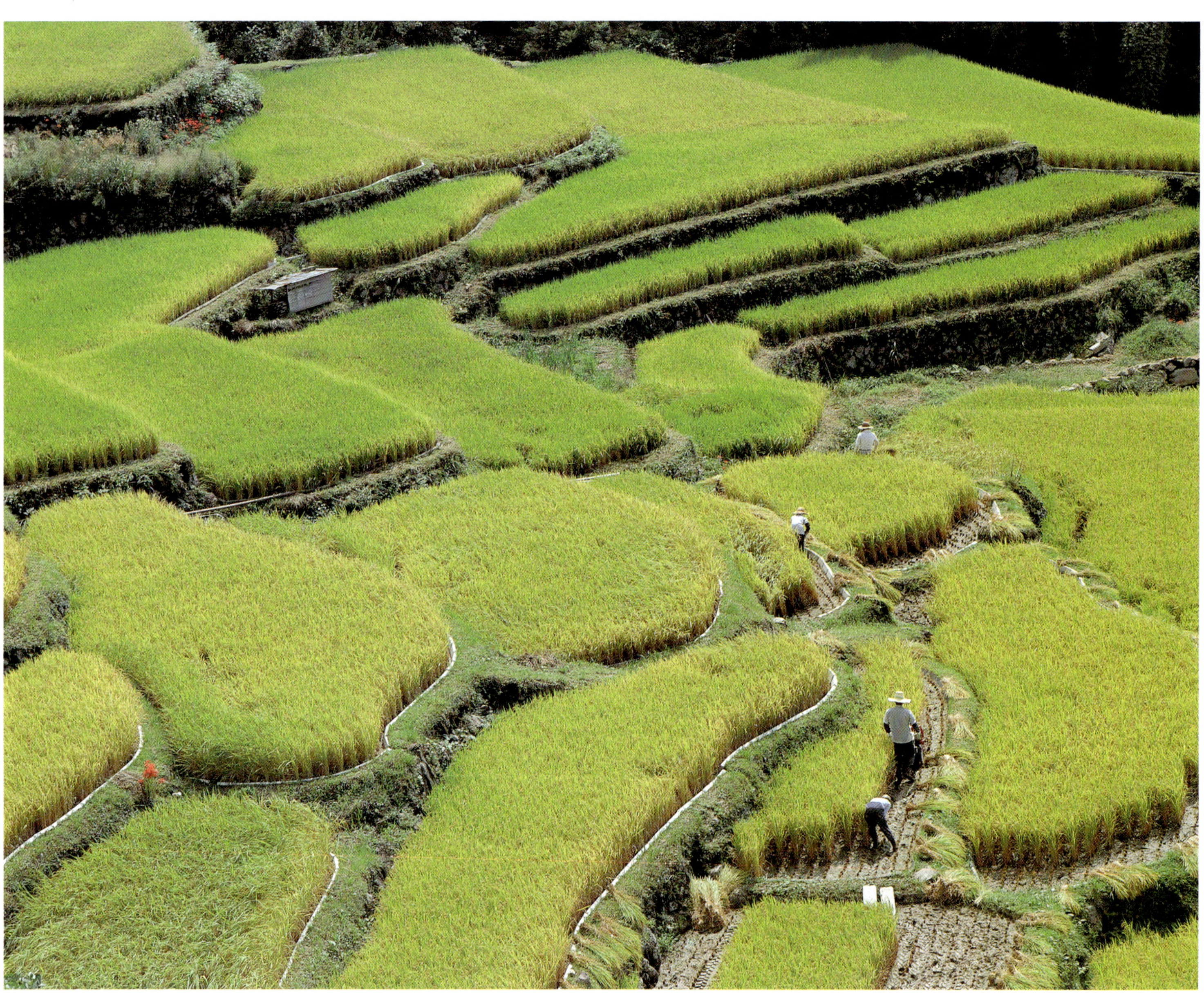

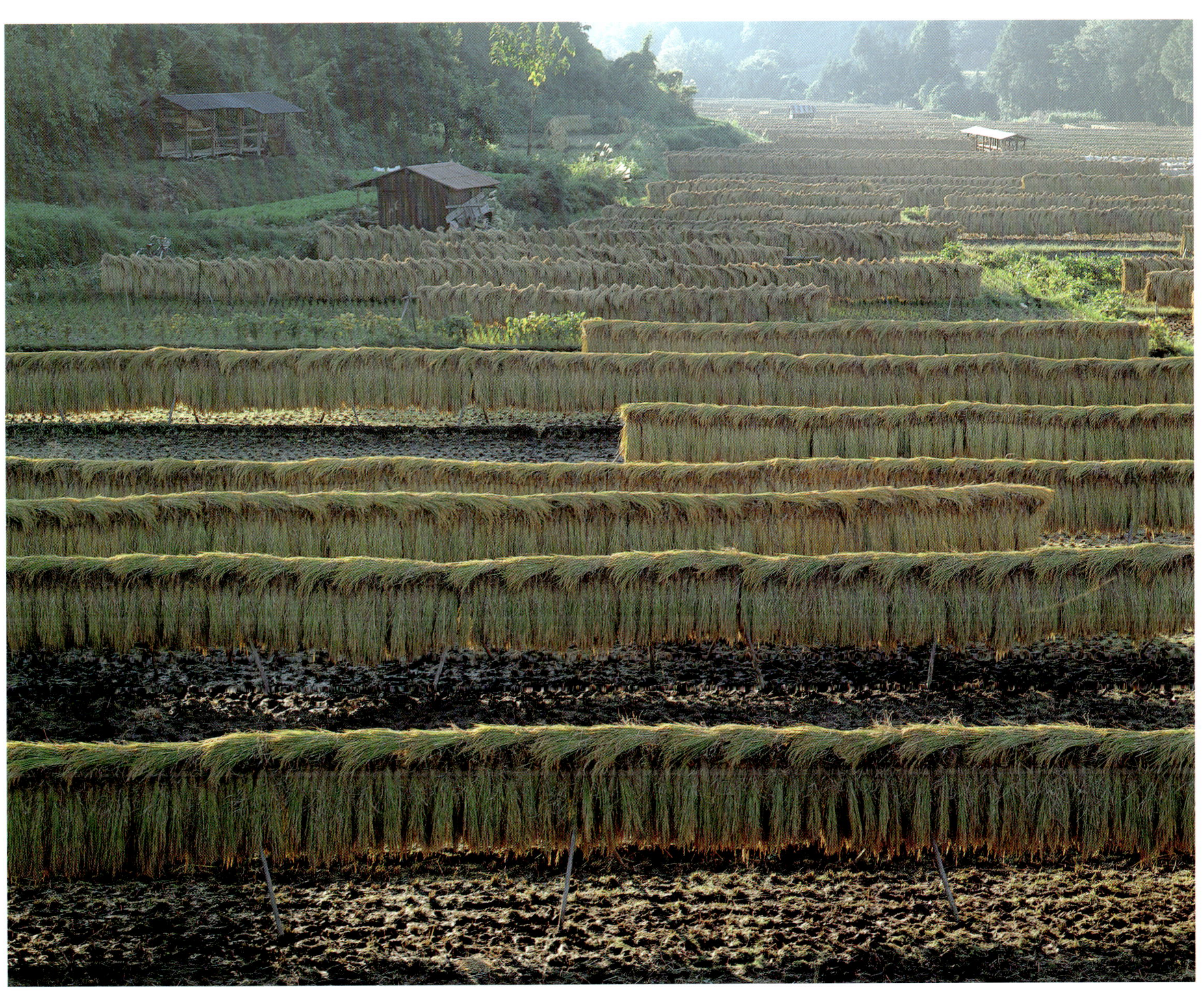

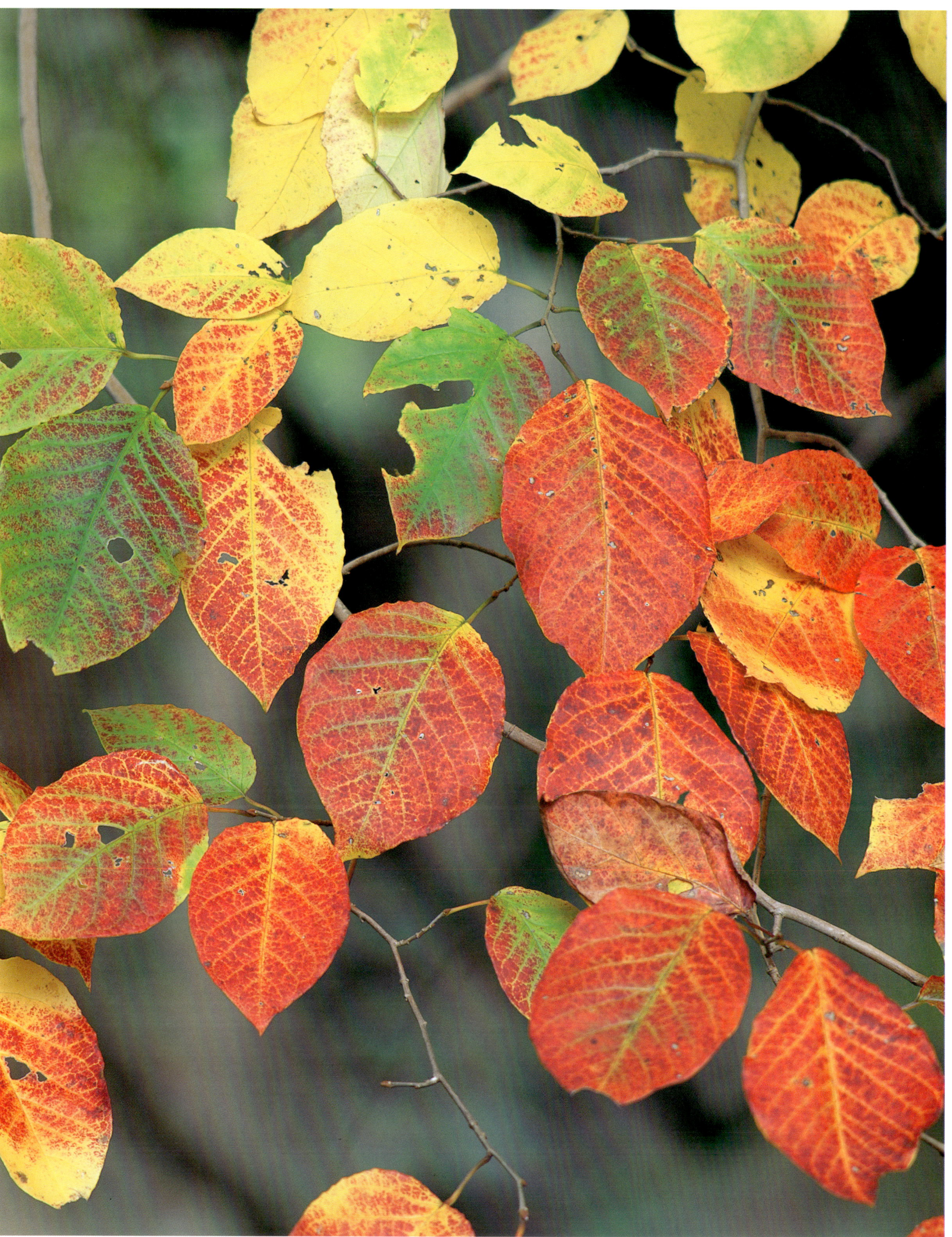

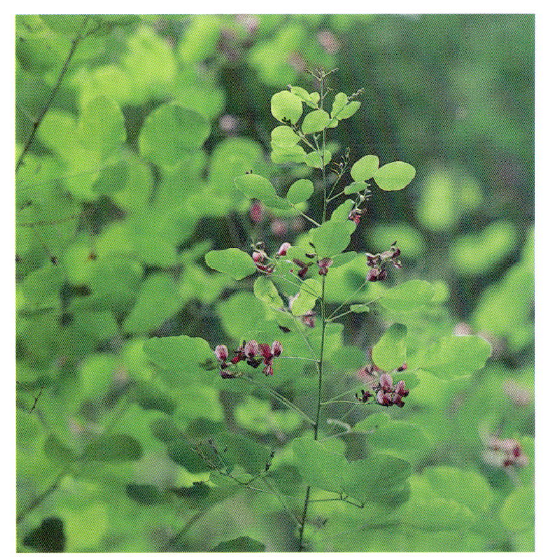

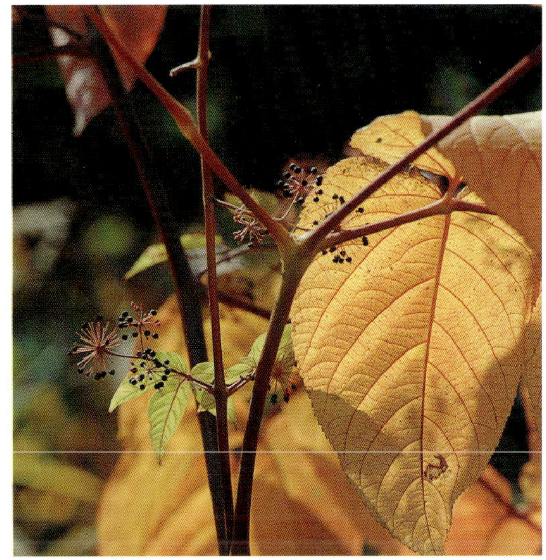

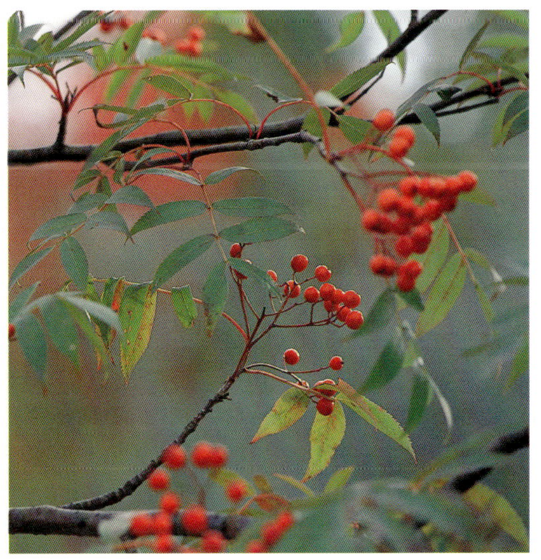

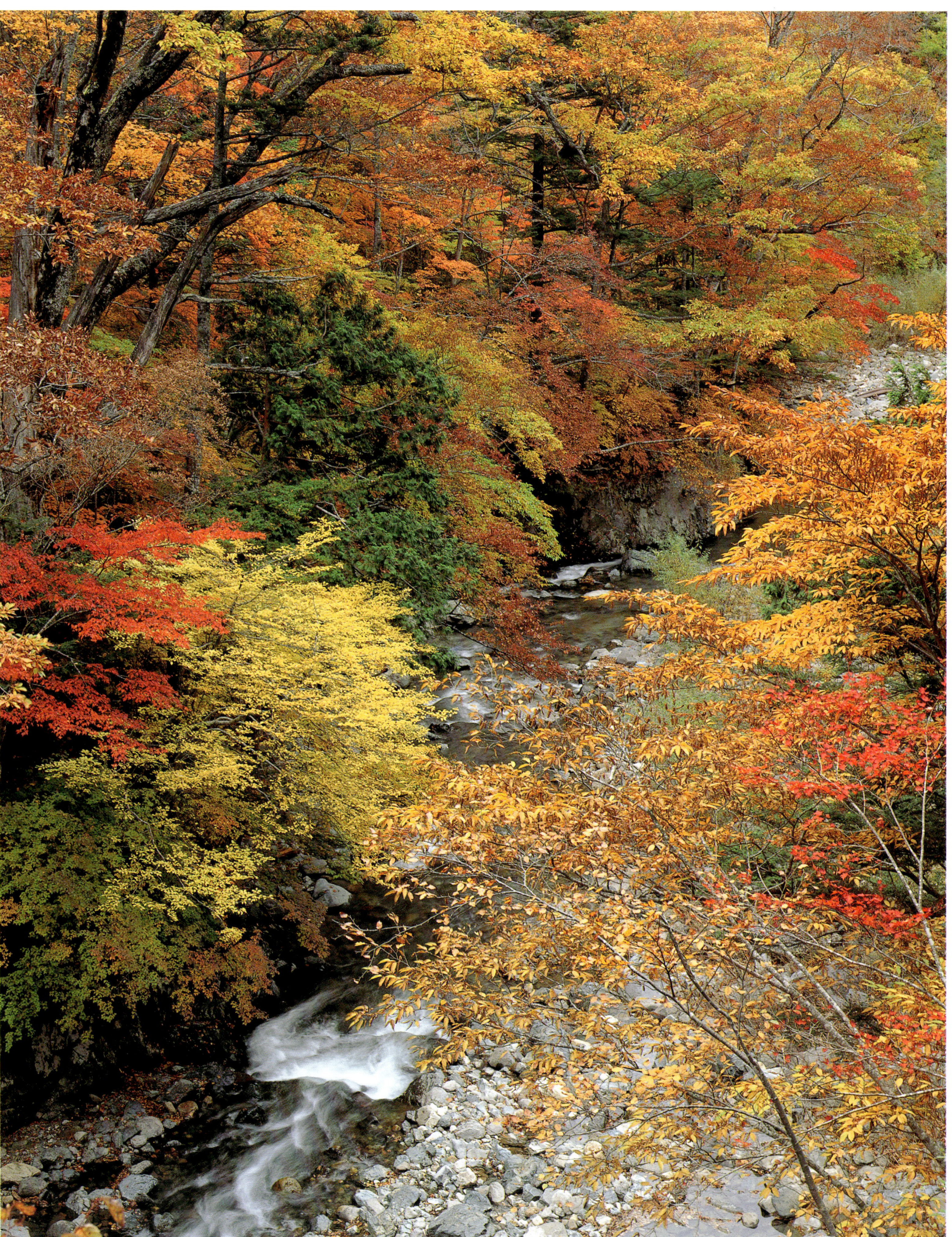

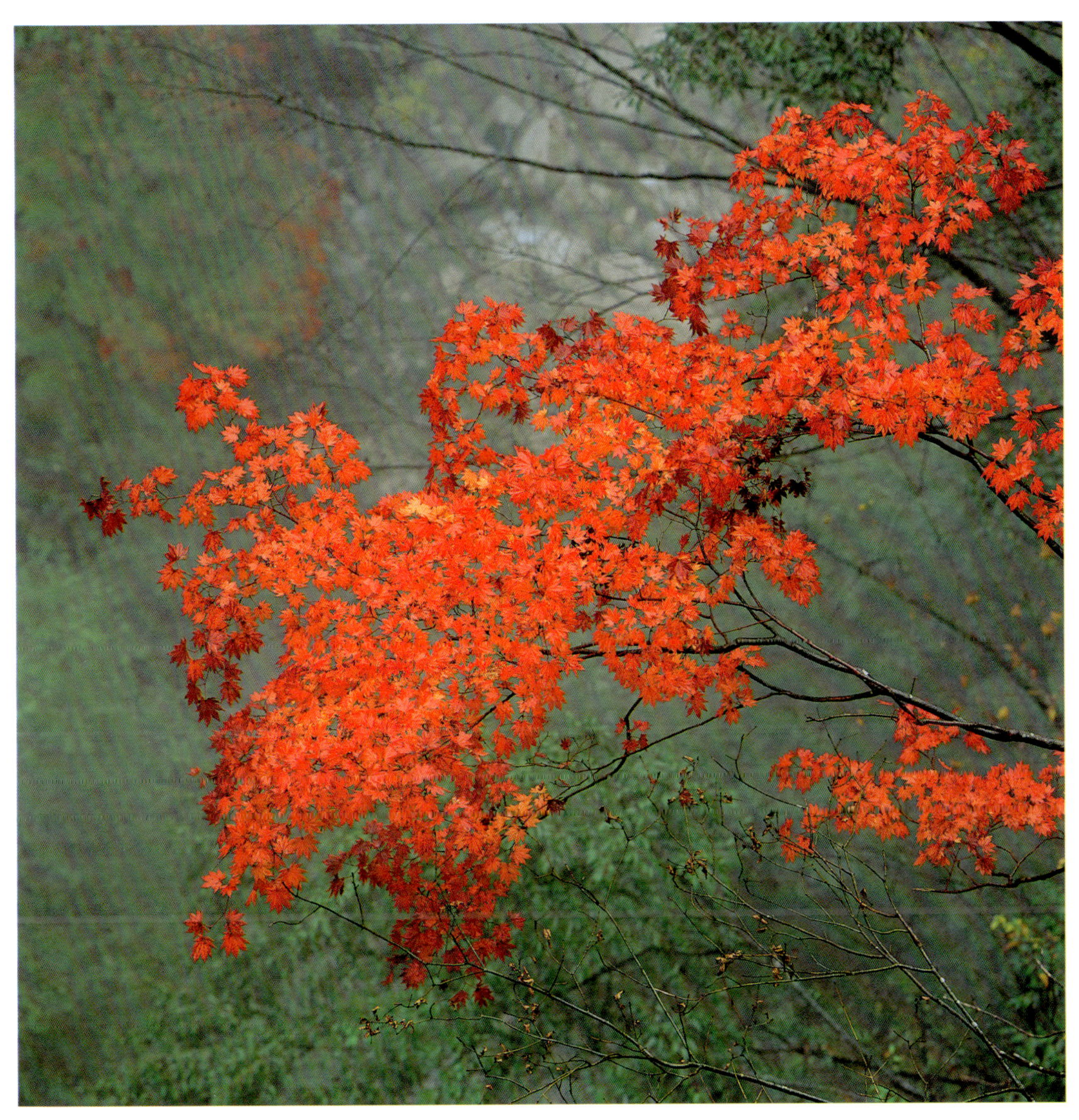

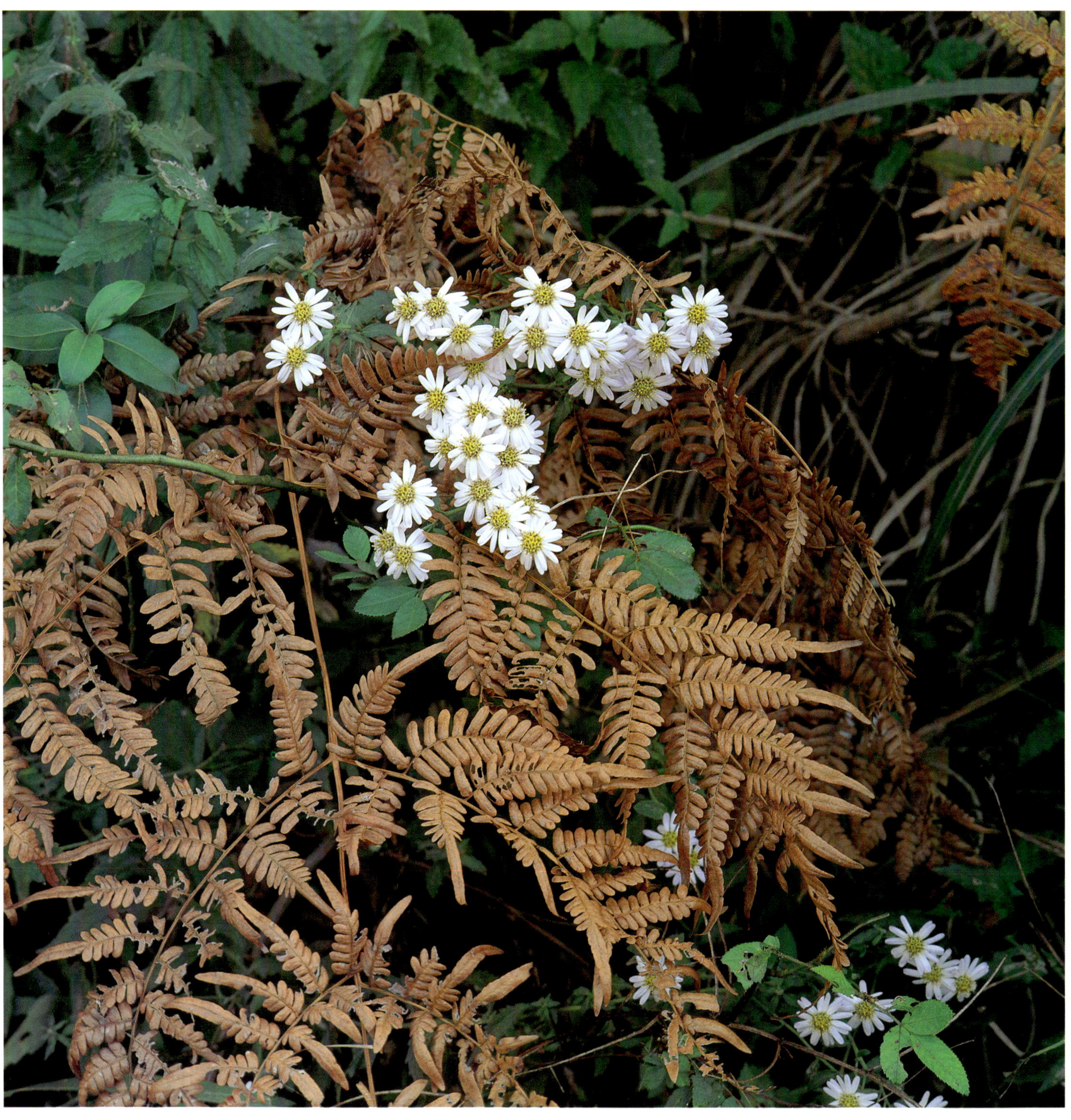

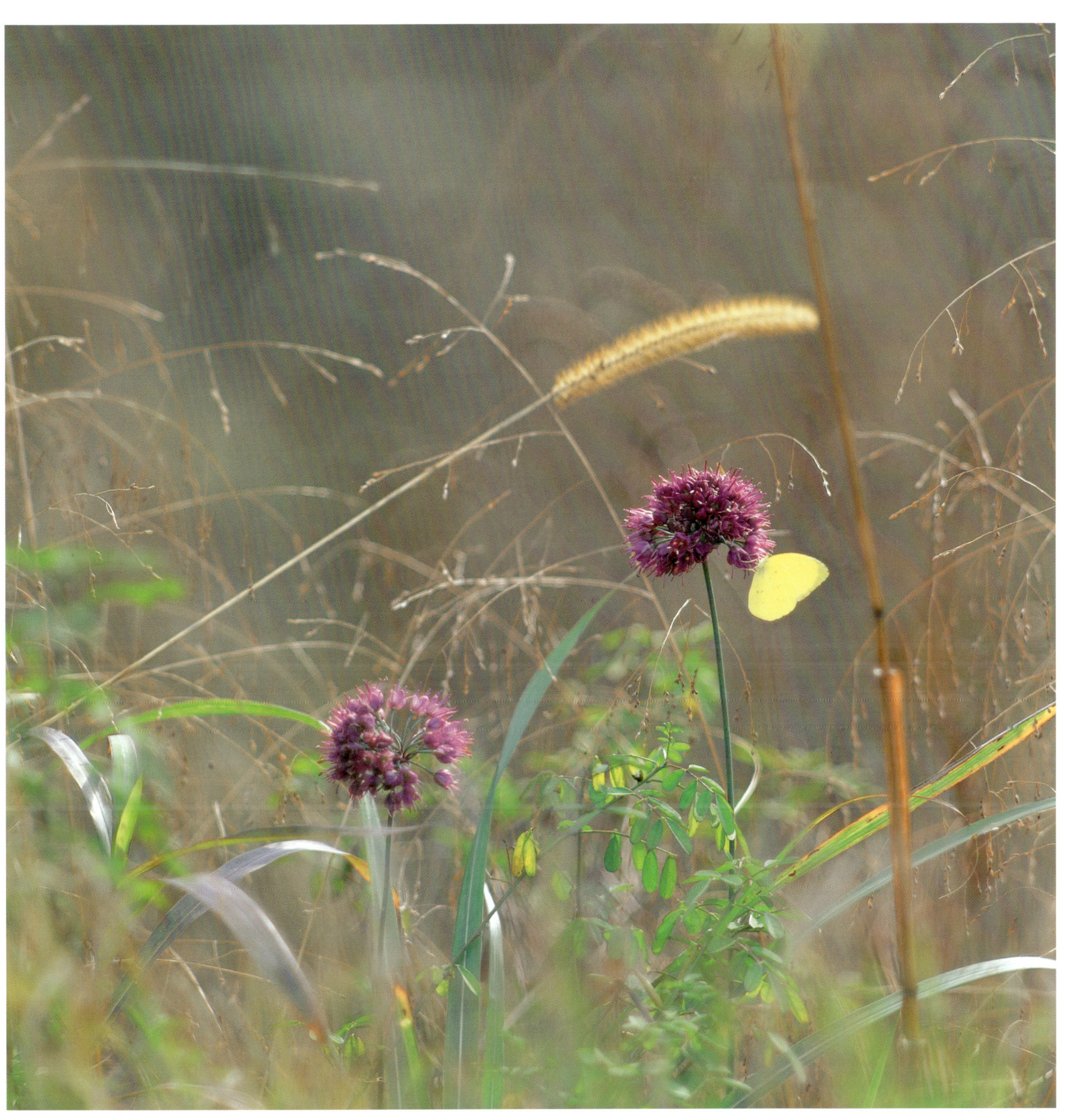

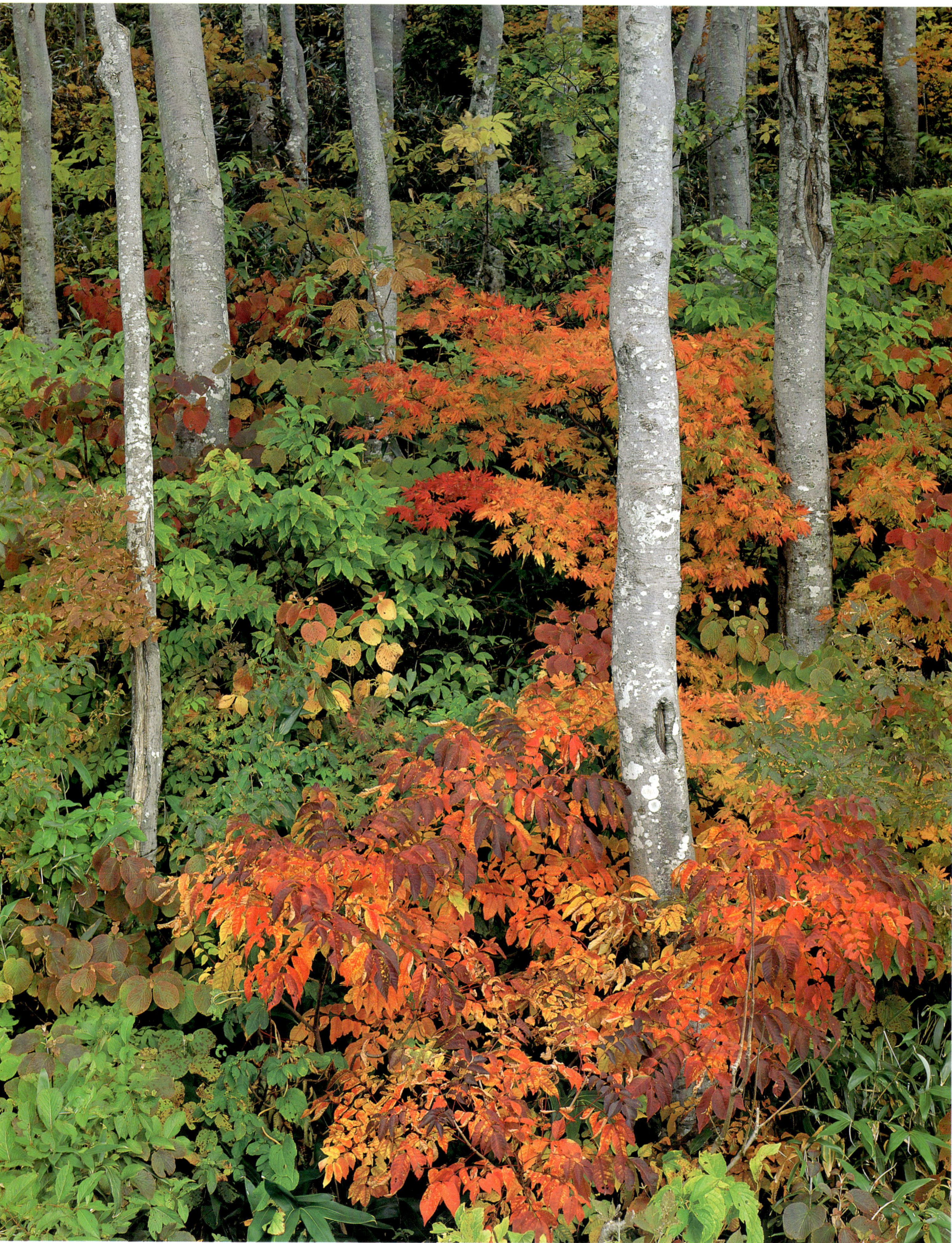

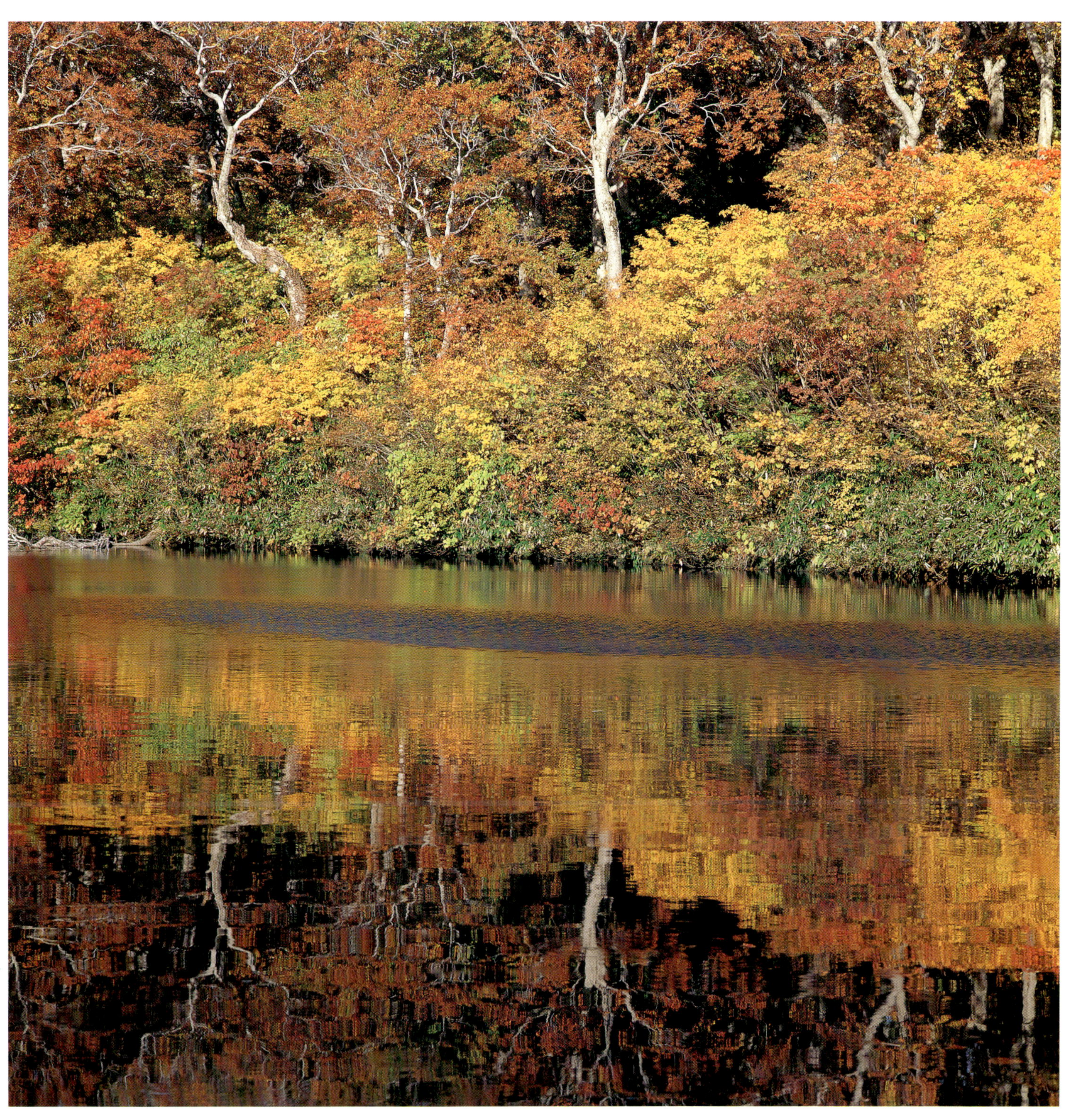

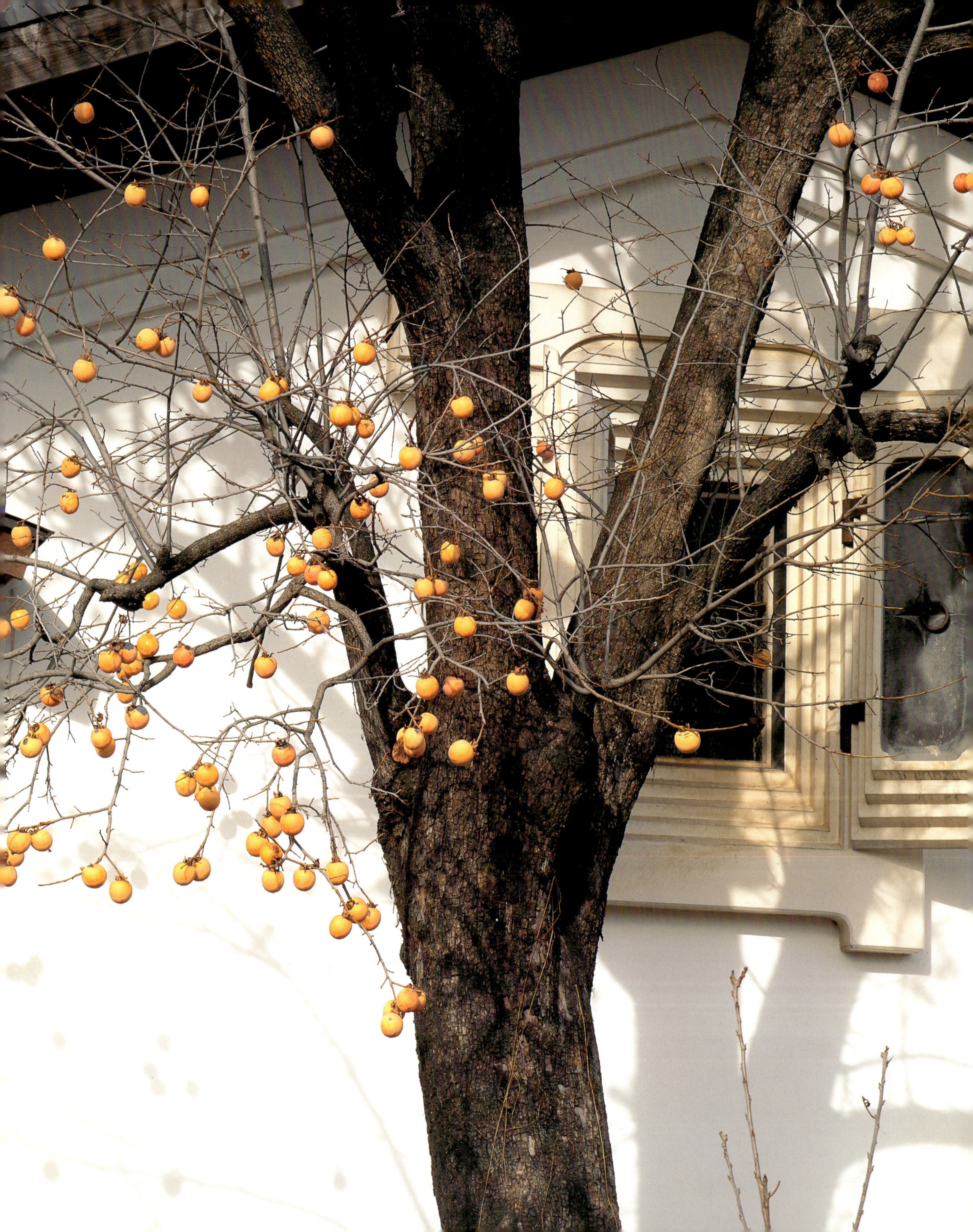

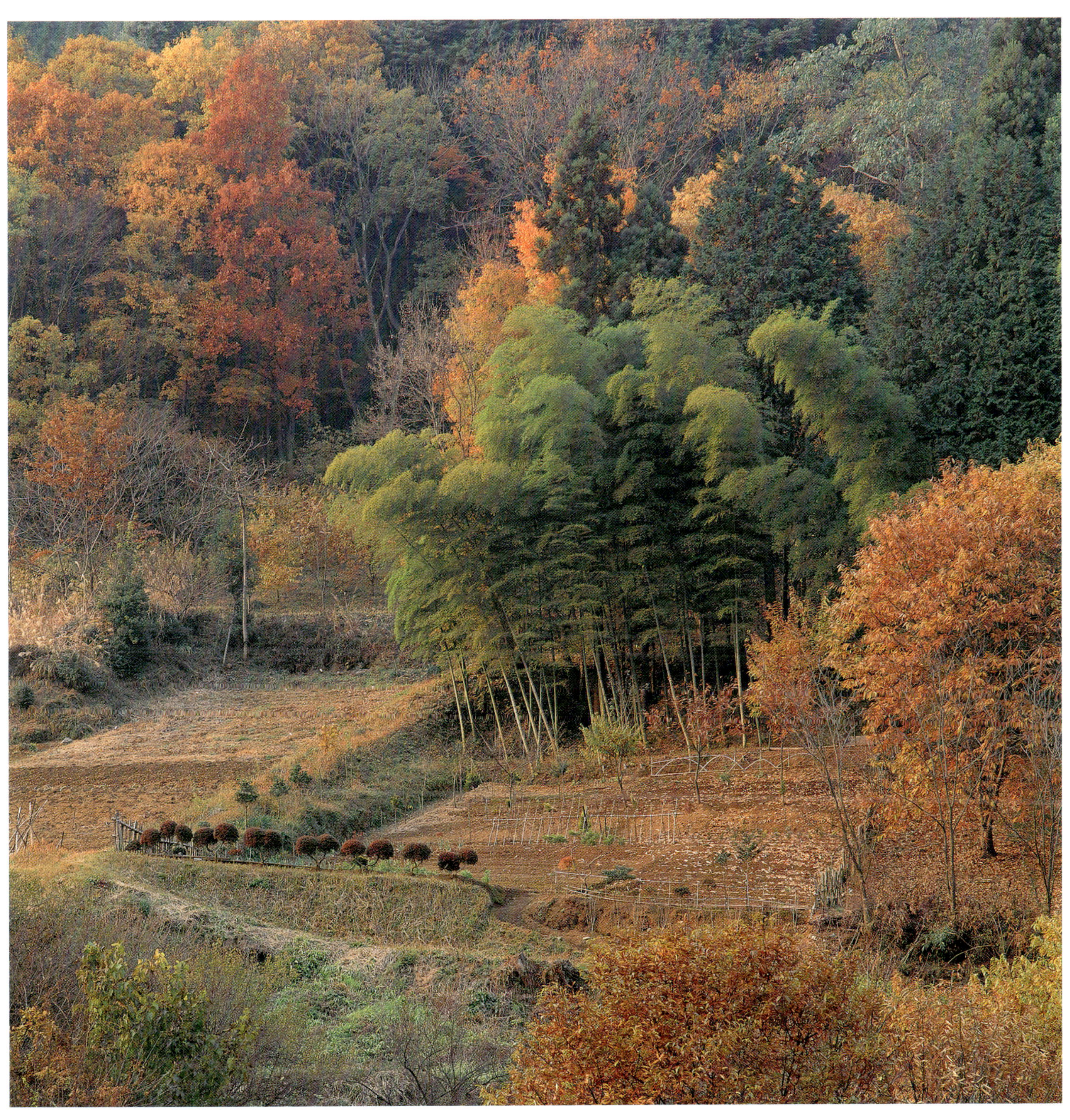

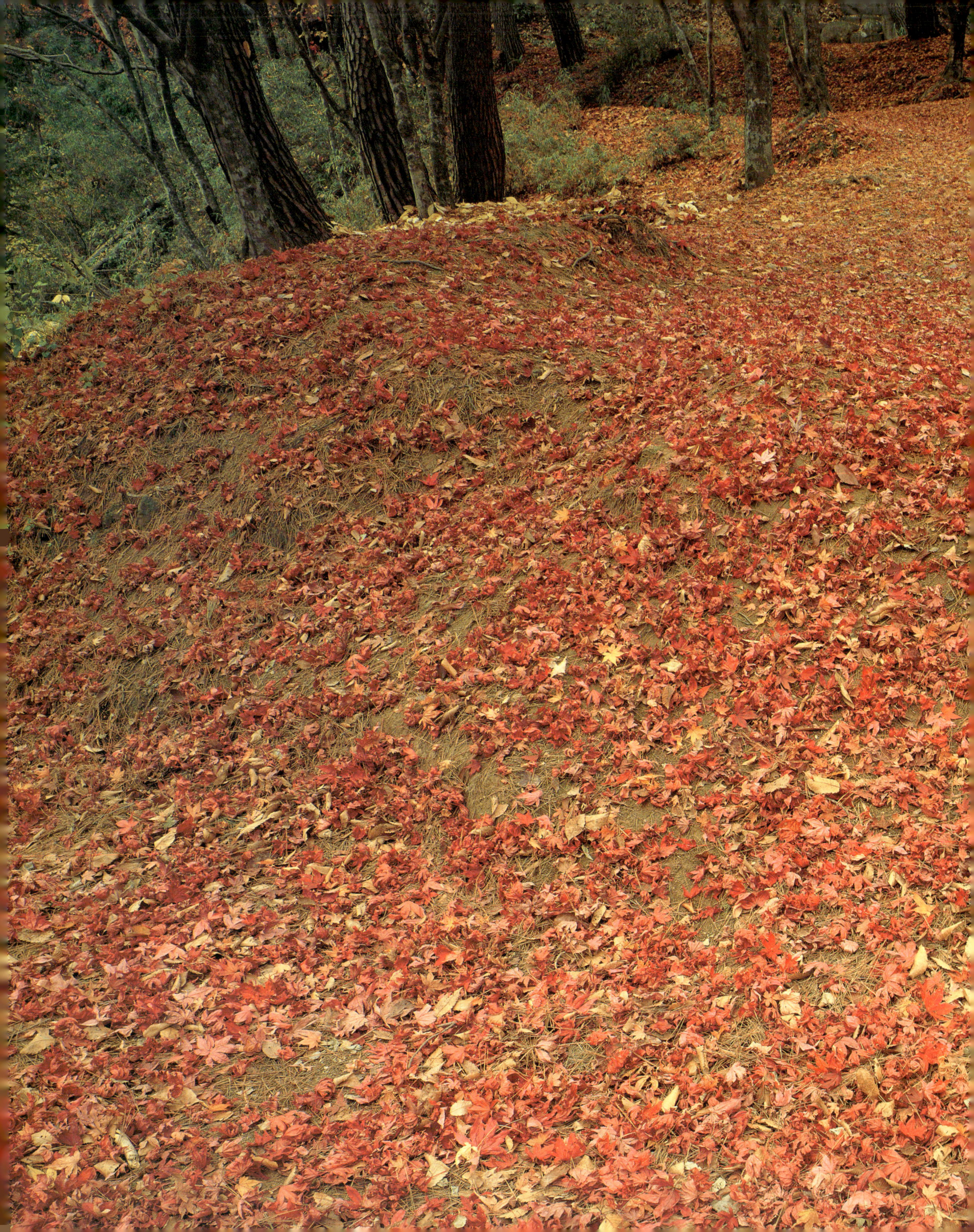

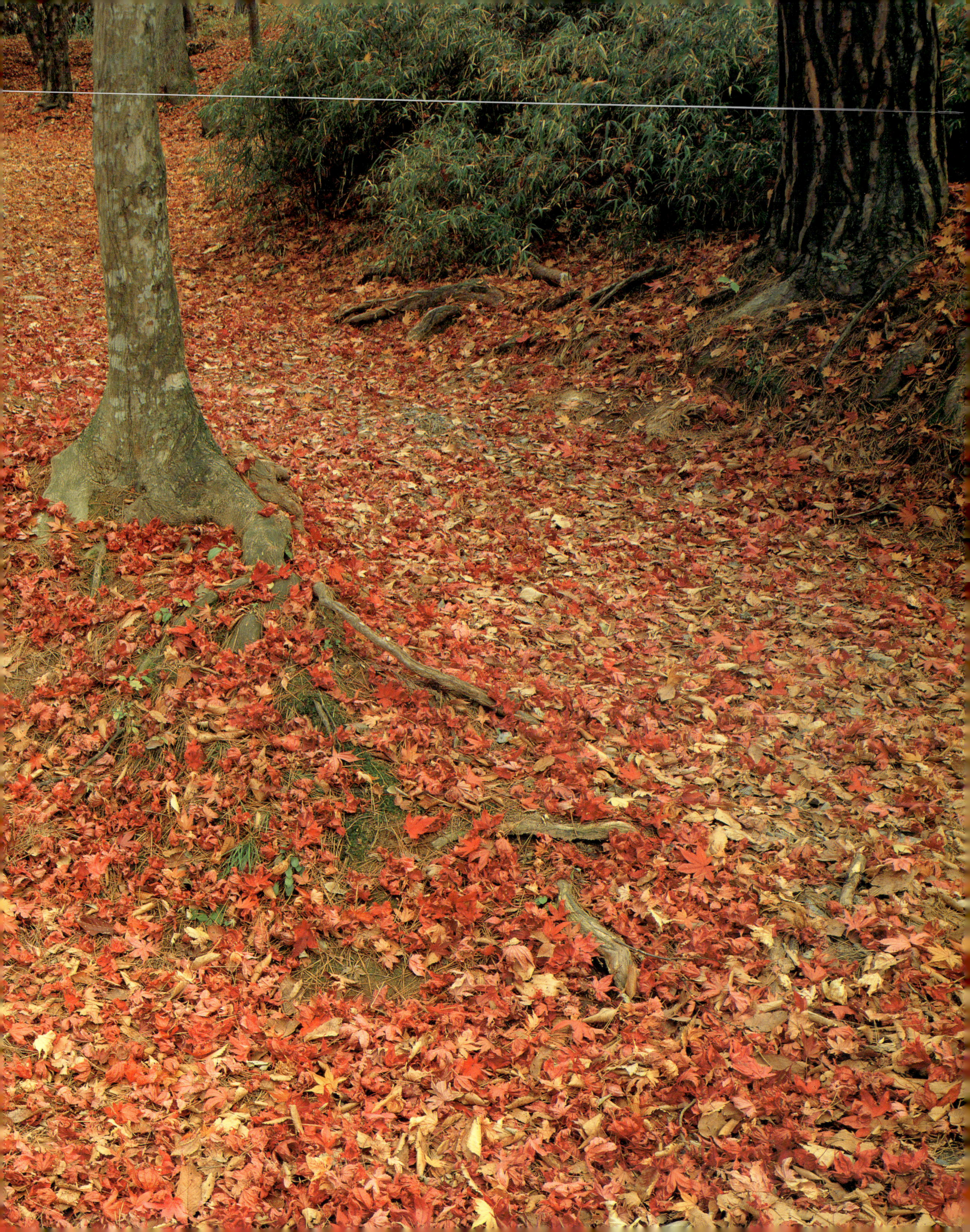

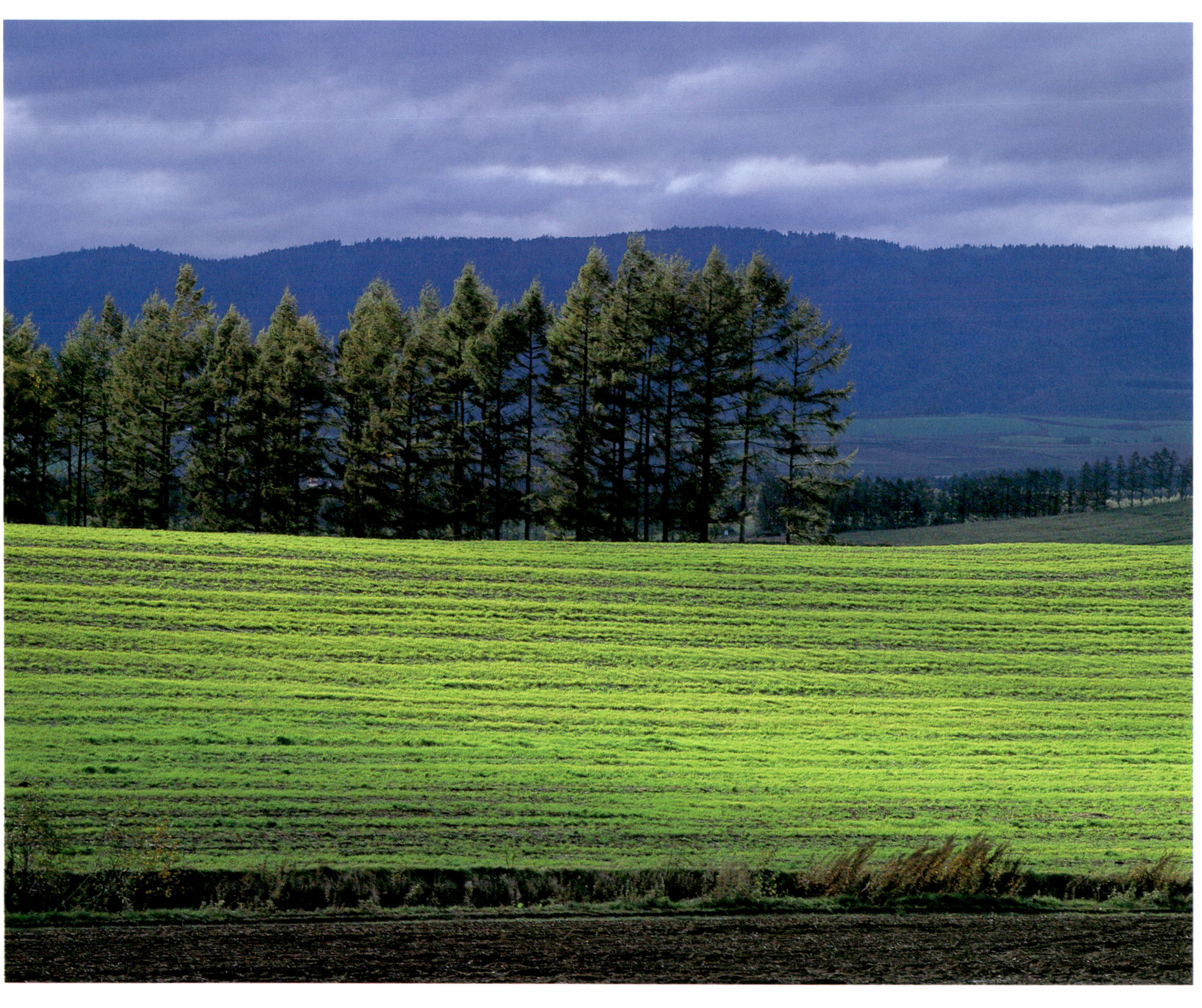

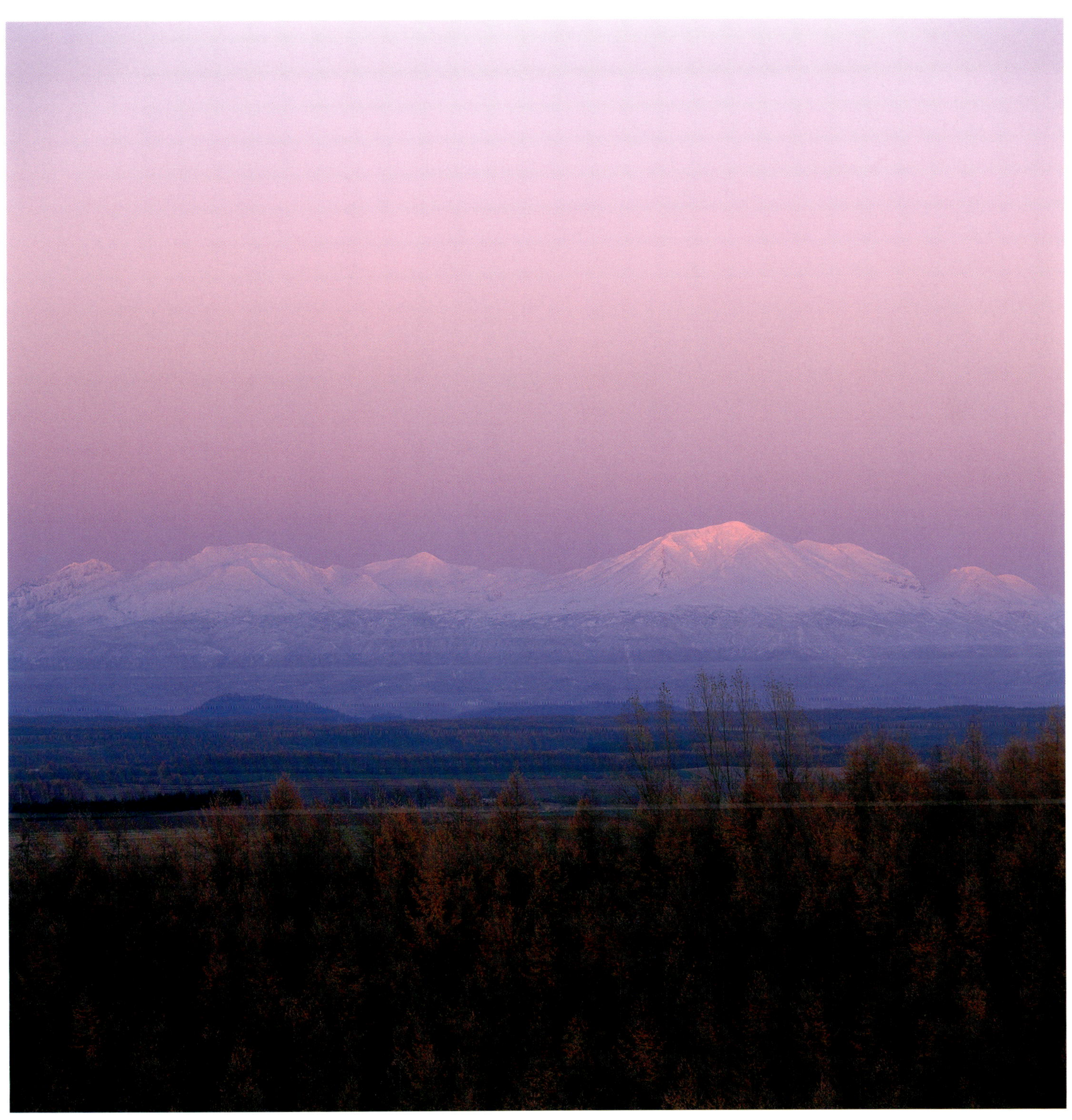

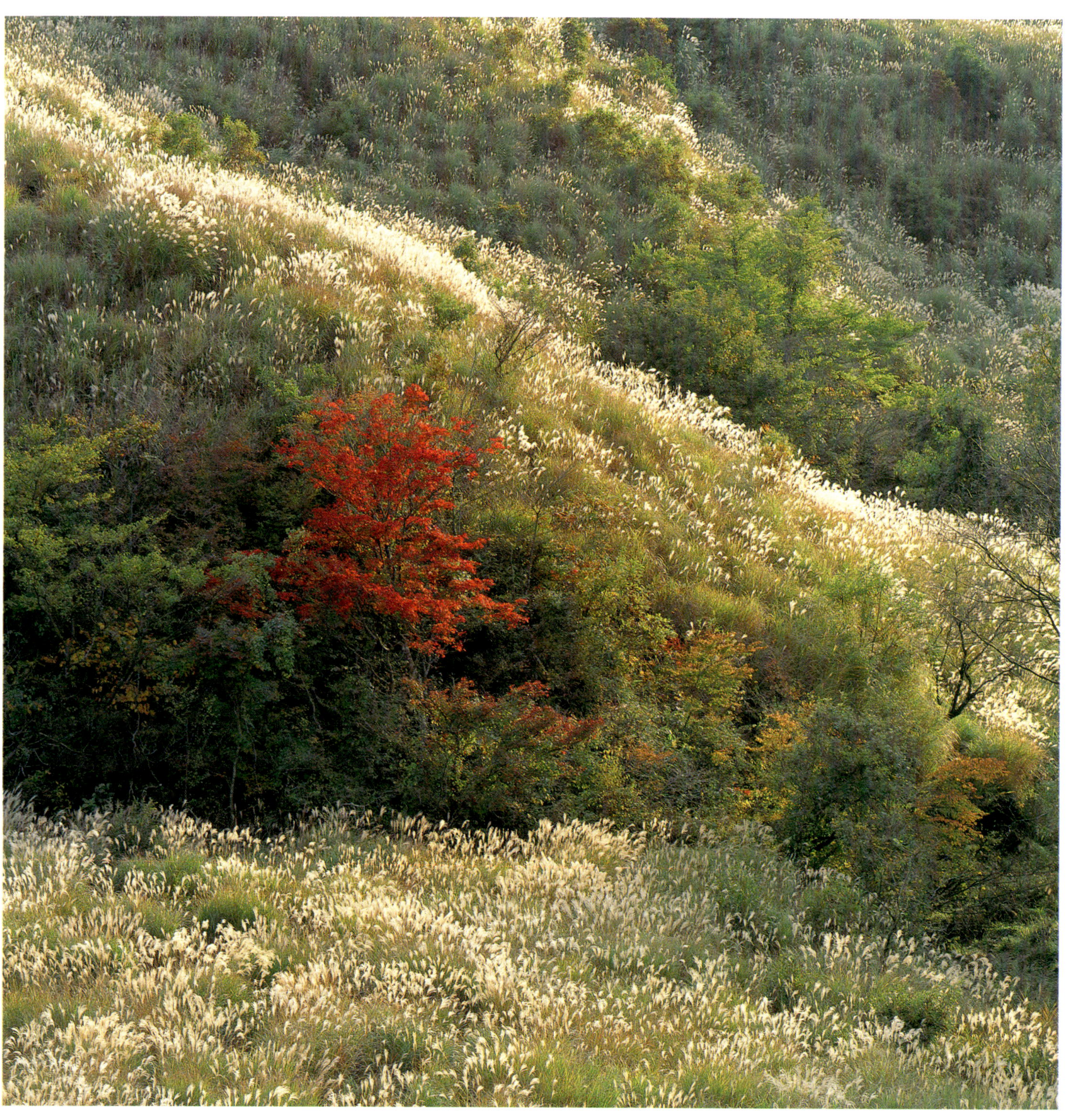

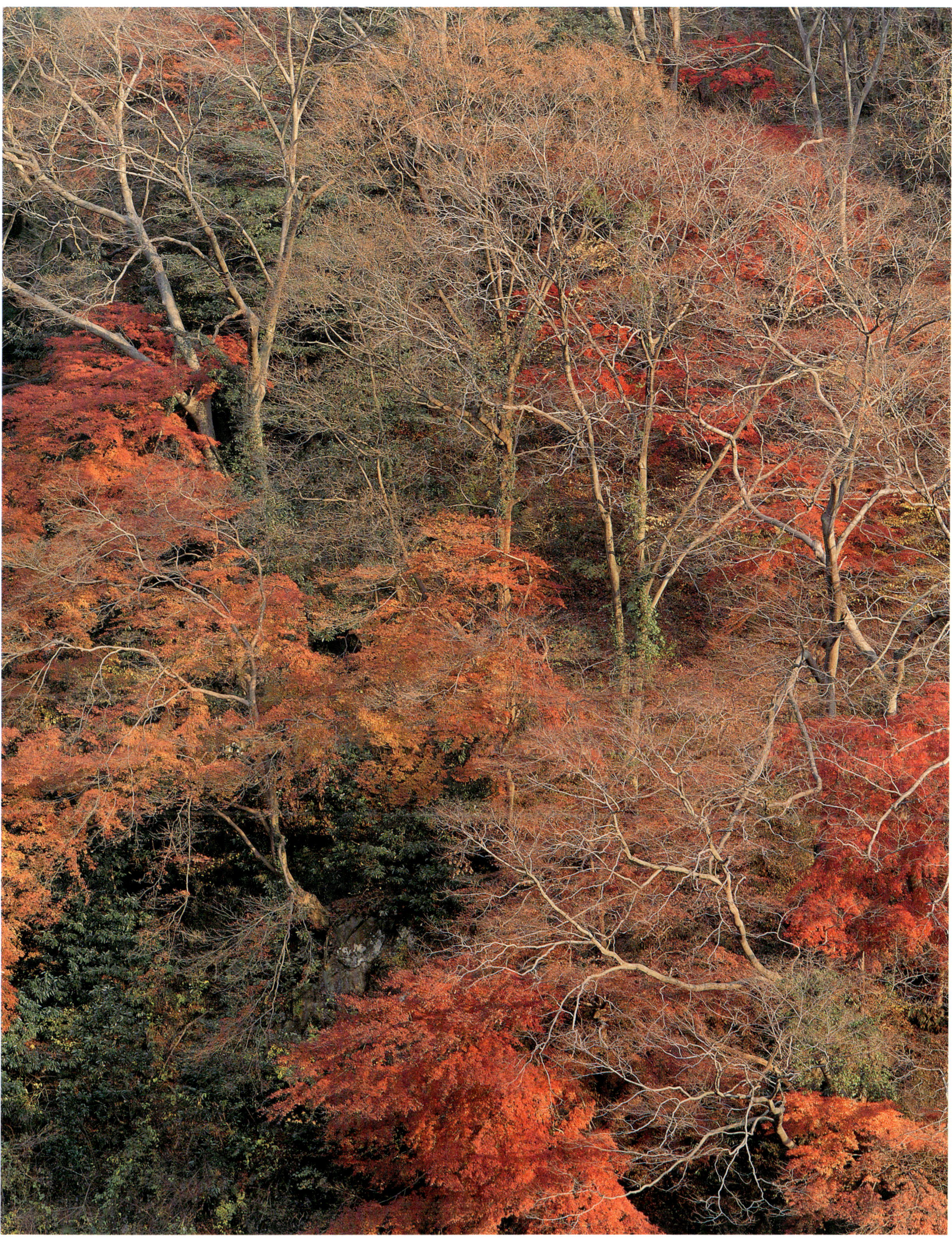

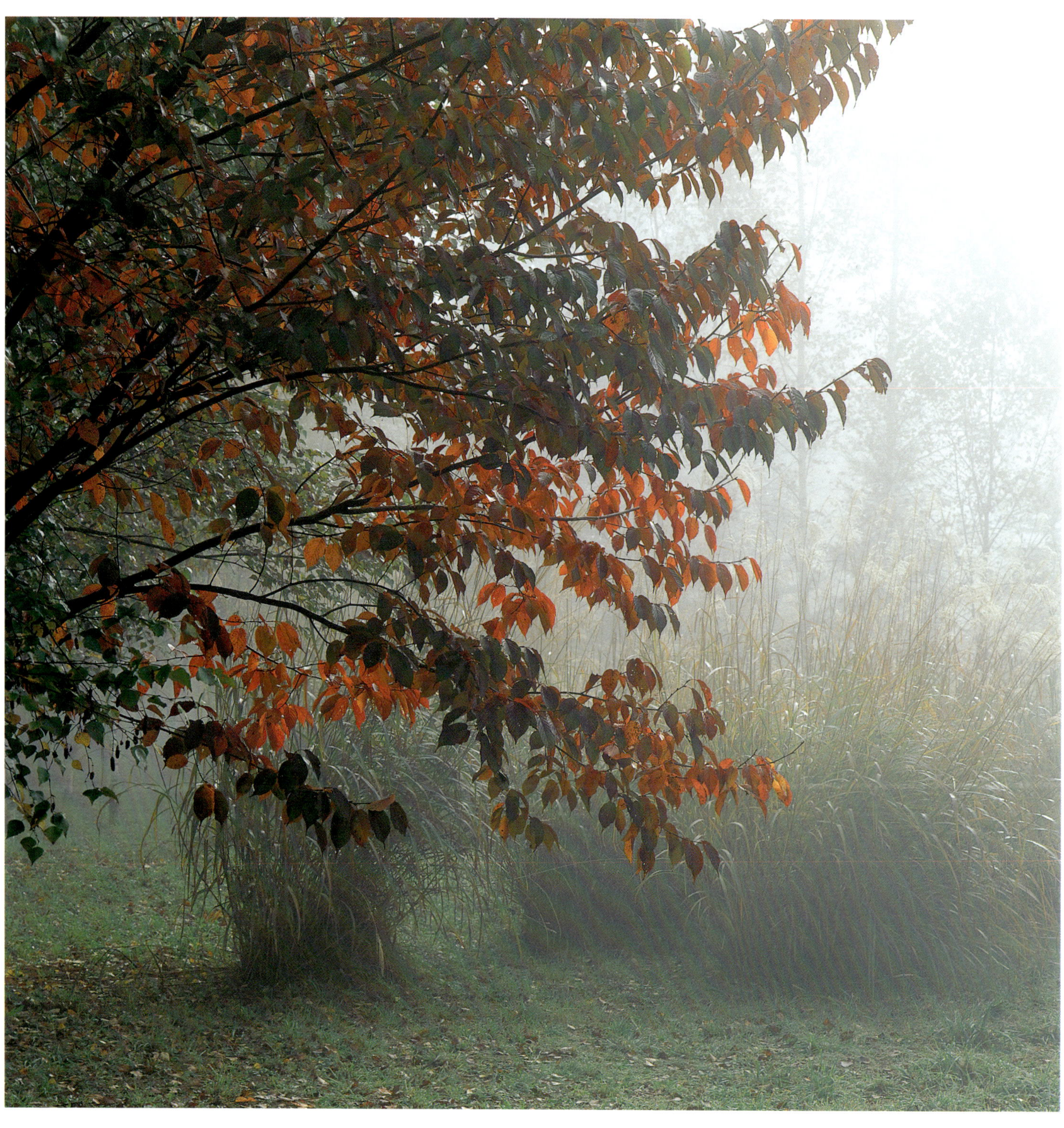

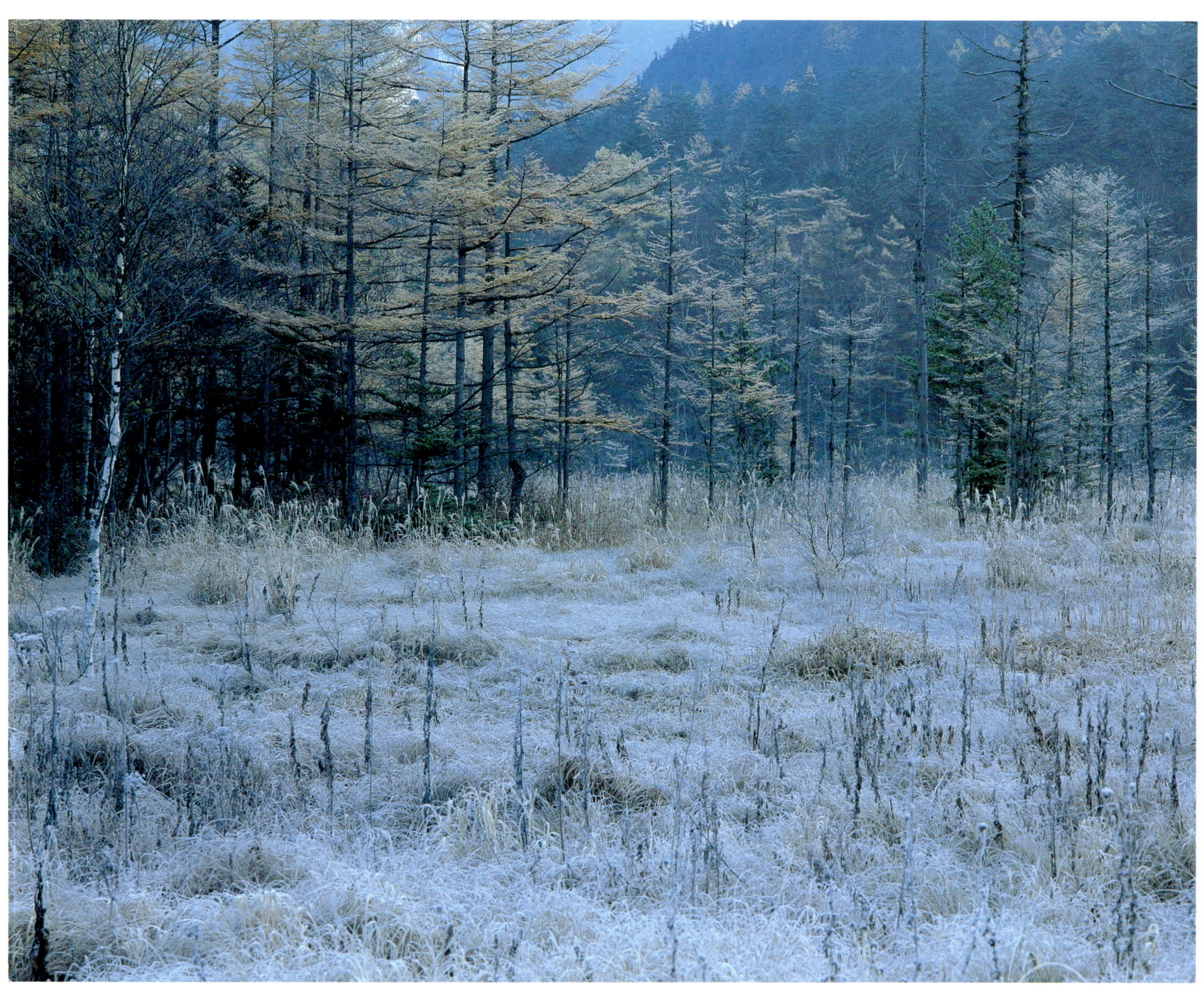

The axe bites
and odour shocks the sense:
the grove in winter.

YOSA BUSON

WINTER 冬

斧入れて
香に驚くや
冬木立

与謝蕪村

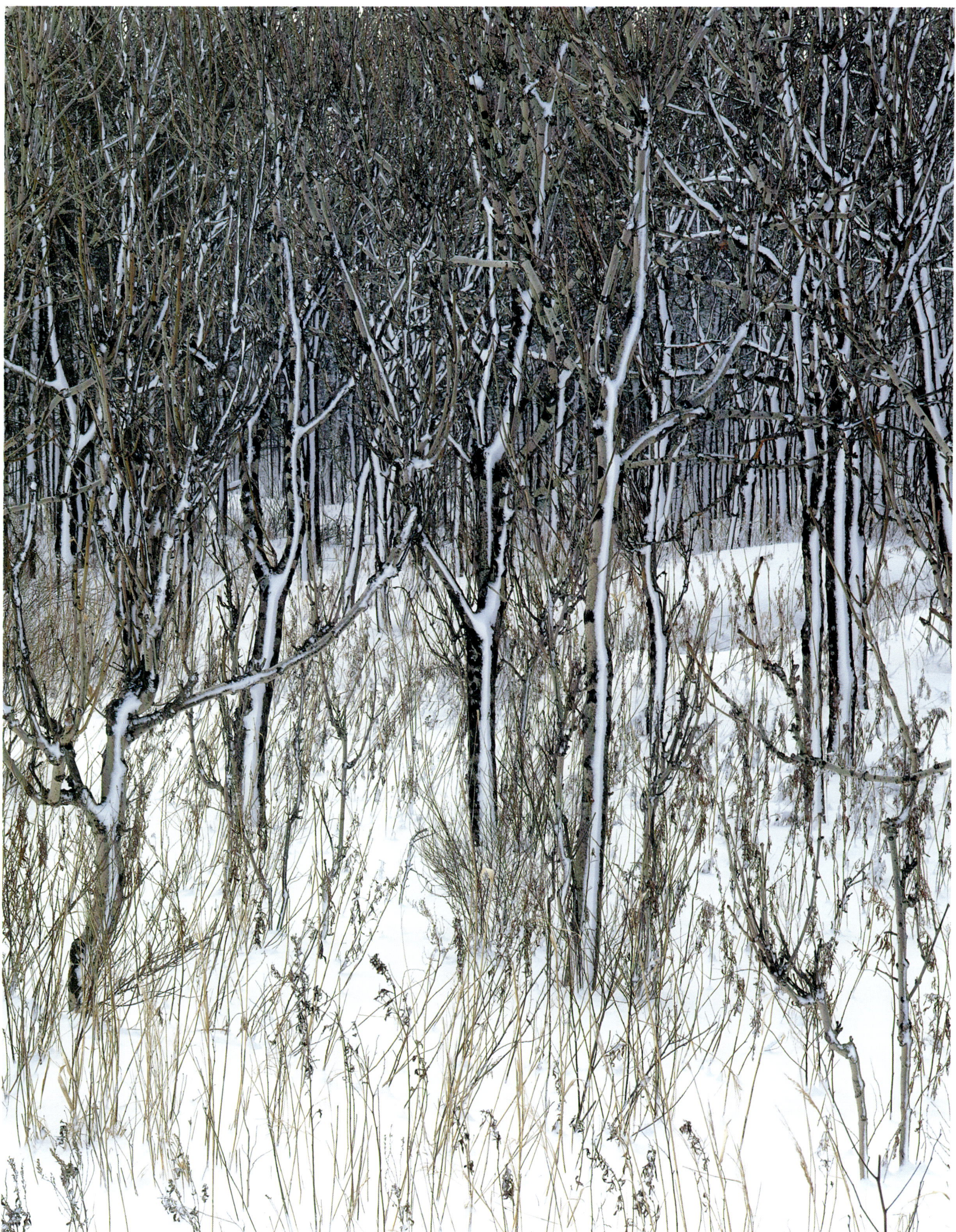

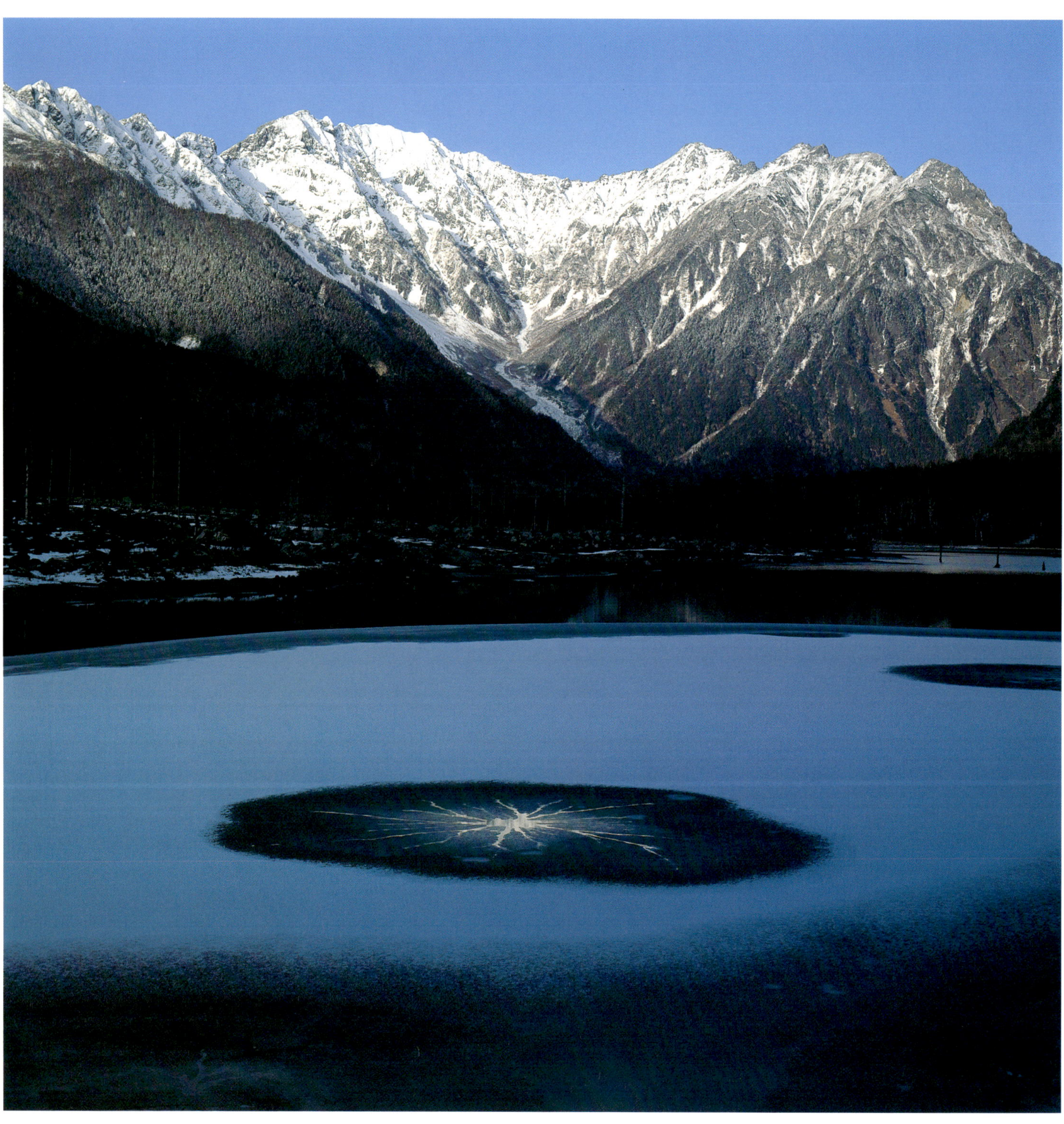

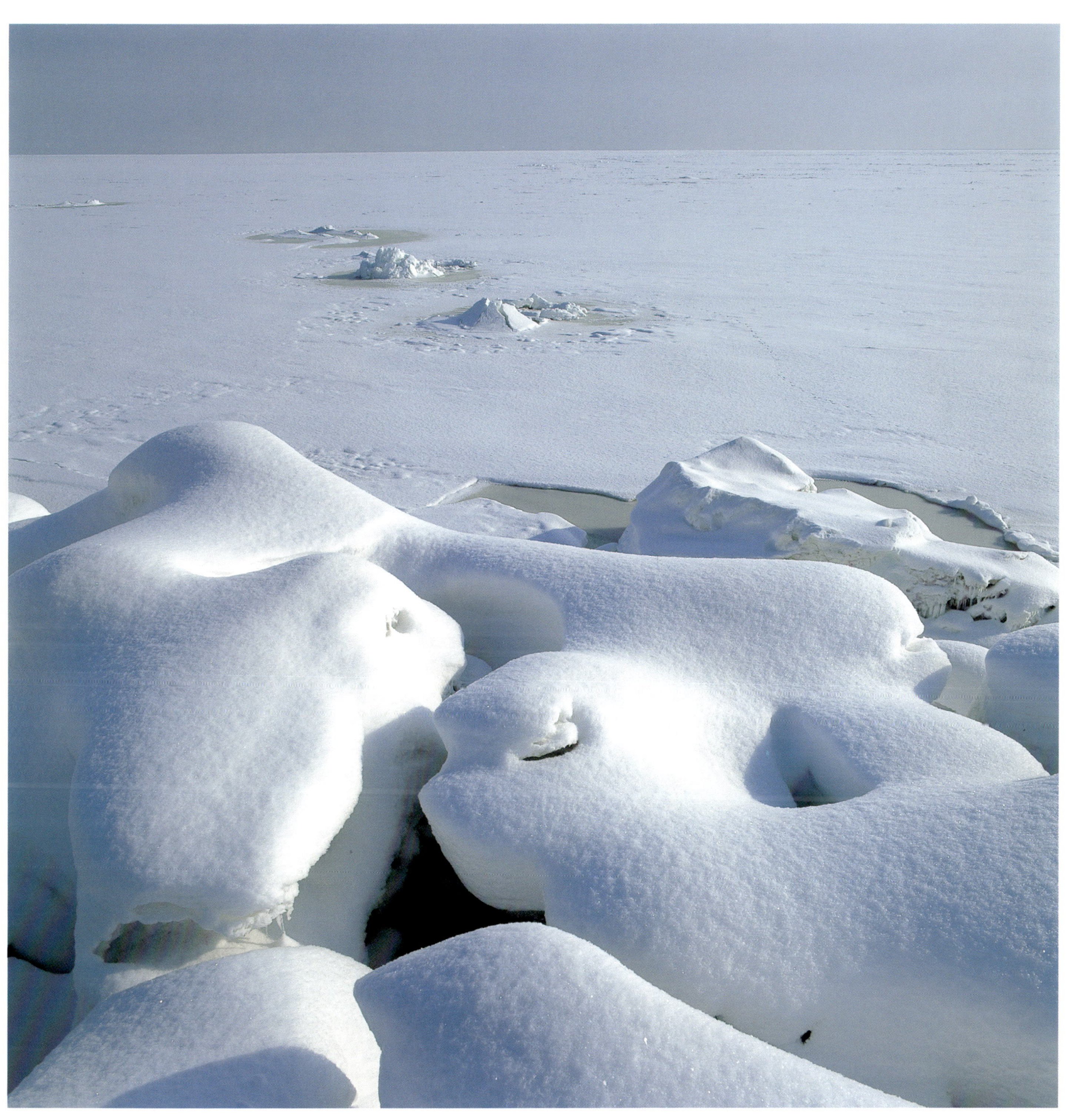

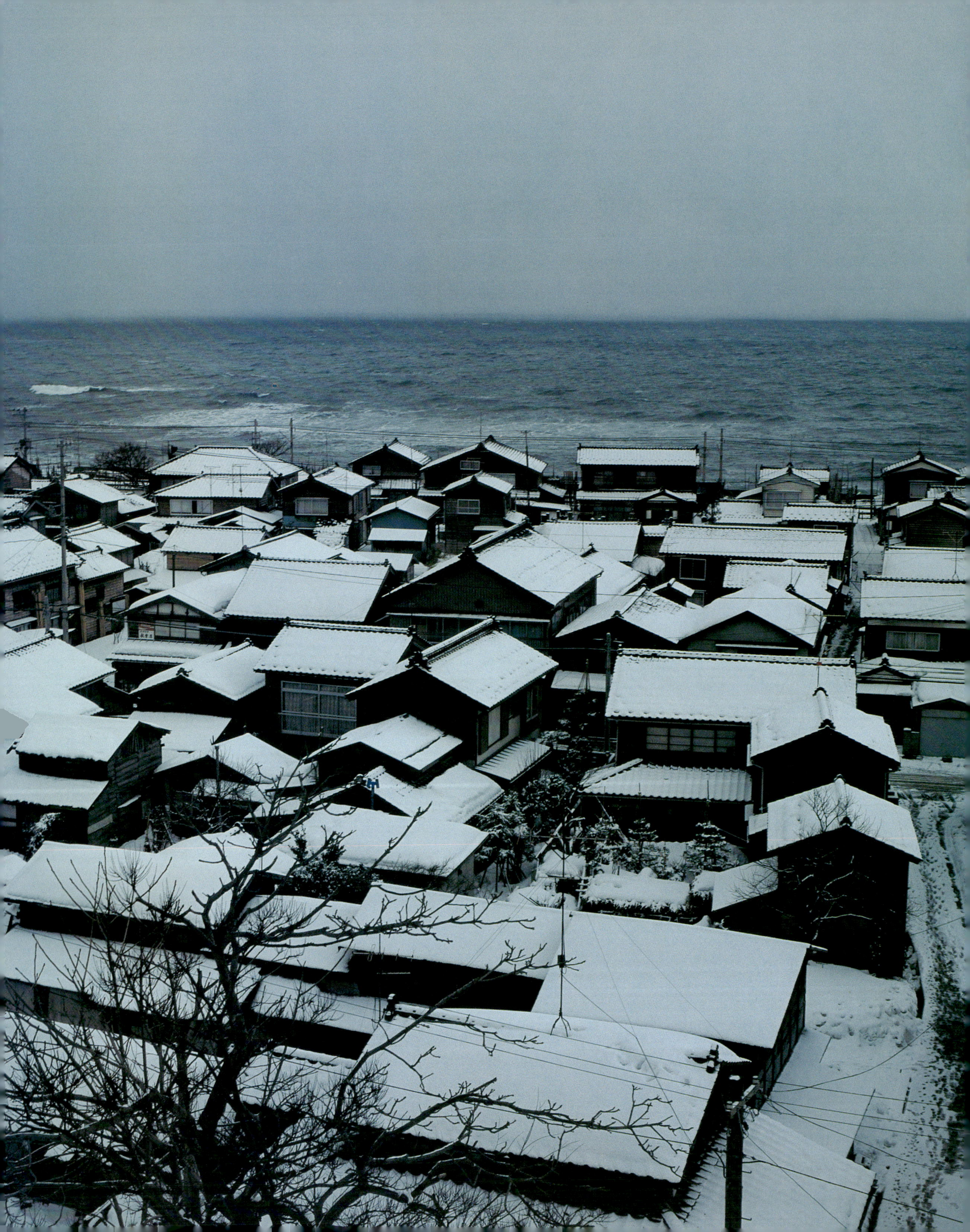

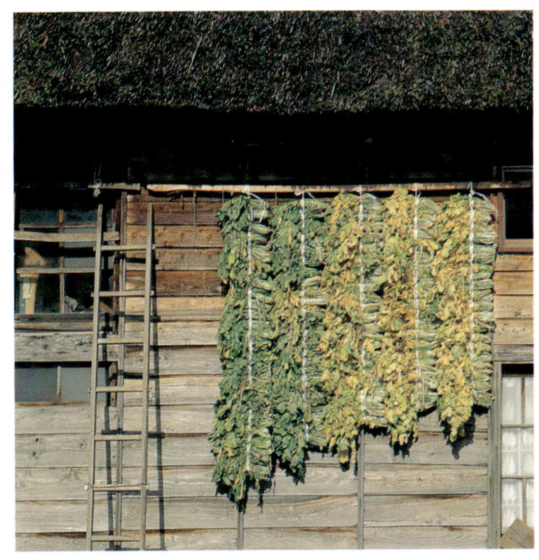

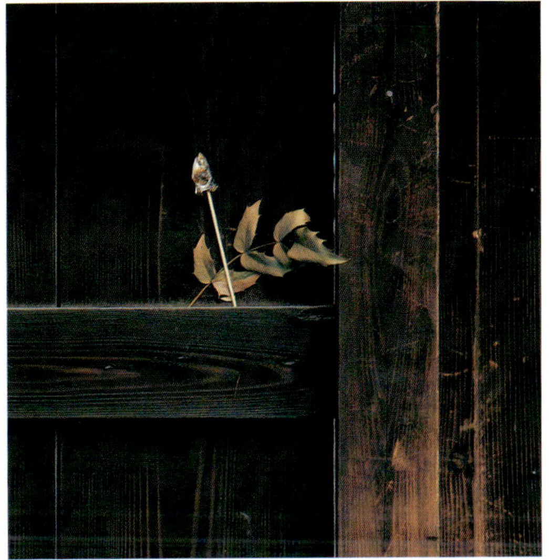

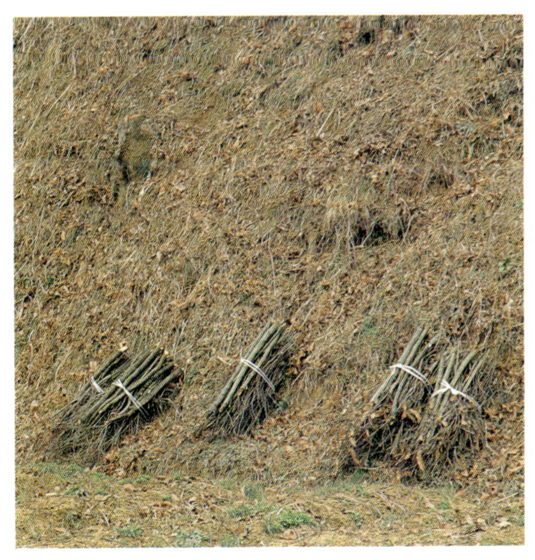

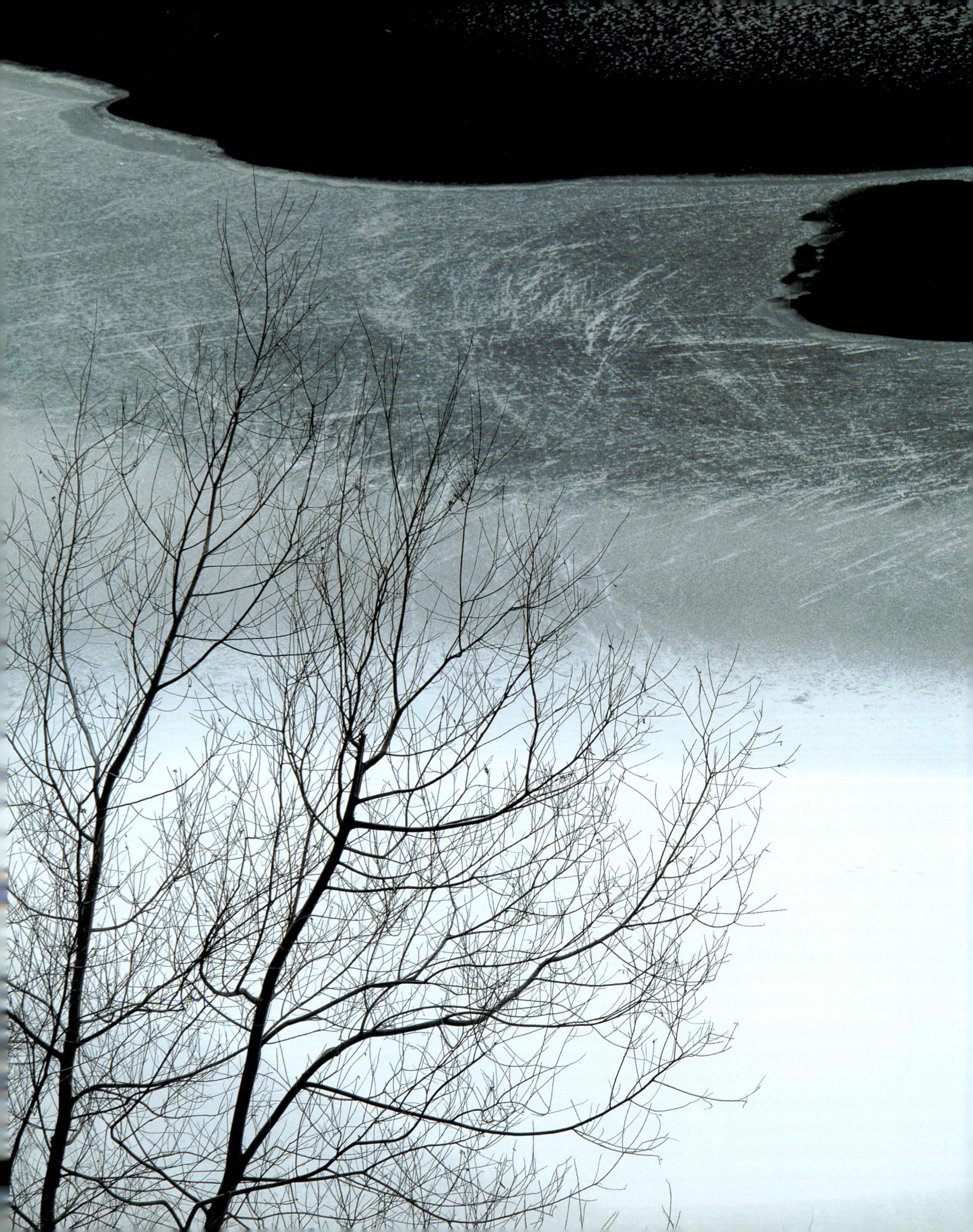

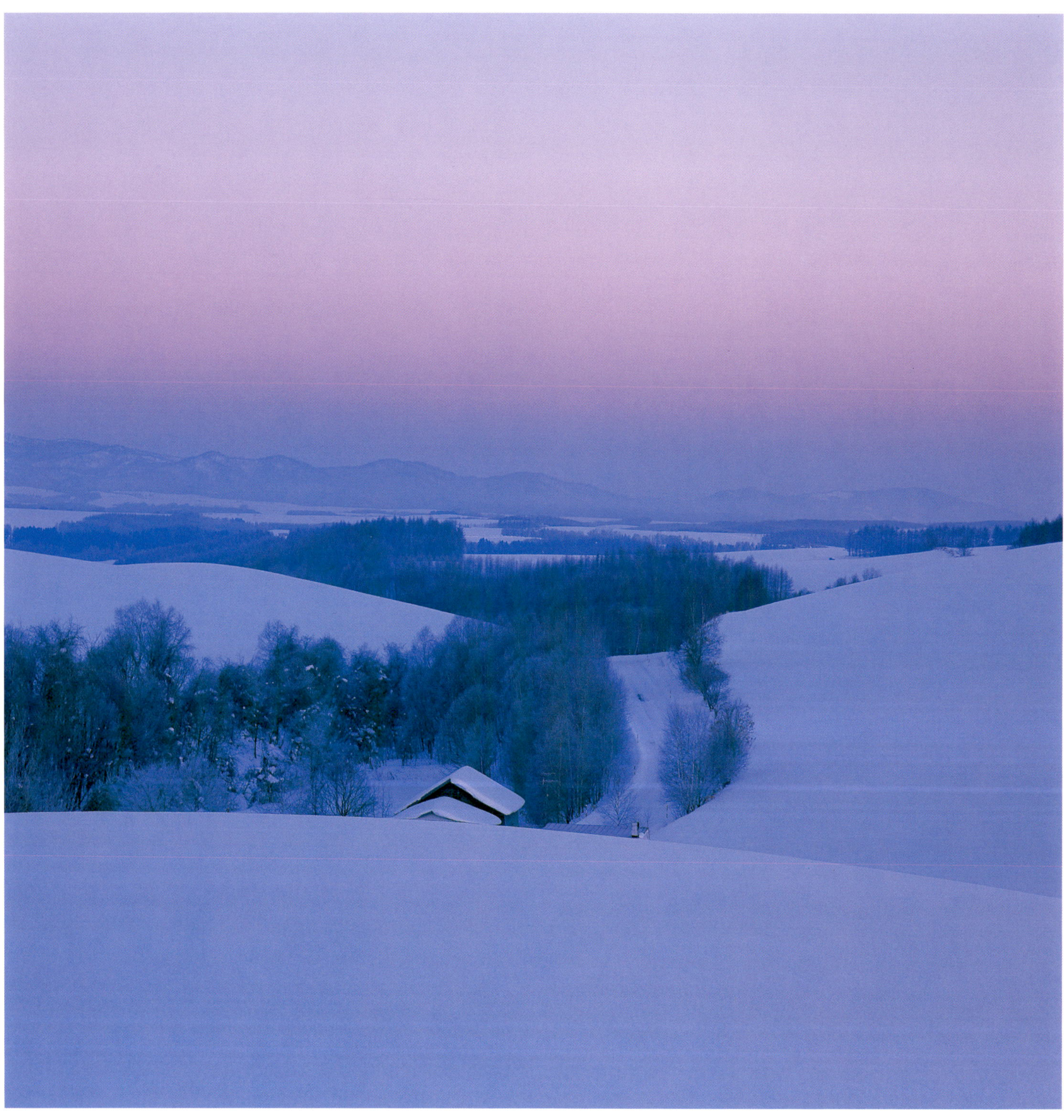

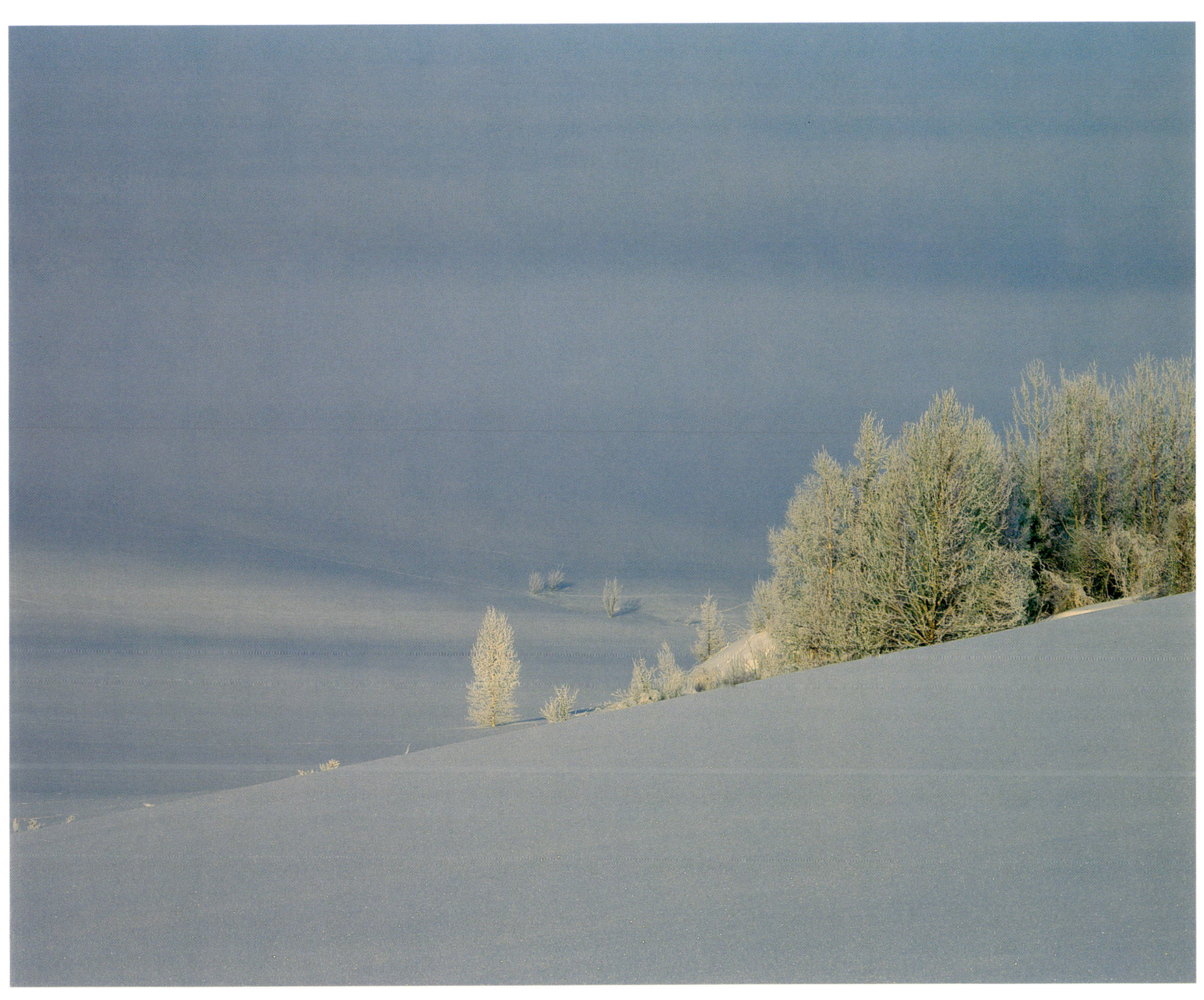

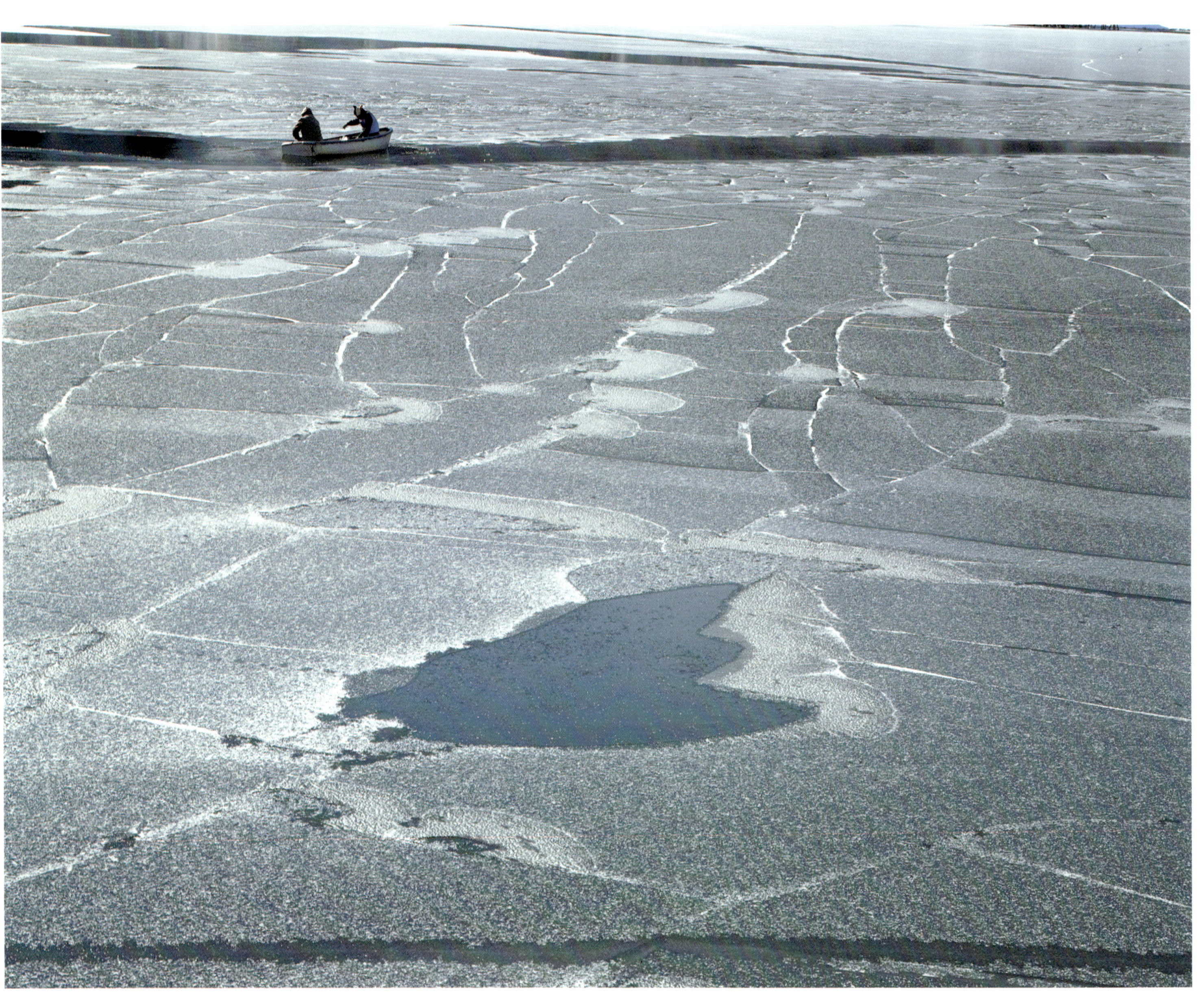

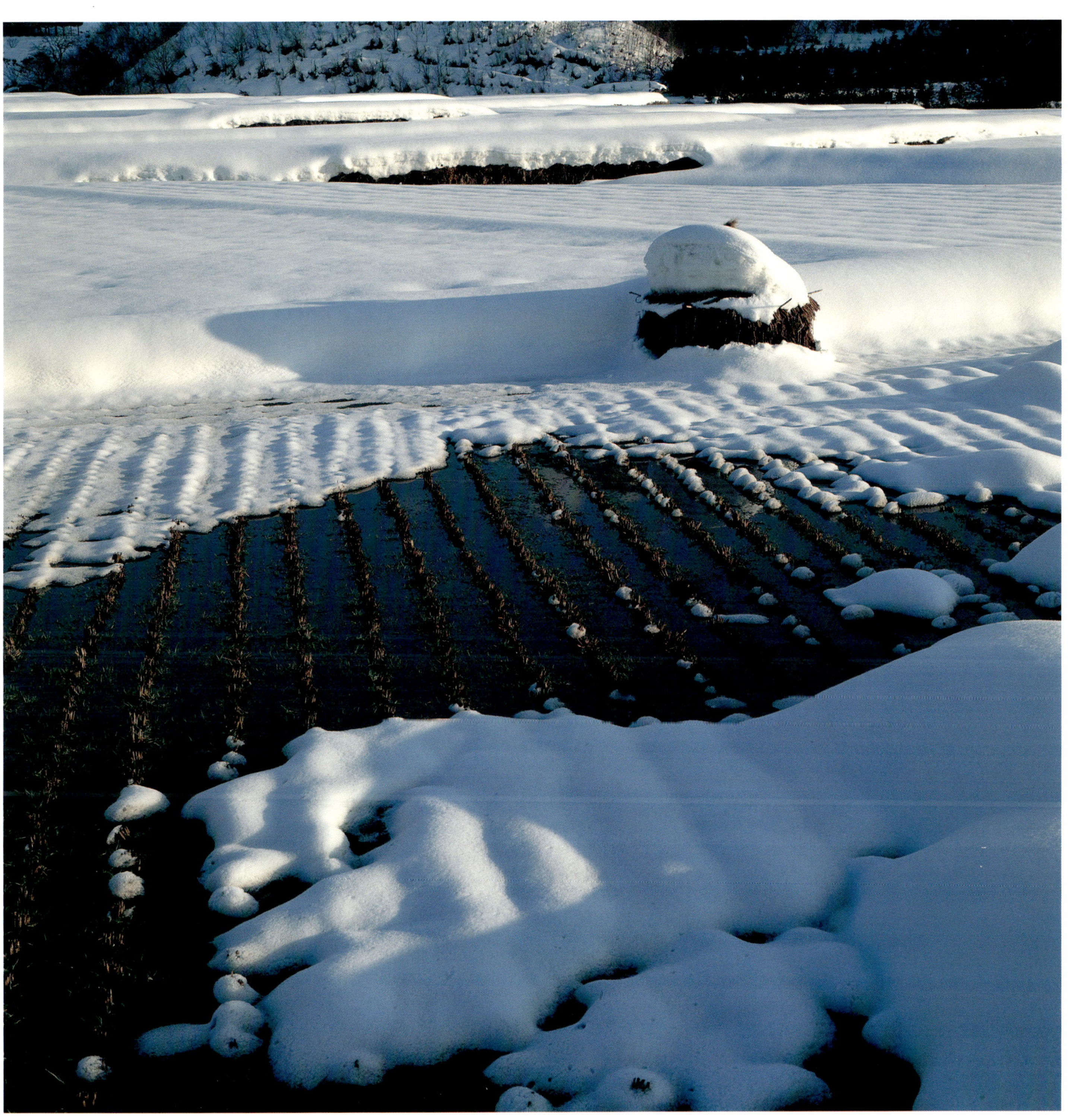

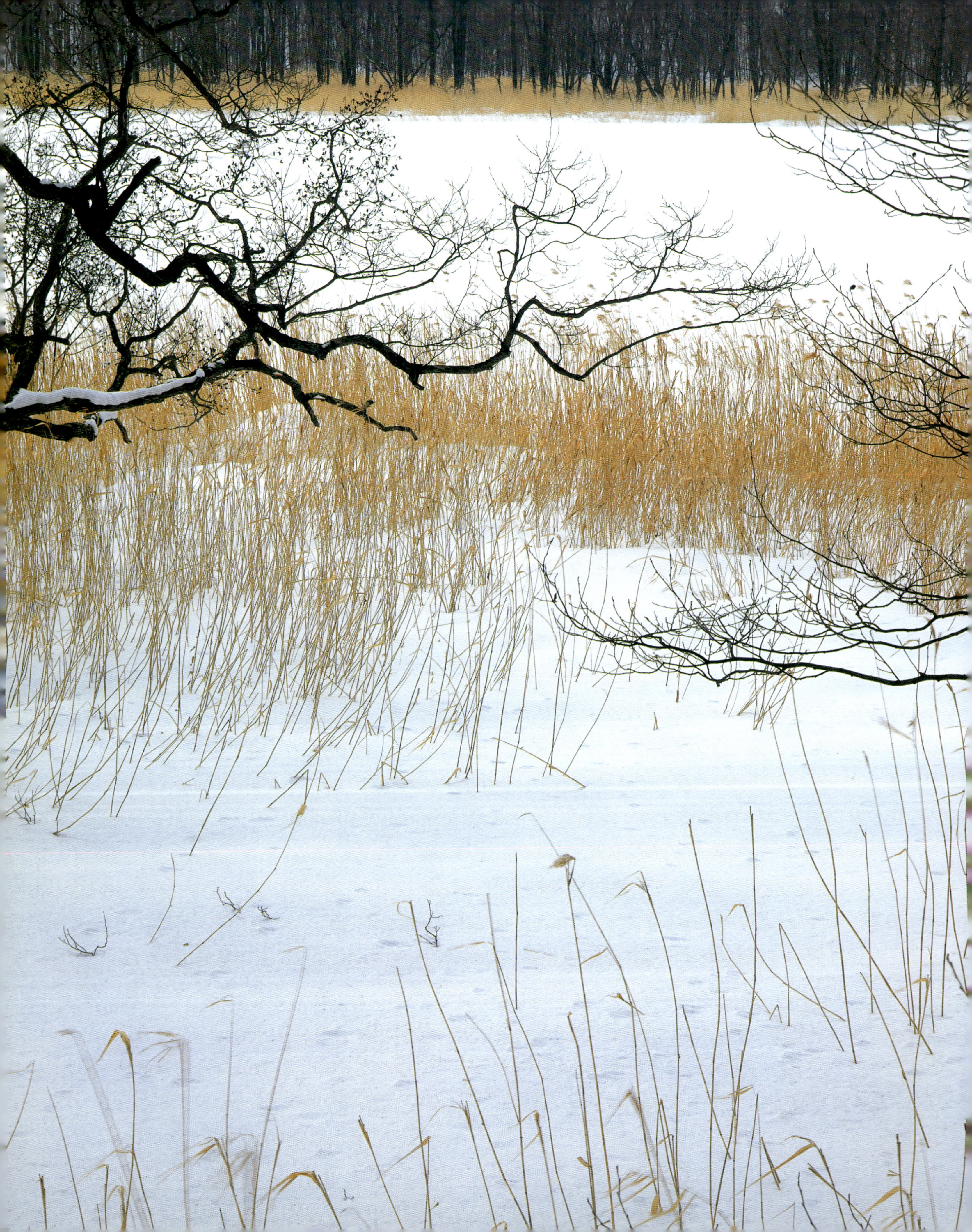

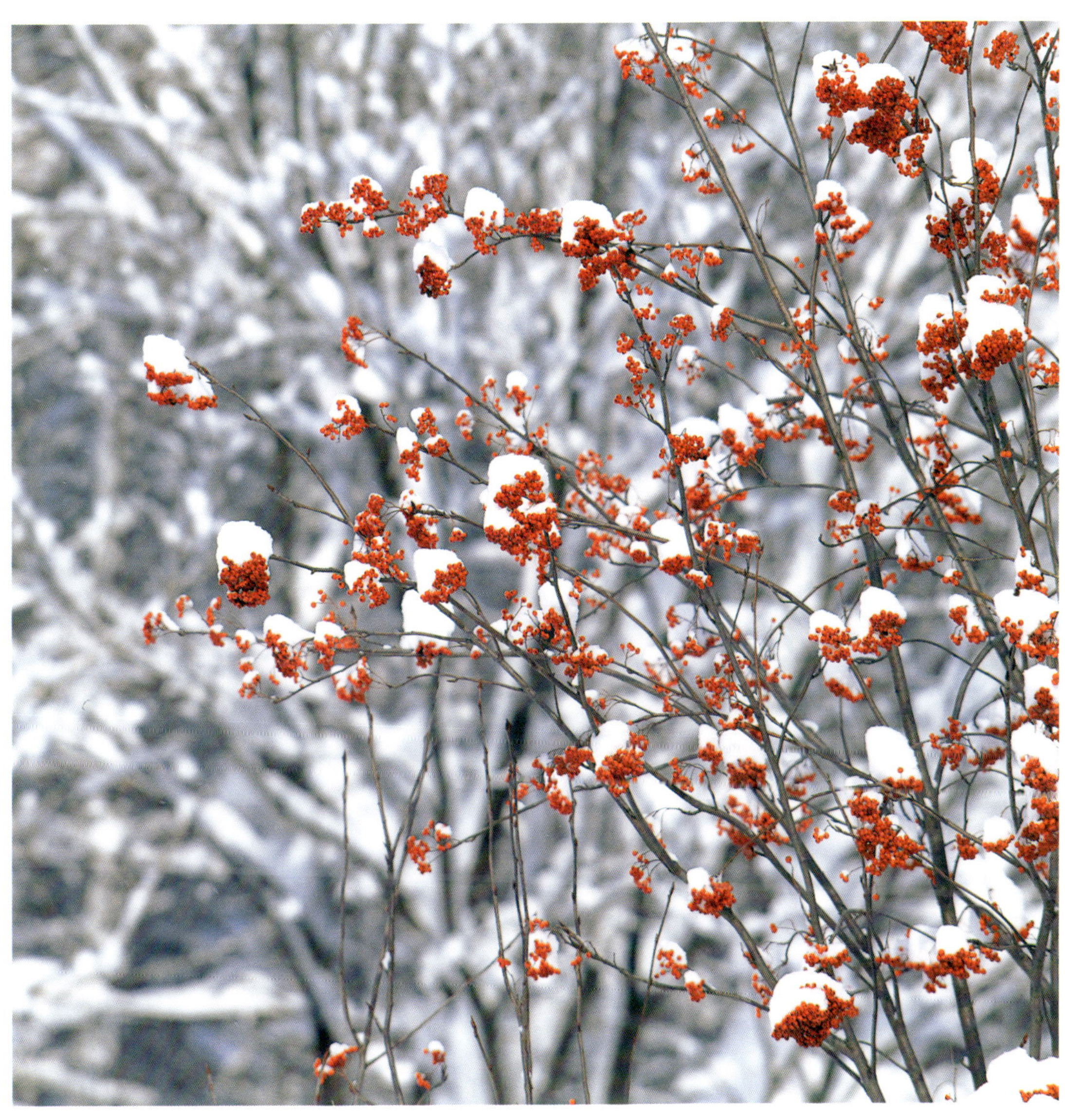

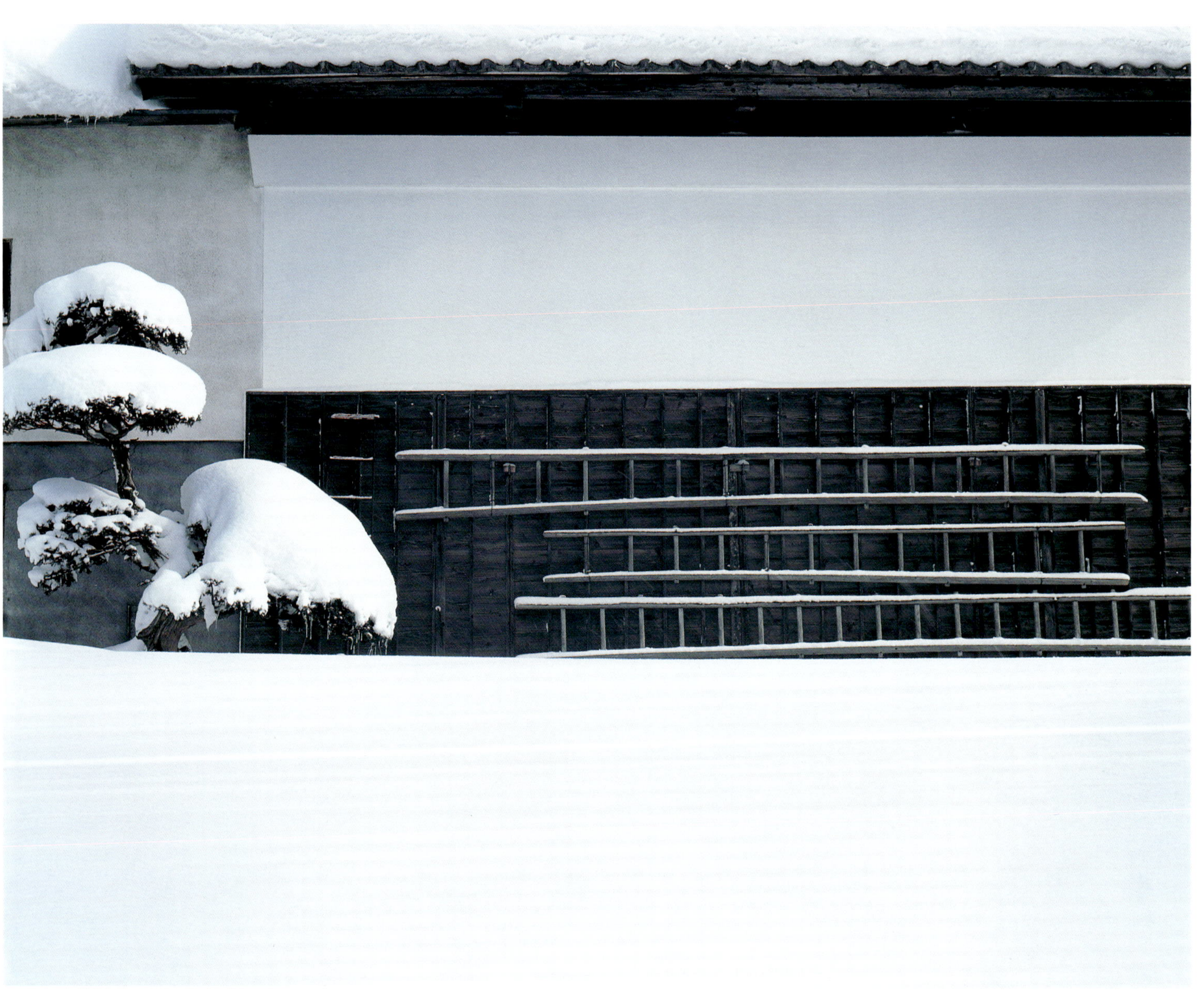

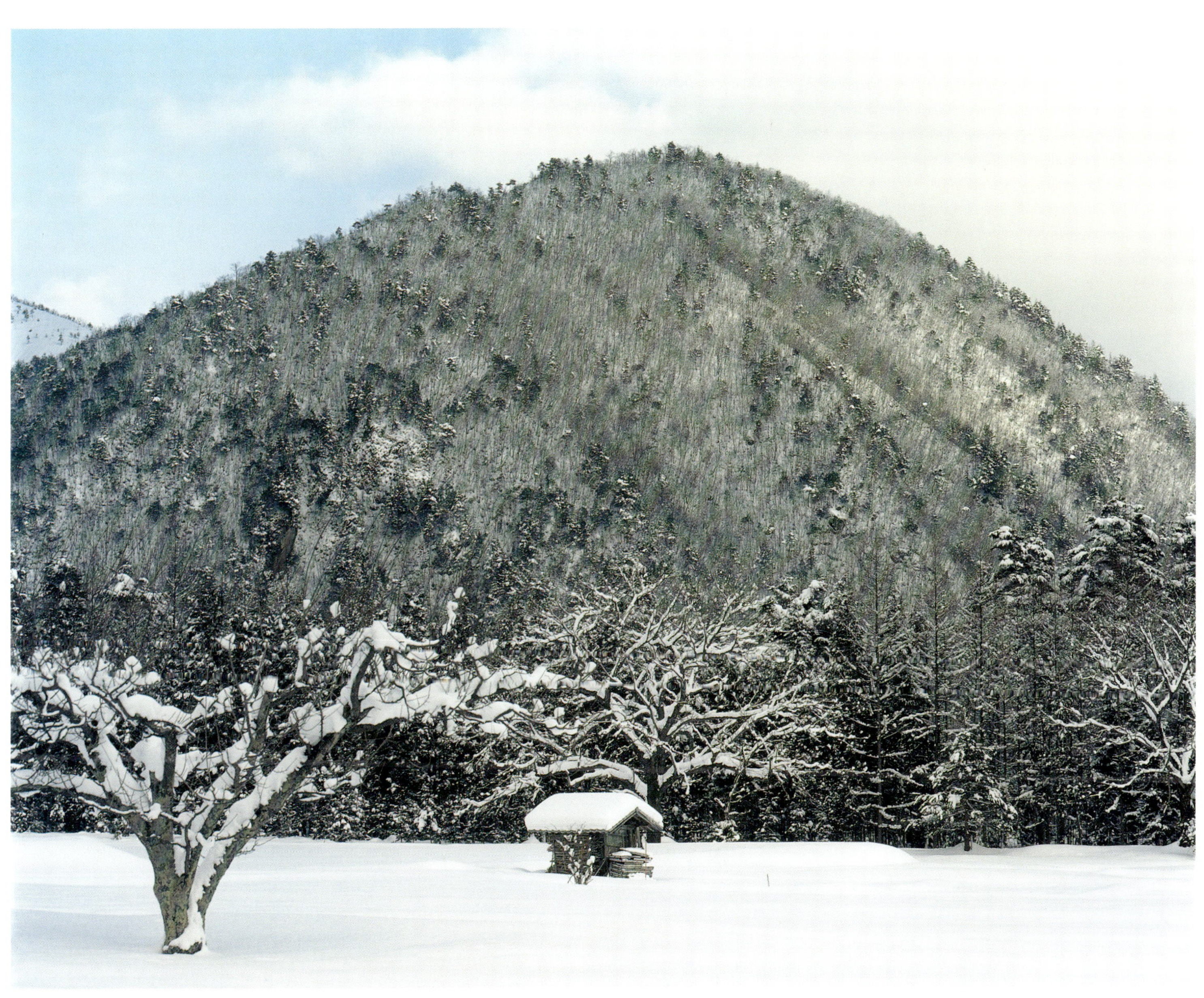

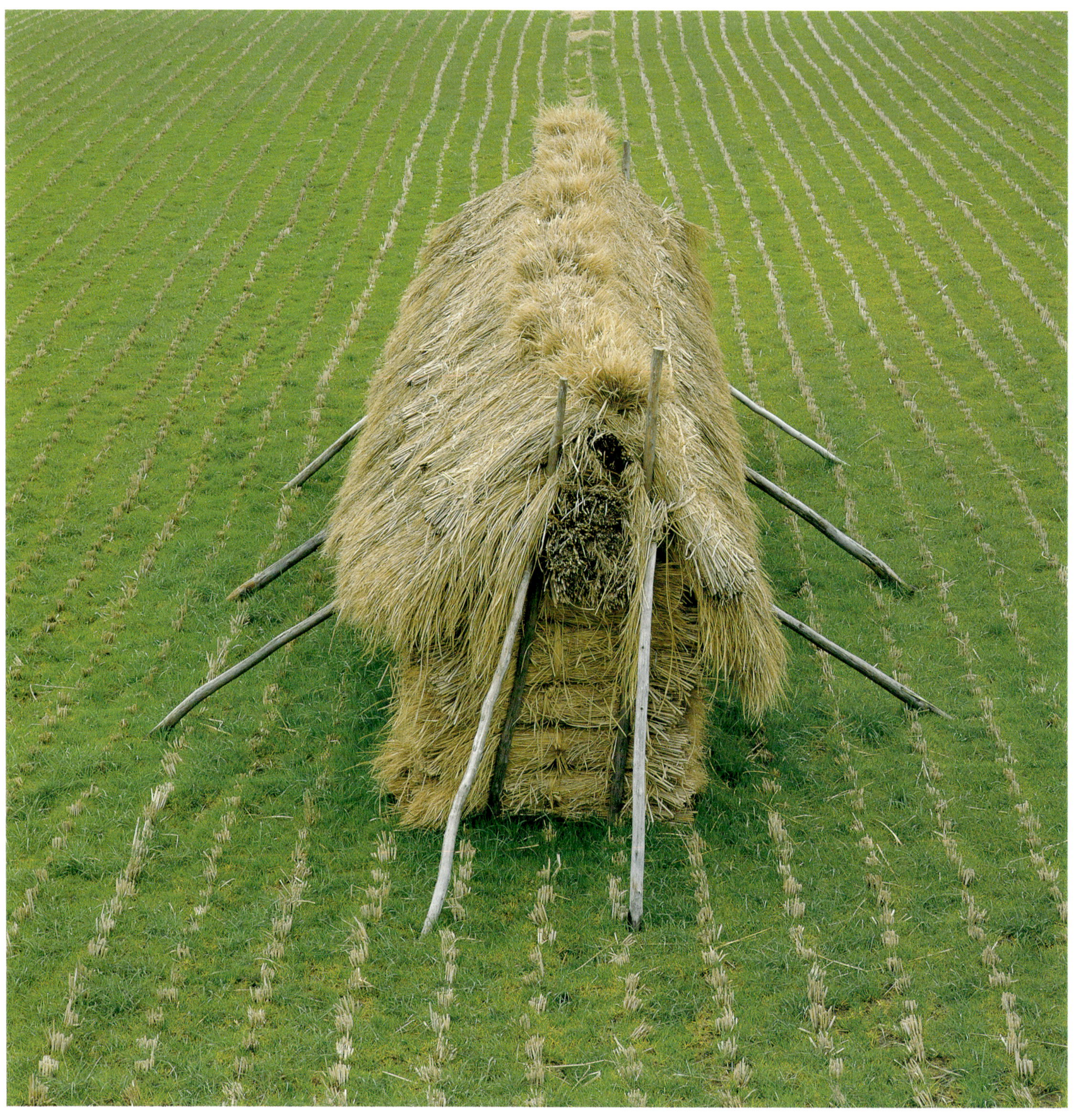

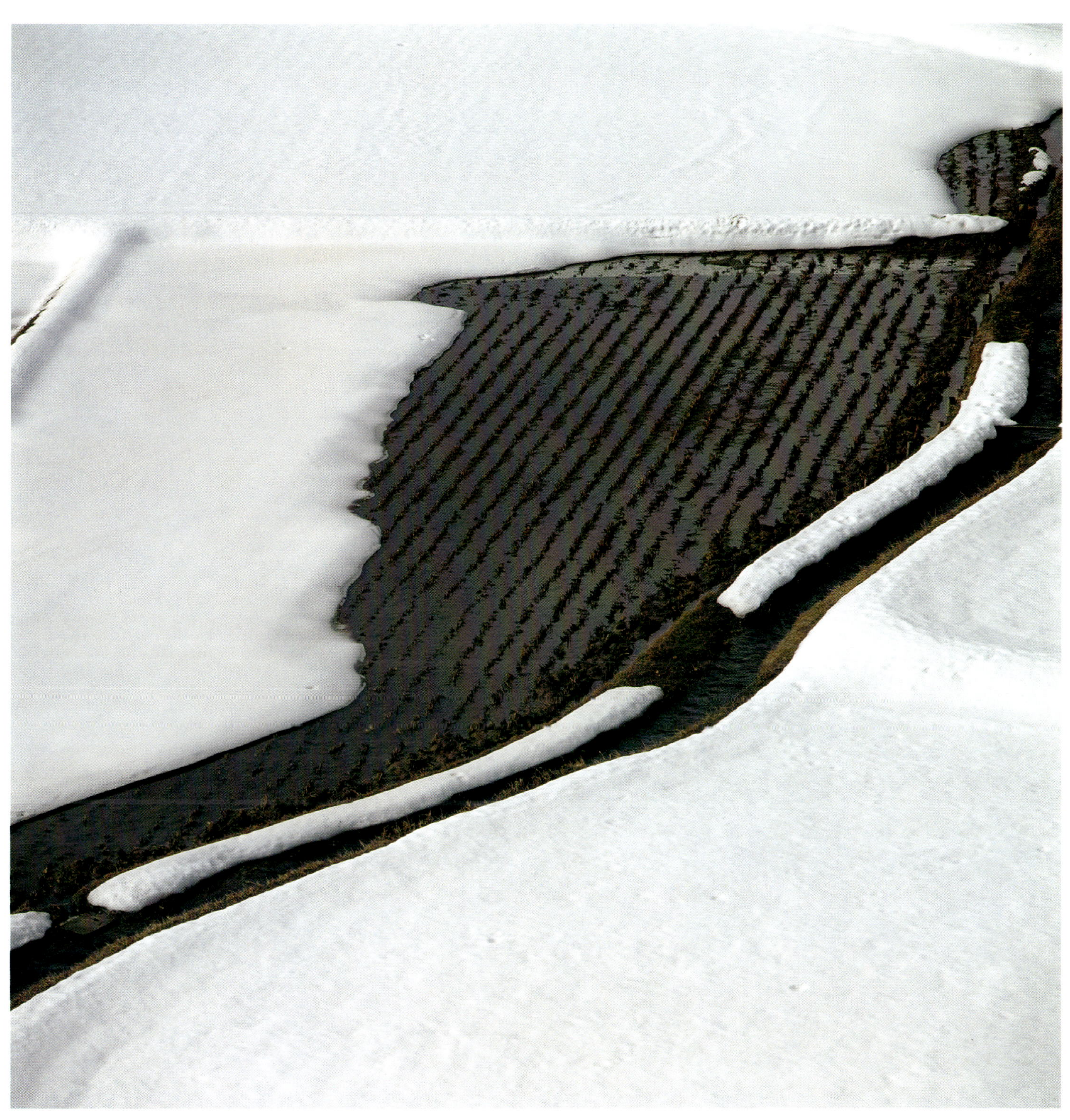

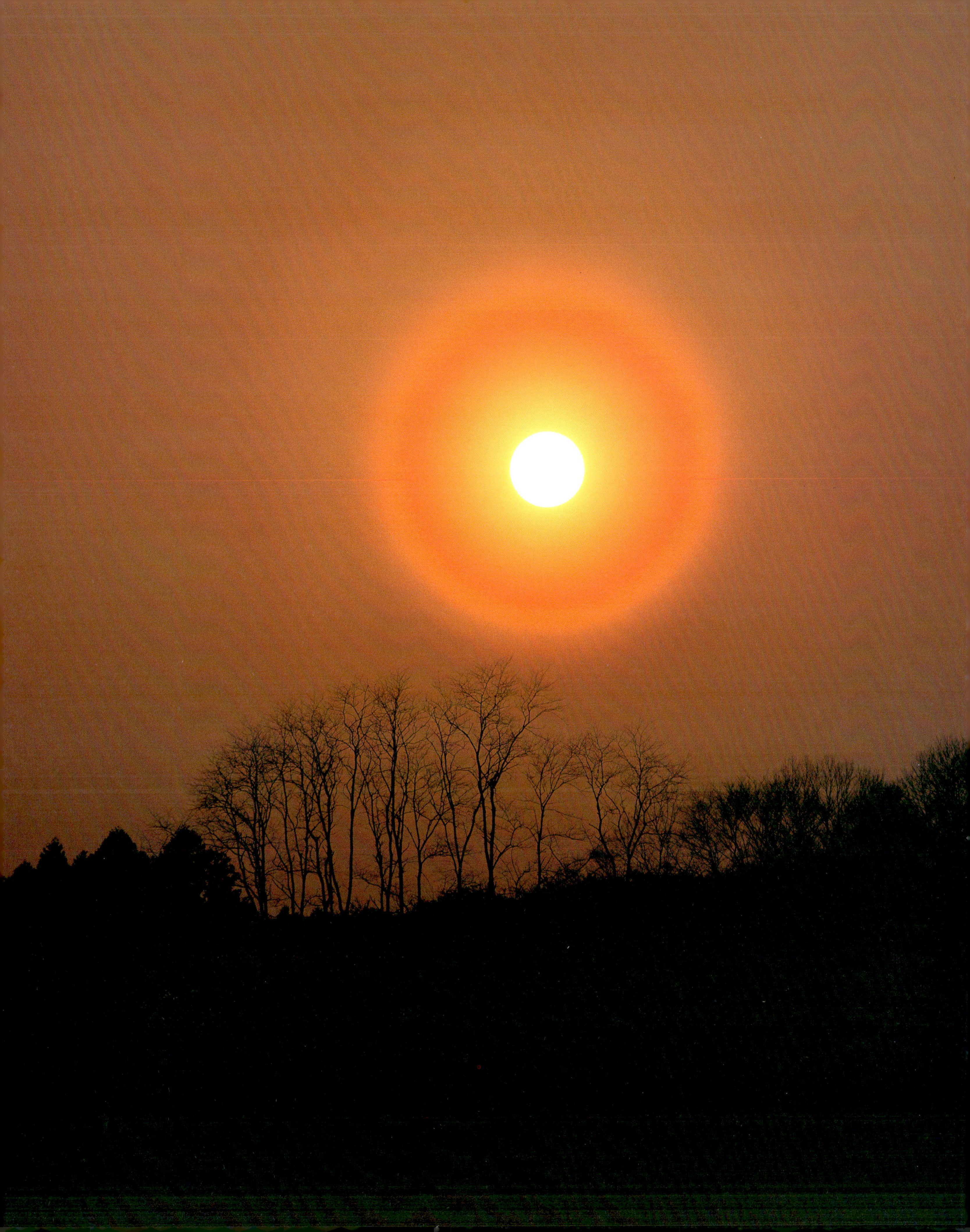

LIST OF PHOTOGRAPHS

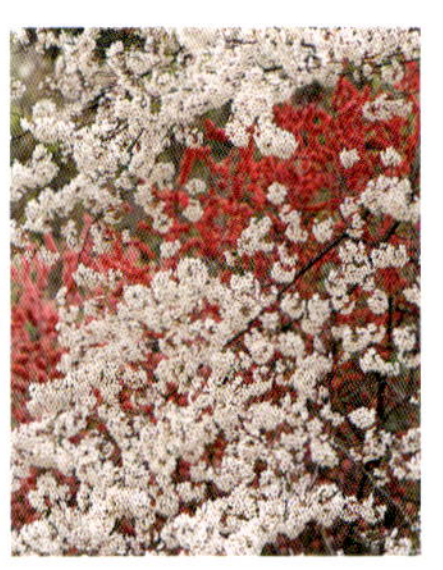
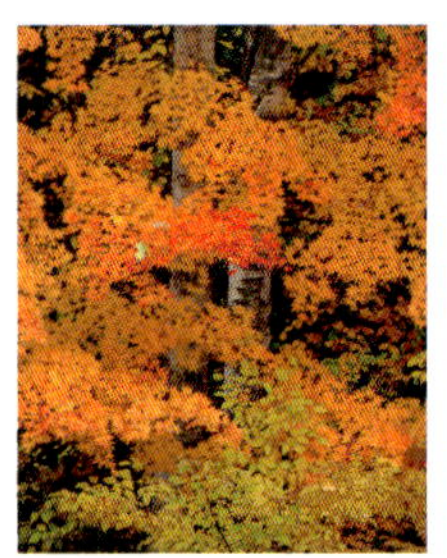
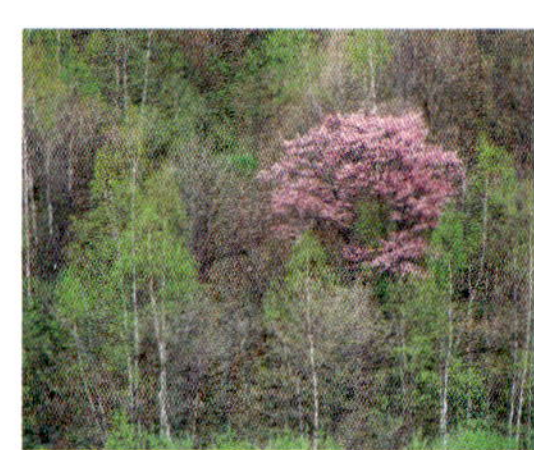
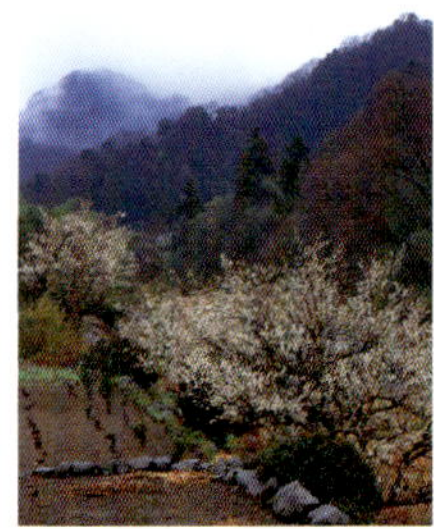
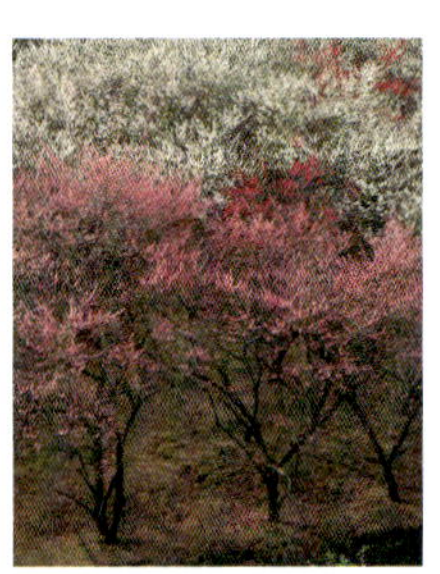
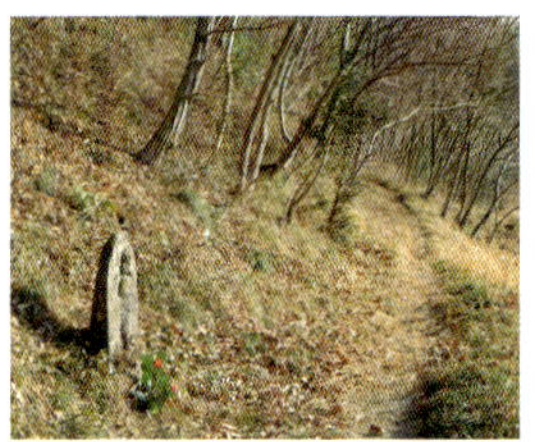
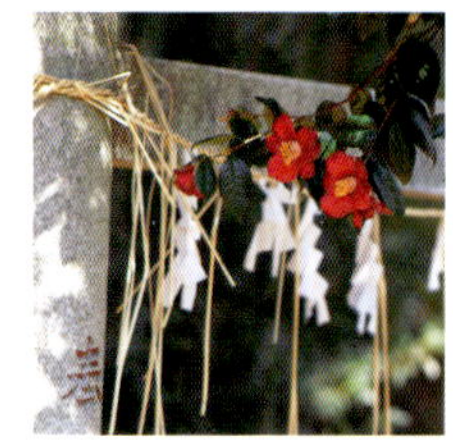
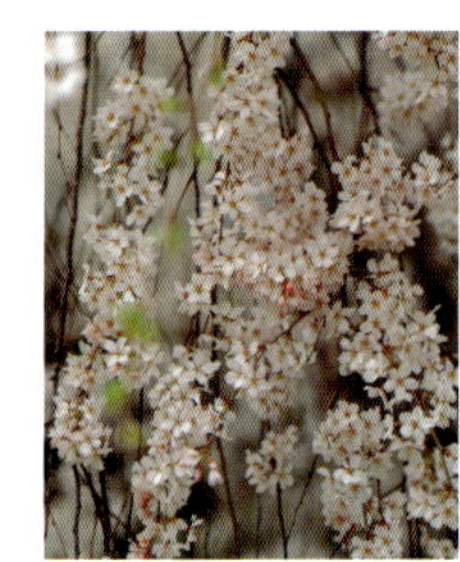
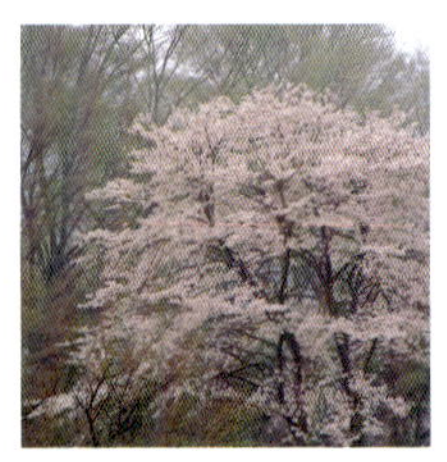
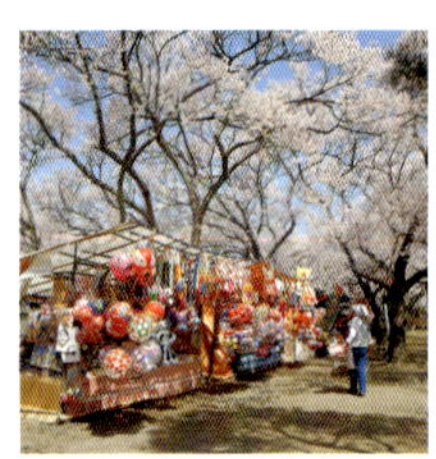
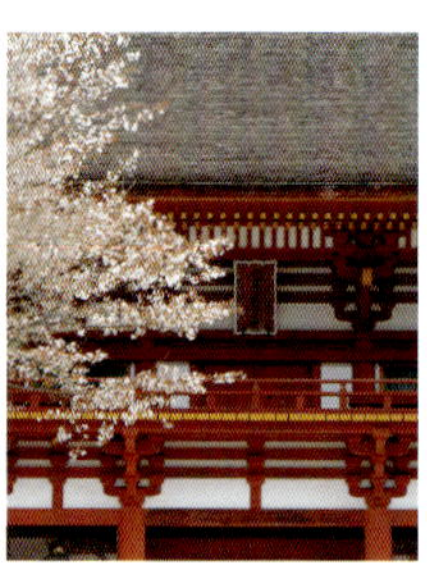
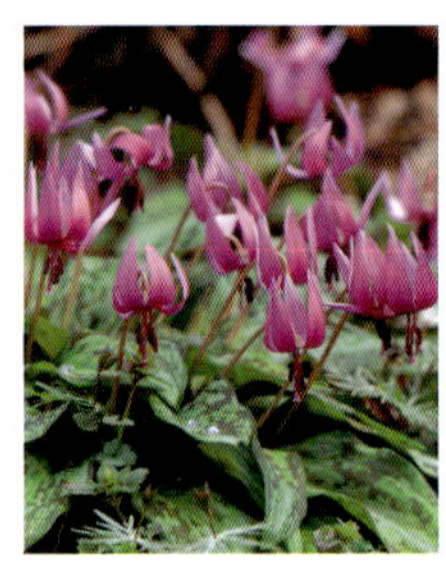
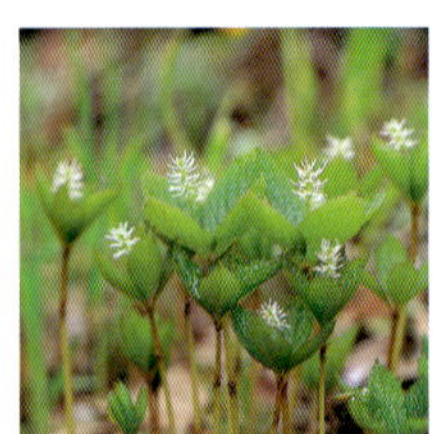
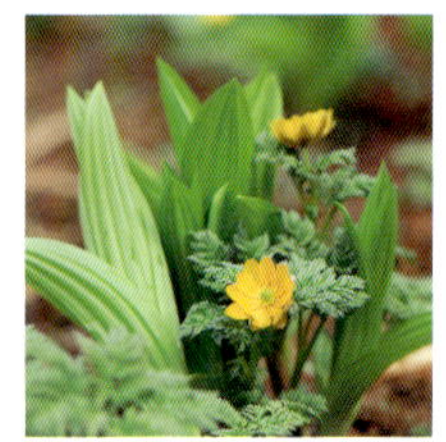
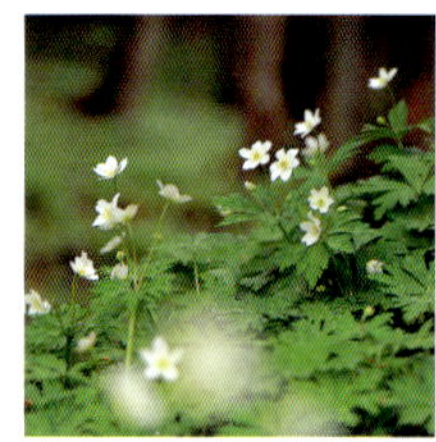
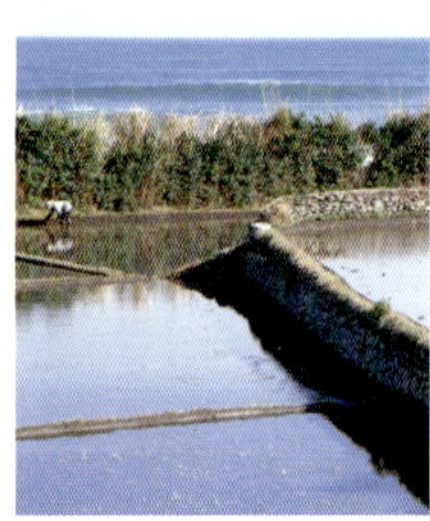

Jacket (front)
Cherry and scarlet peach blossom
Setagaya Ward, Tokyo
Akira Maeda 1998

Jacket (back)
Patterns of maple leaves
Bieicho, Hokkaido
Akira Maeda 1998

P 2–3
A splash of pink on the spring mountainside
Bieicho, Hokkaido
Akira Maeda 1997

P 5
Mist from spring rain
Shimonitamachi, Gunma Prefecture
Shinzo Maeda 1991

P 8
Grove of red and white Japanese apricot blossom
Shuzenjicho, Shizuoka Prefecture
Shinzo Maeda 1991

P 10
A sunny spot in early spring
Naka-izucho, Shizuoka Prefecture
Shinzo Maeda 1981

P 11
Camellia (*yabutsubaki*) at an Inari shrine
Hachiojishi, Tokyo
Akira Maeda 2000

P 12
Old weeping cherry
Onoji Temple, Nara Prefecture
Shinzo Maeda 1989

P 13
Cherry blossom in my home prefecture
Hachiojishi, Tokyo
Shinzo Maeda 1991

P 14
Early flowering cherry on castle ruins
Takatomachi, Nagano Prefecture
Shinzo Maeda 1982

P 15
Wild cherry and temple gate
Muroji Temple, Nara Prefecture
Shinzo Maeda 1989

P 16
Cluster of dogtooth violets
Hachiojishi, Tokyo
Akira Maeda 1998

P 17 (top)
Hitorishizuka (*chloranthus japonicus*)
Bieicho, Hokkaido
Akira Maeda 1997

P 17 (middle)
Pheasant's eye
Bieicho, Hokkaido
Akira Maeda 1998

P 17 (bottom)
Windflowers
Tatsukomachi, Aomori Prefecture
Akira Maeda 2000

P 18
Rice paddies by the sea
Hyugashi, Miyazaki Prefecture
Shinzo Maeda 1978

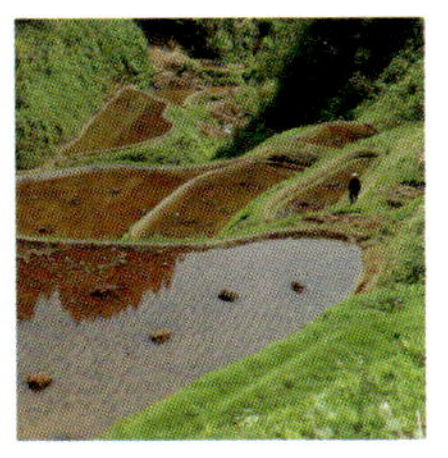
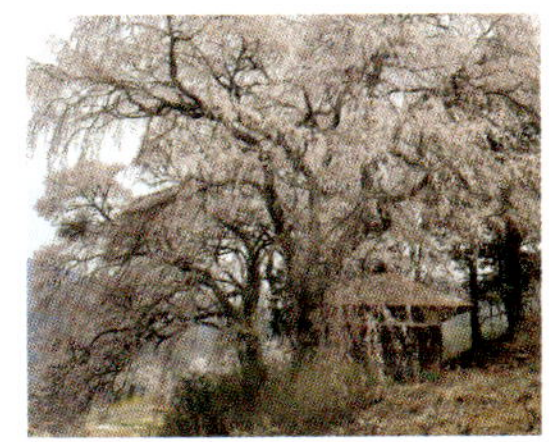
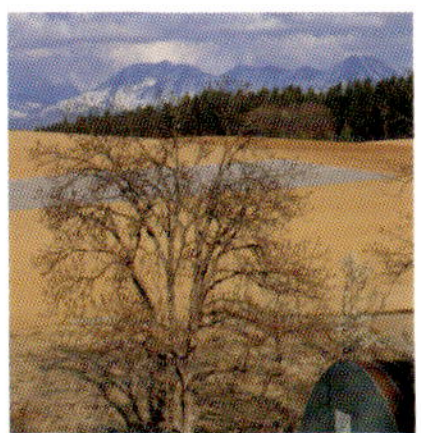
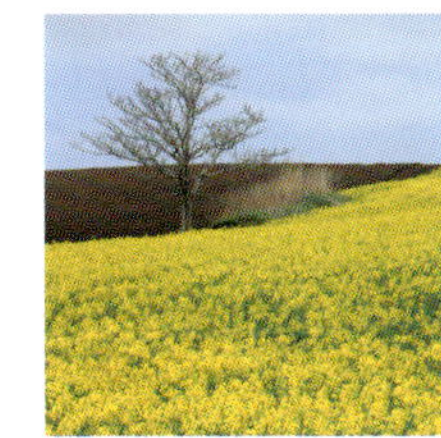
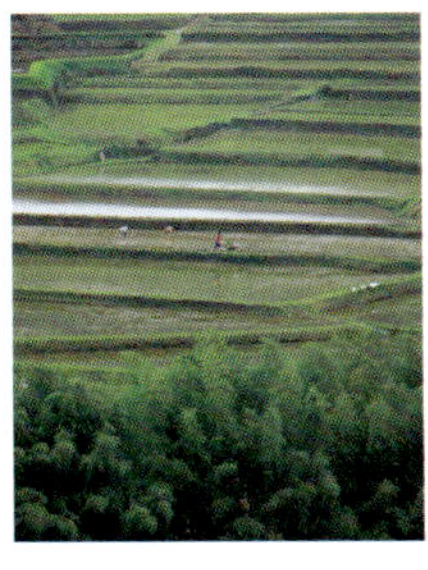
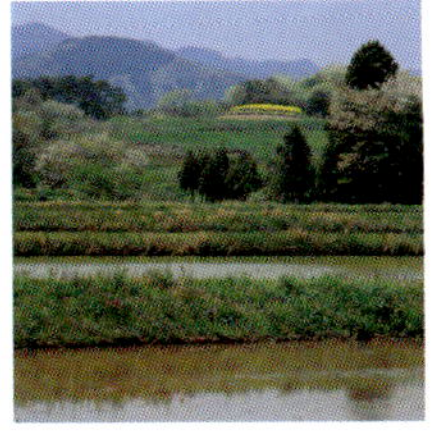
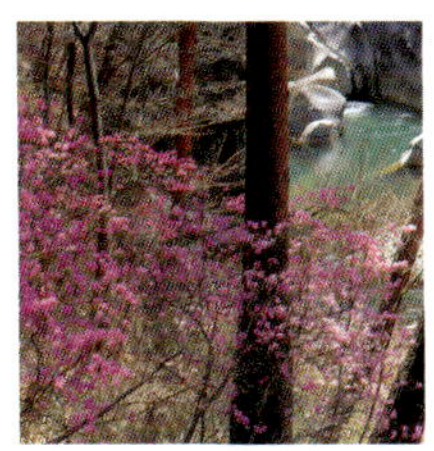
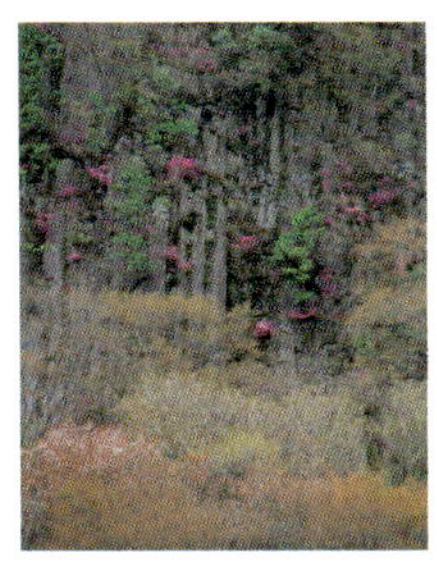
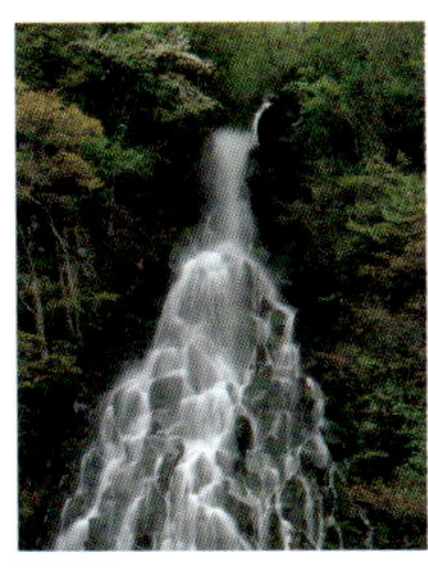
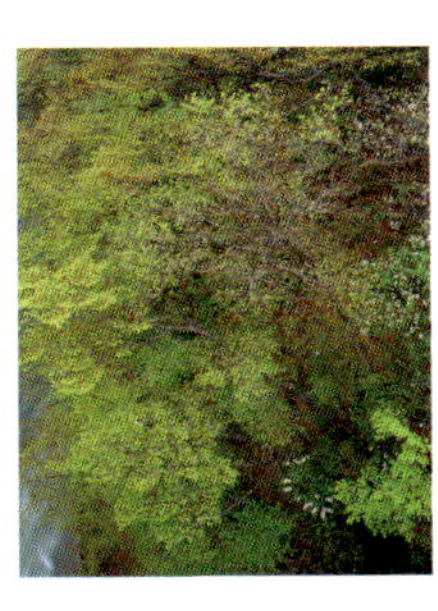
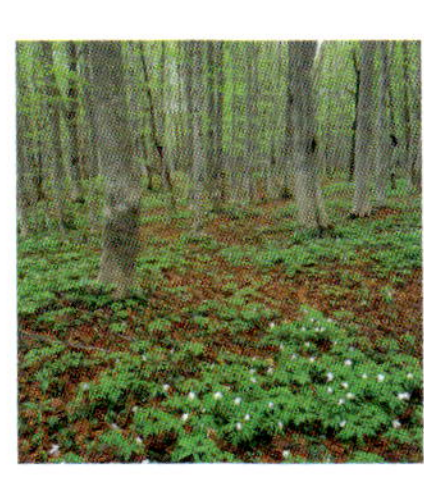
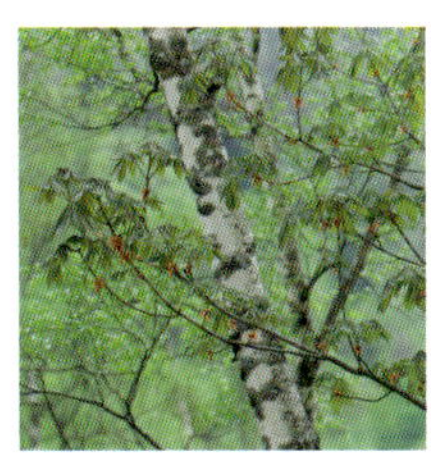
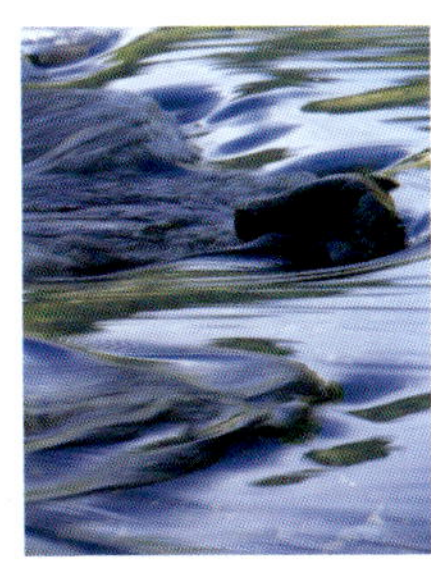
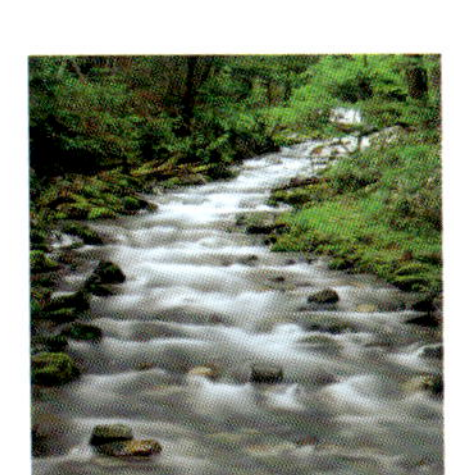
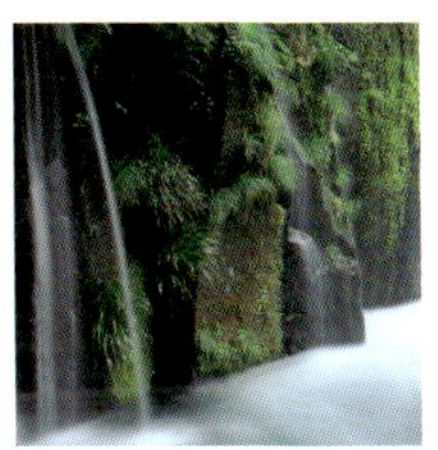
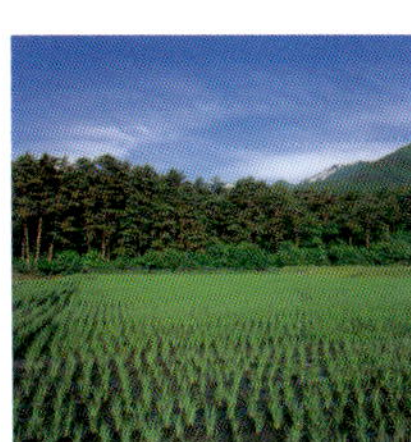

P 19
Man with straw hat
Tokamachishi, Niigata Prefecture
Shinzo Maeda 1979

P 20–21
Weeping cherry blossom and shrine
Takatomachi, Nagano Prefecture
Shinzo Maeda 1982

P 22
Hillside magnolia kobus in bloom
Bieicho, Hokkaido
Akira Maeda 2000

P 23
Field of rape flowers
Yokohamamachi, Aomori Prefecture
Akira Maeda 2000

P 24
Rice planting in terraced paddies
Kikuchishi, Kumamoto Prefecture
Akira Maeda 2000

P 25
Full springtime in the country
Koriyamashi, Fukushima Prefecture
Akira Maeda 2000

P 26
Azaleas (*mitsubatsutsuji*) by a gorge
Shosenkyo, Yamanashi Prefecture
Shinzo Maeda 1993

P 27
Azalea blossoms on Byobuiwa Cliff
Sonimura, Nara Prefecture
Shinzo Maeda 1991

P 28
The refreshing sight of Tarudaki Waterfall
Kijimadairamura, Nagano Prefecture
Shinzo Maeda 1979

P 29
Trees in bud
Sendaishi, Miyagi Prefecture
Akira Maeda 2000

P 30
Kikusaki anemones in beech woods
Tatsukomachi, Aomori Prefecture
Akira Maeda 2000

P 31
Young horse-chestnut foliage
Hirayutoge, Gifu Prefecture
Shinzo Maeda 1982

P 33
Blue stream
Chokaimachi, Akita Prefecture
Akira Maeda 2000

P 34
Dakesawa in the rain
Kamikochi, Nagano Prefecture
Akira Maeda 2000

P 35
Rock springs
Kikuchi Gorge, Kumamoto Prefecture
Akira Maeda 2000

P 36
Paddy field in early summer
Omachishi, Nagano Prefecture
Akira Maeda 1999

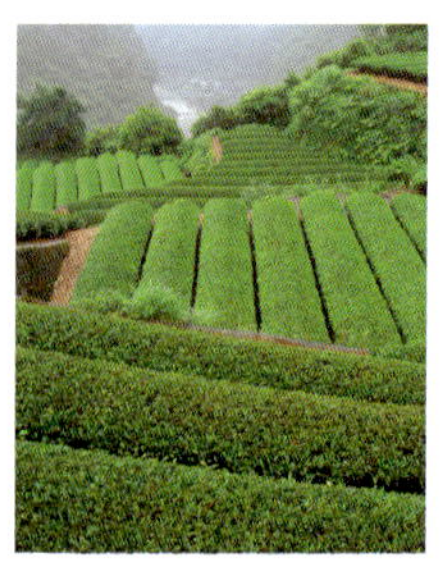
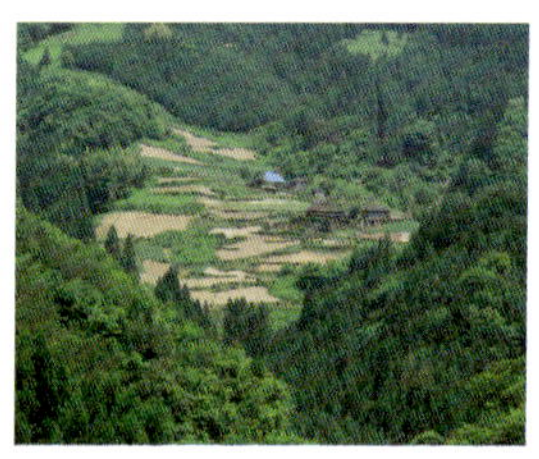
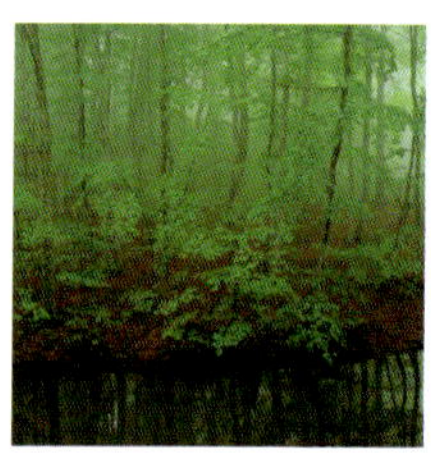
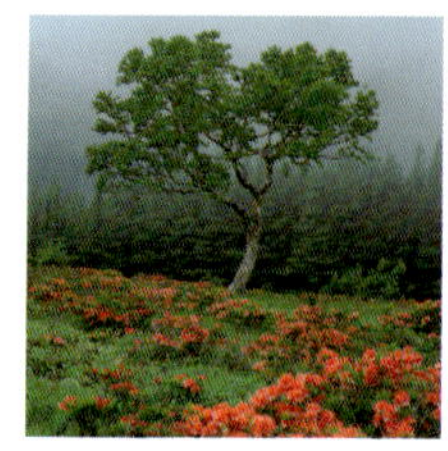
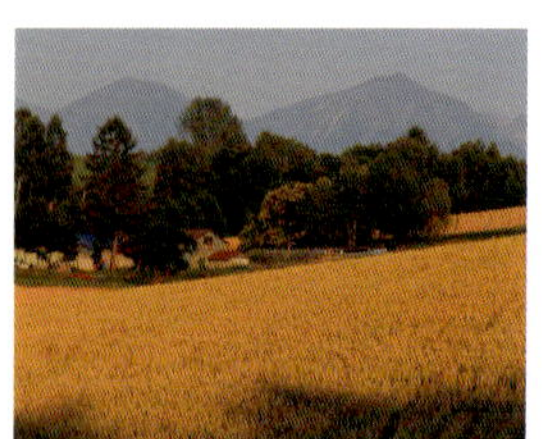
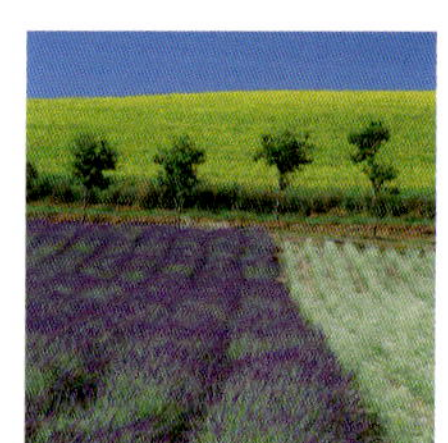
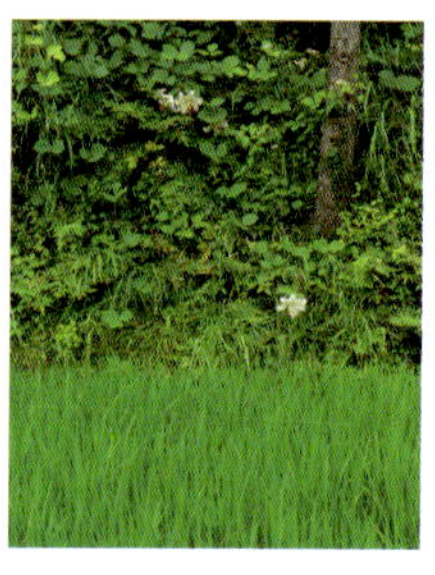
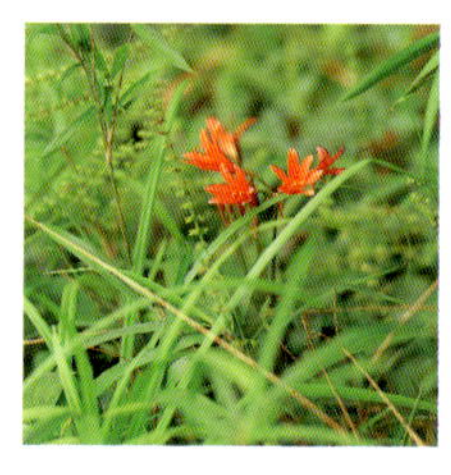
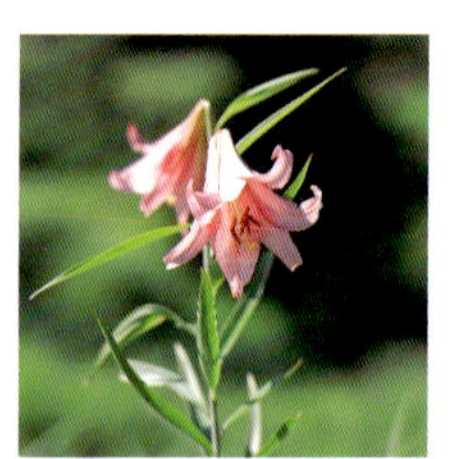
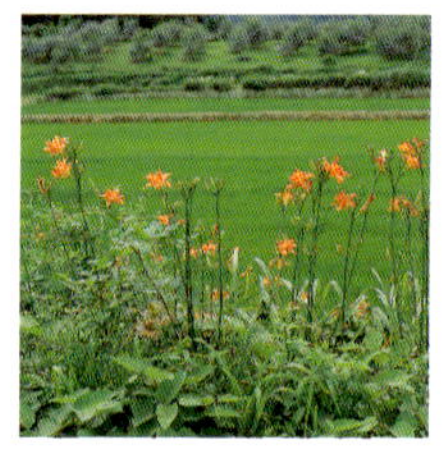
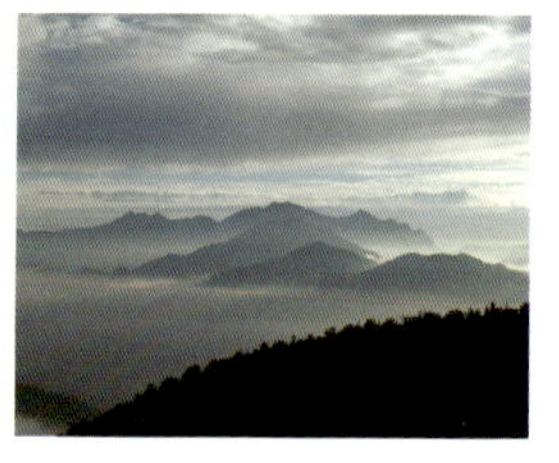
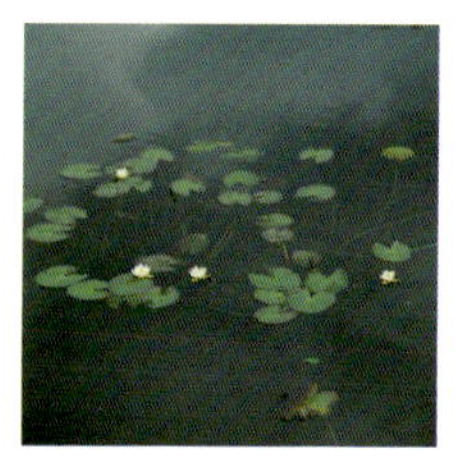
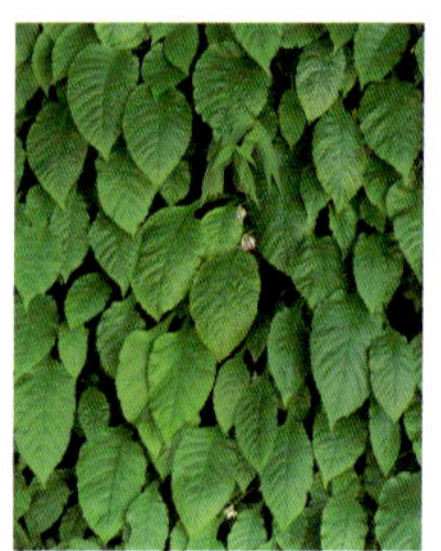
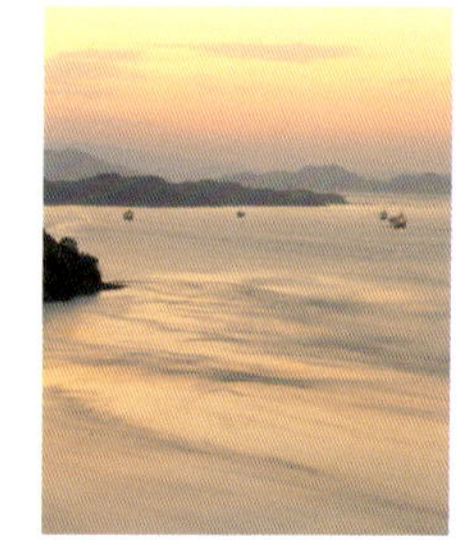
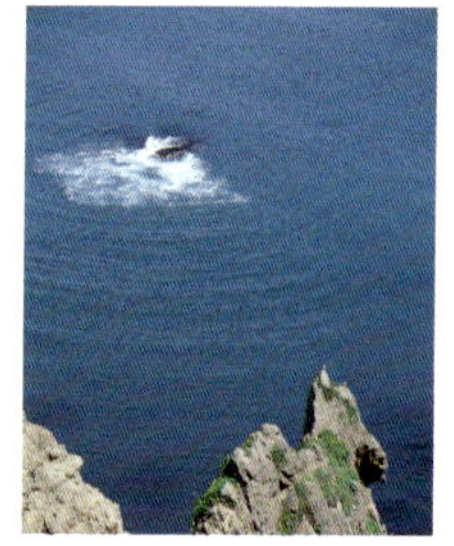
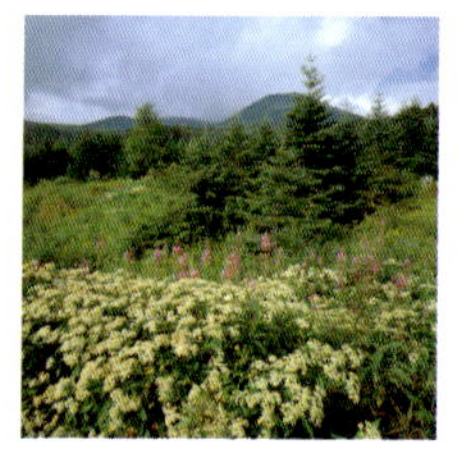
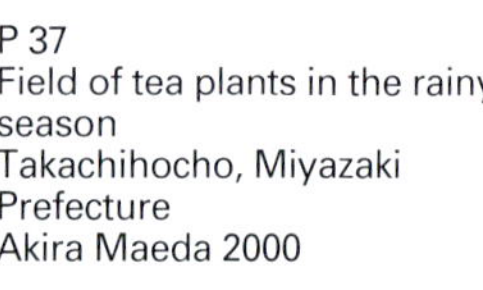
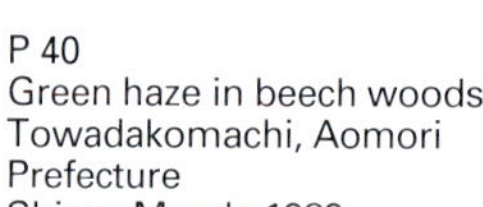

P 37
Field of tea plants in the rainy season
Takachihocho, Miyazaki Prefecture
Akira Maeda 2000

P 38–39
Terraced fields and farmhouses
Higashiiyayamamura, Tokushima Prefecture
Shinzo Maeda 1986

P 40
Green haze in beech woods
Towadakomachi, Aomori Prefecture
Shinzo Maeda 1989

P 41
Hazy highlands
Utsukushigahara, Nagano Prefecture
Shinzo Maeda 1983

P 42
Wheat field at dusk
Bieicho, Hokkaido
Akira Maeda 1998

P 43
Flowerbeds in primary colors
Bieicho, Hokkaido
Akira Maeda 1997

P 44
Green paddy and golden-rayed lily
Shitaracho, Aichi Prefecture
Shinzo Maeda 1980

P 45 (top)
Kitsunenokamisori ("foxes' razor")
Hachiojishi, Tokyo
Akira Maeda 1997

P 45 (middle)
Sasa lily
Muromura, Nara Prefecture
Shinzo Maeda 1991

P 45 (bottom)
Tawny day lilies
Toyotamura, Nagano Prefecture
Shinzo Maeda 1989

P 46–47
Mountain ridge in a sea of clouds
Northern Alps, Gifu Prefecture
Shinzo Maeda 1980

P 48
Water lily pads
Onumakoen, Hokkaido
Shinzo Maeda 1978

P 49
Dense growth of conandron
Toeicho, Aichi Prefecture
Shinzo Maeda 1986

P 50
Kurushima Straits at dusk
Imabarishi, Ehime Prefecture
Shinzo Maeda 1986

P 51
Cliff and blue sea
Muroranshi, Hokkaido
Shinzo Maeda, 1978

P 52
Highland flowers
Kitayatsugatake, Nagano Prefecture
Shinzo Maeda 1985

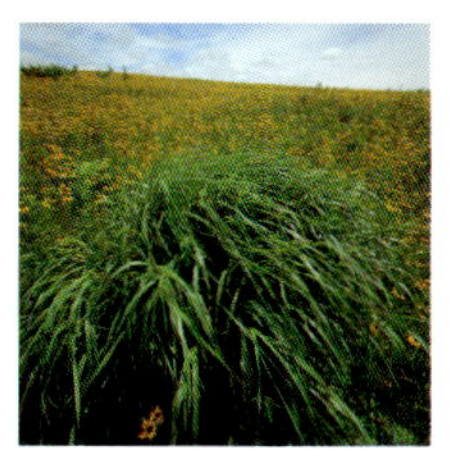
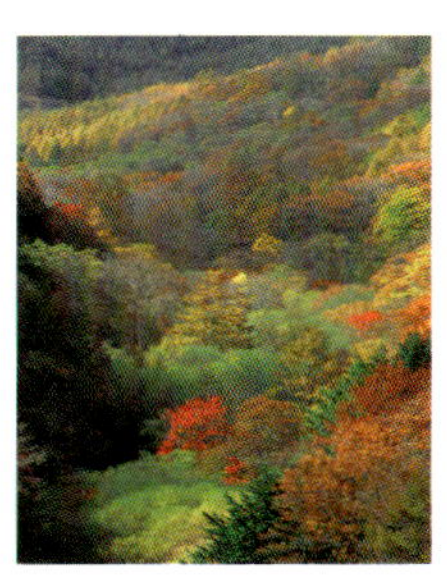
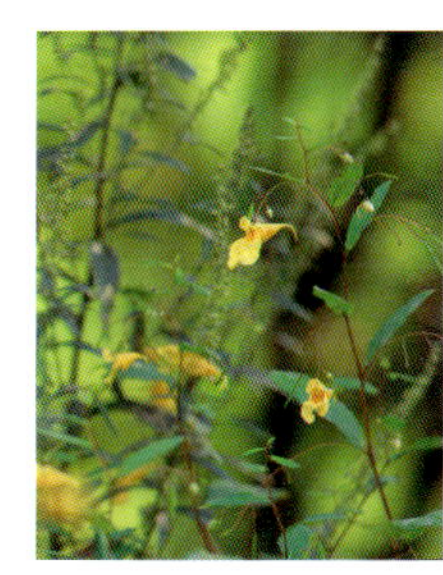
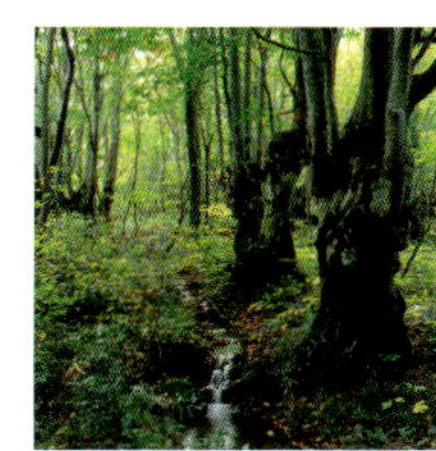
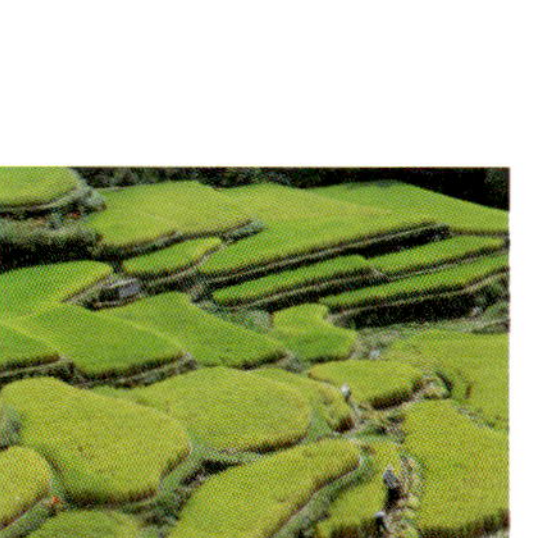
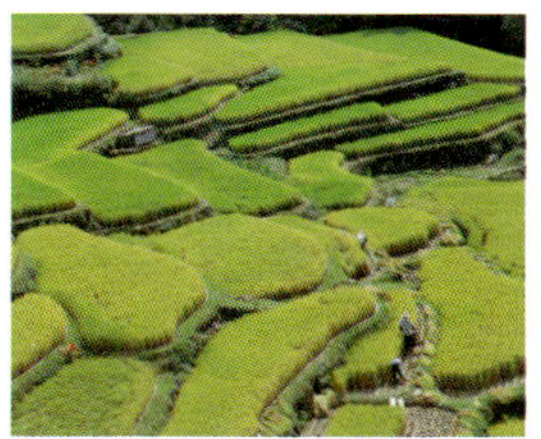
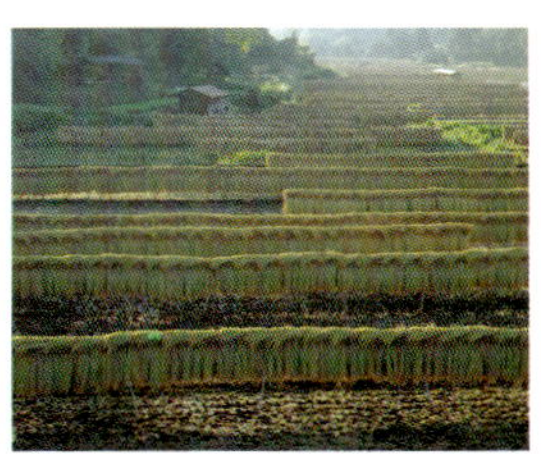
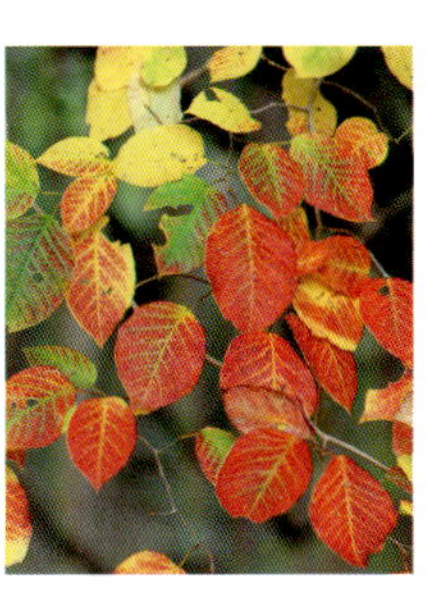
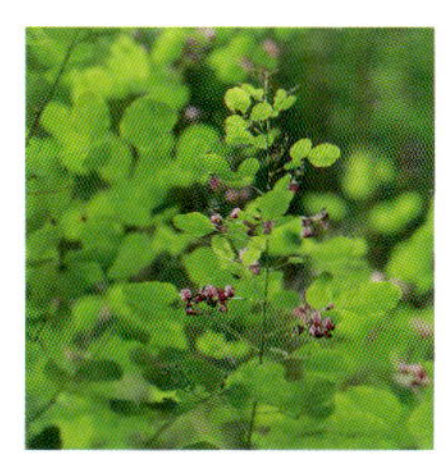
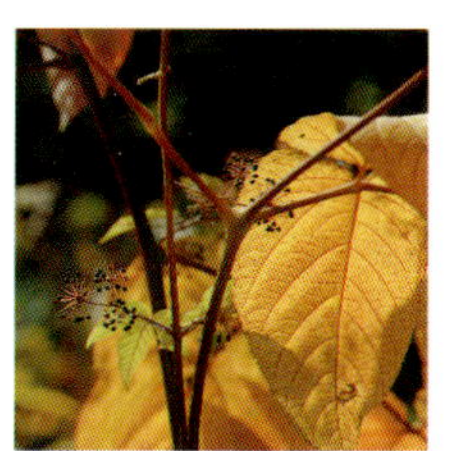
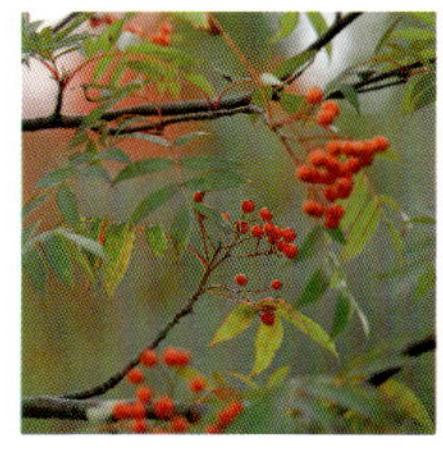
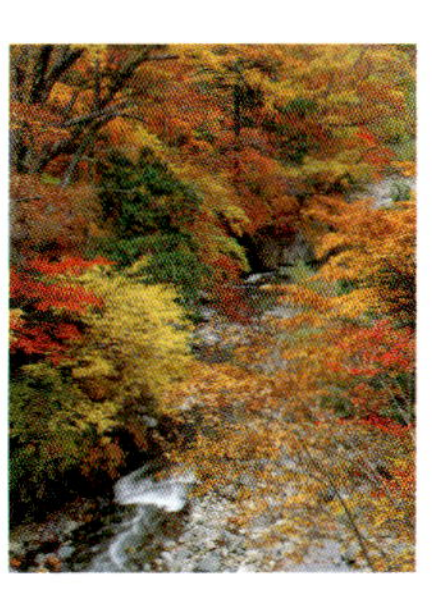
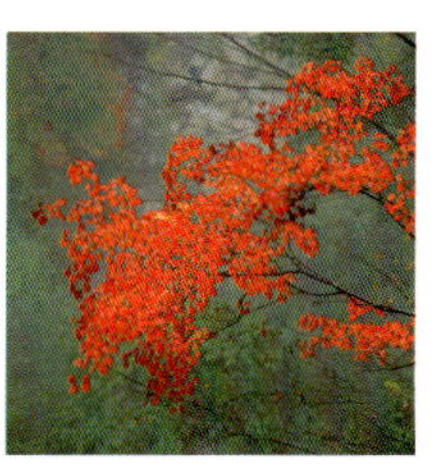
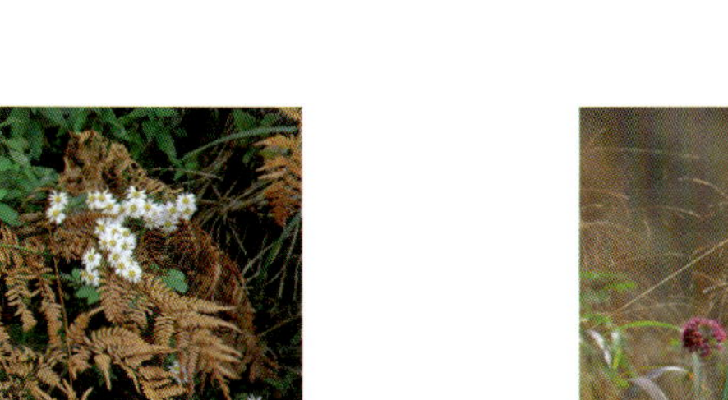
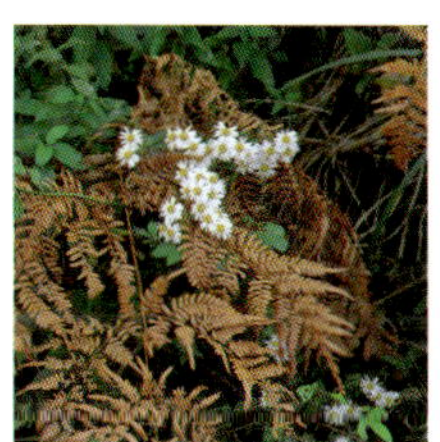
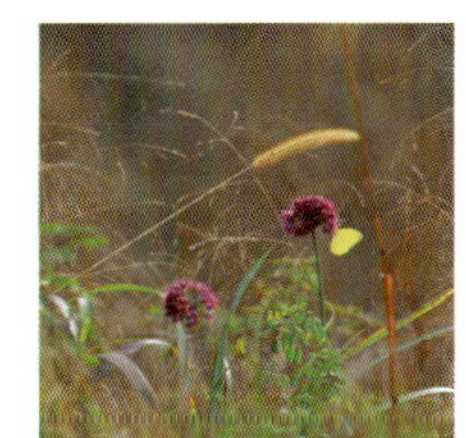
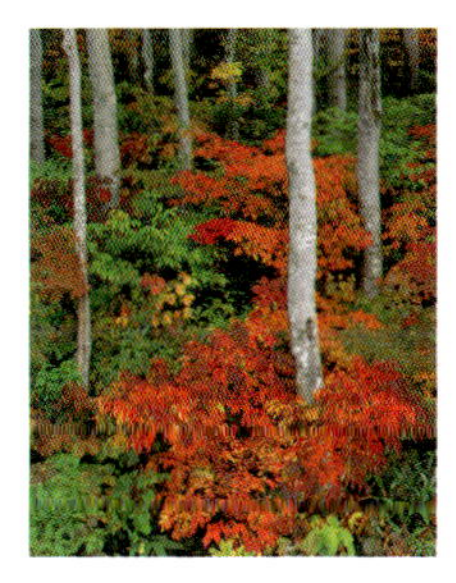
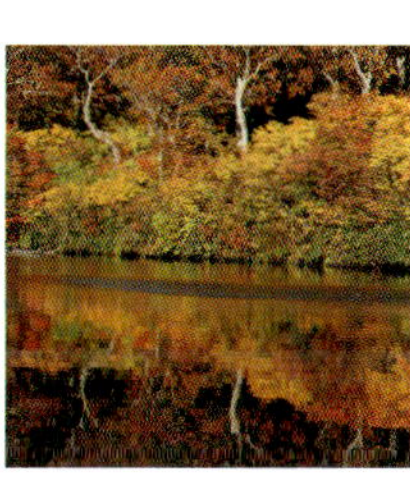

P 53
Summer growth on the plain
Nemuroshi, Hokkaido
Shinzo Maeda 1980

P 54
Light and shadow on an autumn mountain
Oizumimura, Yamanashi Prefecture
Akira Maeda 2000

P 56
Marshside touch-me-nots
Bieicho, Hokkaido
Akira Maeda 2000

P 57
Beech grove in early autumn
Kisakatamachi, Akita Prefecture
Akira Maeda 2000

P 58
Harvesting terraced paddies
Horaicho, Aichi Prefecture
Shinzo Maeda 1984

P 59
Ranks of rice-drying frames
Nyukawamura, Gifu Prefecture
Shinzo Maeda 1978

P 60
Beginning to turn color
Ubuyamamura, Kumamoto Prefecture
Akira Maeda 2000

P 61 (top)
First bushclover flowers of the year
Bieicho, Hokkaido
Akira Maeda 1995

P 61 (middle)
Yellow-leaved udo
Bieicho, Hokkaido
Shinzo Maeda 1990

P 61 (bottom)
Mountain ash
Bieicho, Hokkaido
Shinzo Maeda 1989

P 62
Autumn colors in Kasashinagawa
Katashinamura, Gunma Prefecture
Shinzo Maeda 1990

P 63
Fiery color in deep ravine
Nakabusadani, Nagano Prefecture
Akira Maeda 2000

P 64
Bracken and asters
Kuginomura, Kumamoto Prefecture
Akira Maeda 2000

P 65
Yamarakkyo ("mountain shallots") and yellow butterfly
Naminoson, Kumamoto Prefecture
Akira Maeda 2000

P 66
Beech woods changing color
Yawatamachi, Yamagata Prefecture
Akira Maeda 2000

P 67
Yellow leaves reflected
Yashimamachi, Akita Prefecture
Akira Maeda 2000

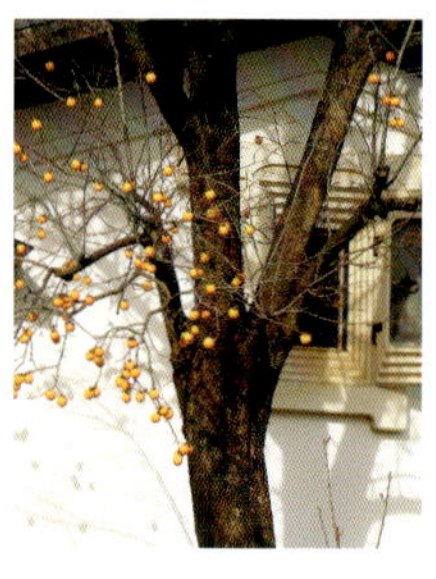
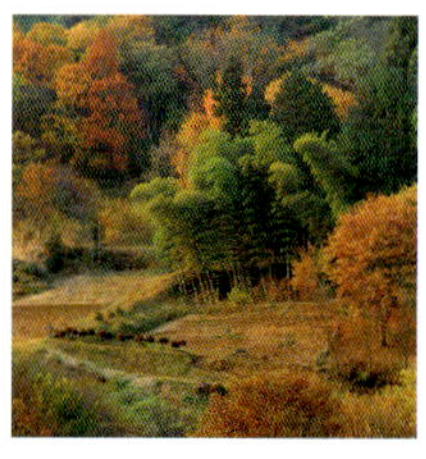
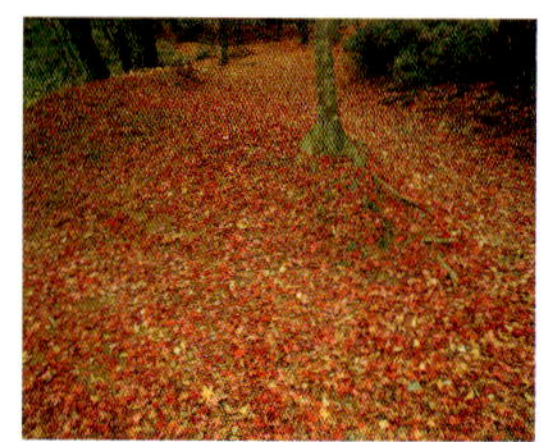
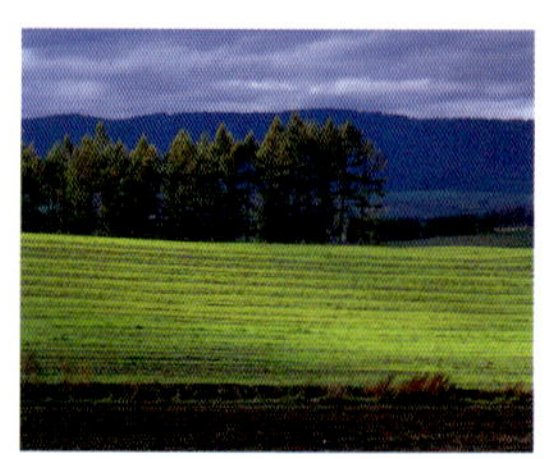
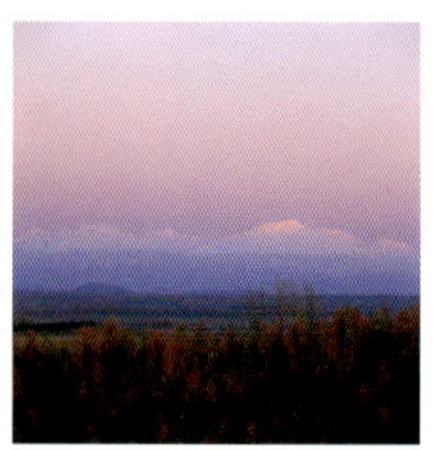
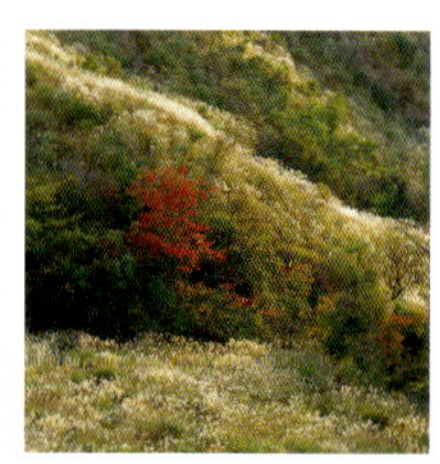
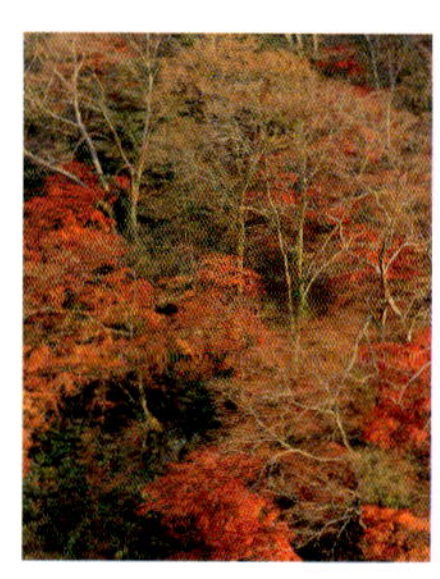
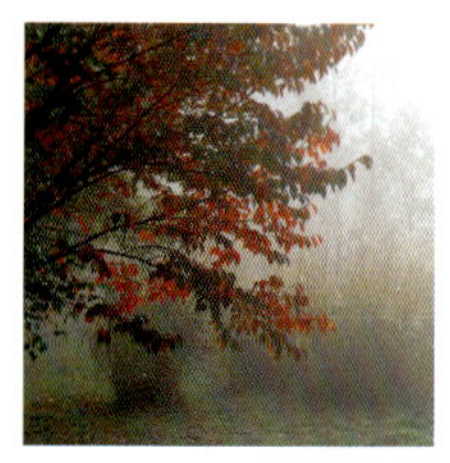
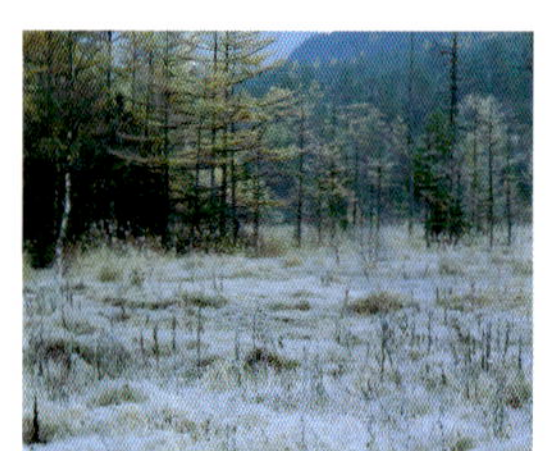
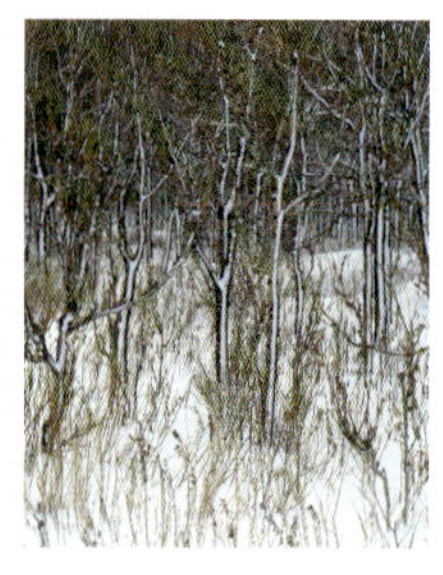
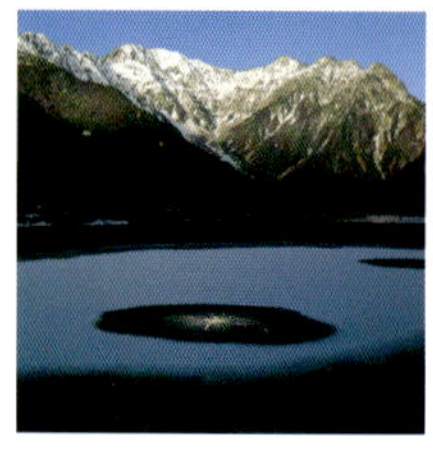
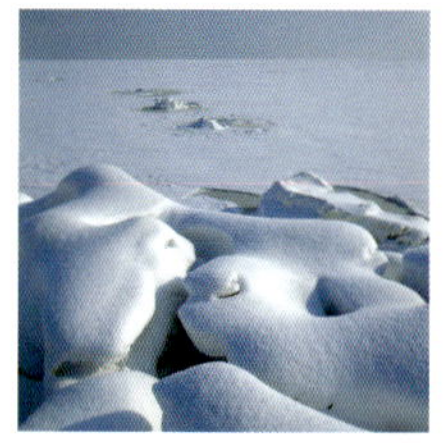
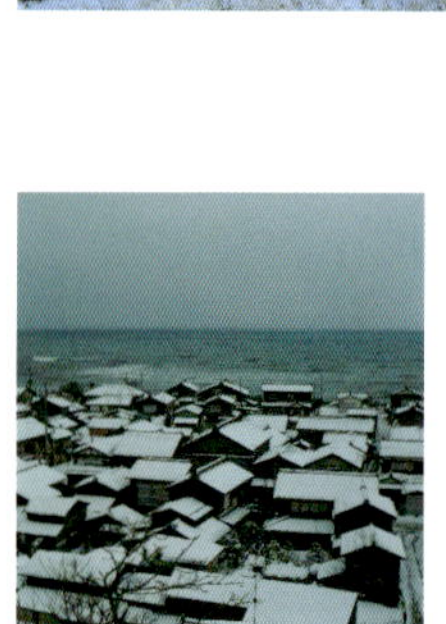
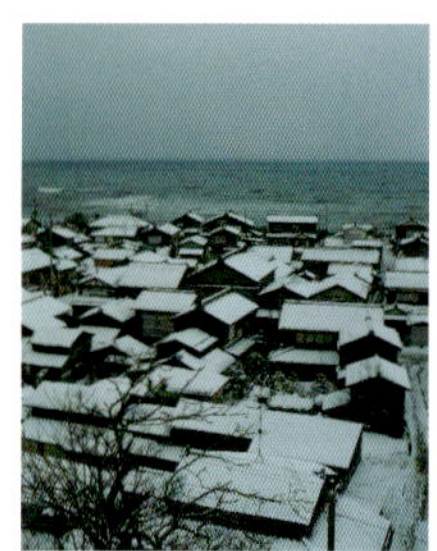
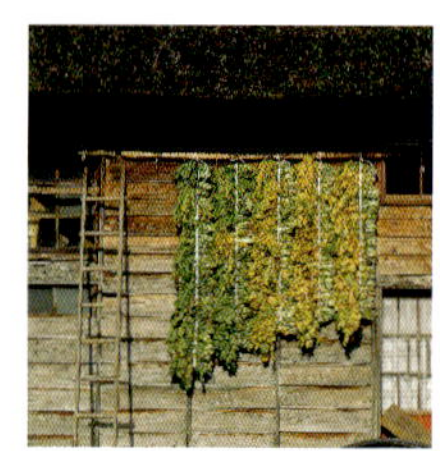
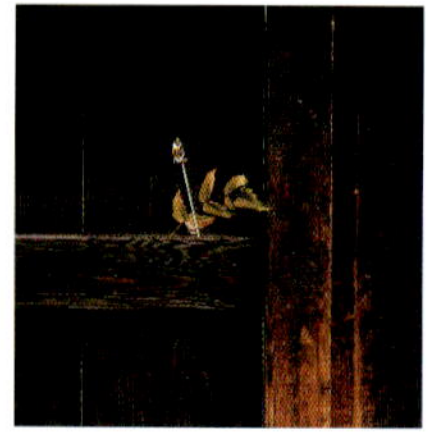
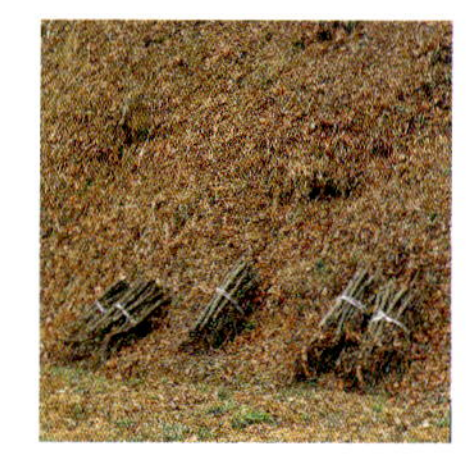
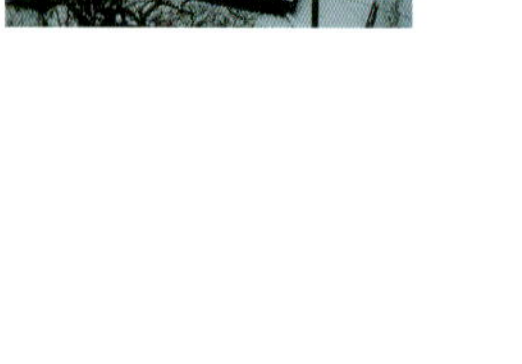
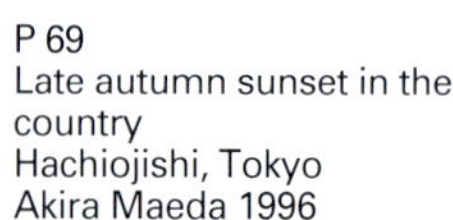
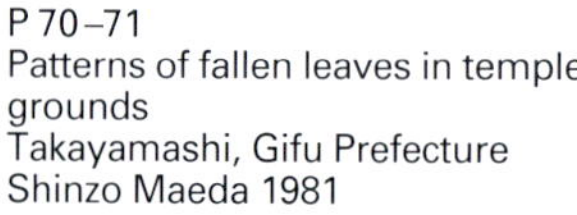

P 68
Persimmon tree and storehouse
Shirasawamura, Gunma Prefecture
Akira Maeda 1997

P 69
Late autumn sunset in the country
Hachiojishi, Tokyo
Akira Maeda 1996

P 70–71
Patterns of fallen leaves in temple grounds
Takayamashi, Gifu Prefecture
Shinzo Maeda 1981

P 72
Flowing autumn light
Bieicho, Hokkaido
Akira Maeda 1998

P 73
Last light on Mt. Daisetsuzan
Bieicho, Hokkaido
Akira Maeda 1996

P 74
Pampas grass in the foothills
Ubuyamamura, Kumamoto Prefecture
Akira Maeda 2000

P 75
Last maple leaves
Kurohonemura, Gunma Prefecture
Shinzo Maeda 1990

P 76
Morning mist with cherry and maple trees
Bieicho, Hokkaido
Akira Maeda 1998

P 77
Frosty moorlands
Kamikochi, Nagano Prefecture
Shinzo Maeda 1982

P 79
Elegant grove of snowclad trees
Koshimizucho, Hokkaido
Akira Maeda 2001

P 80
Ice patterns on Taishoike Lake
Kamikochi, Nagano Prefecture
Shinzo Maeda 1982

P 81
Forms in the frozen sea
Abashirishi, Hokkaido
Akira Maeda 2001

P 82
Rows of snow-covered roofs
Kakizakimachi, Niigata Prefecture
Shinzo Maeda 1980

P 83 (top)
Giant radish leaves drying under the eaves
Matsunoyamamachi, Niigata Prefecture
Shinzo Maeda 1986

P 83 (middle)
An arrangement of holly
Hachiojishi, Tokyo
Akira Maeda 1998

P 83 (bottom)
Bundles of firewood at the foot of the mountain
Muromura, Nara Prefecture
Shinzo Maeda 1989

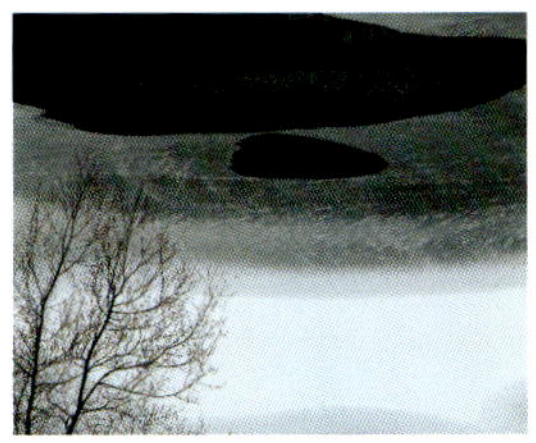
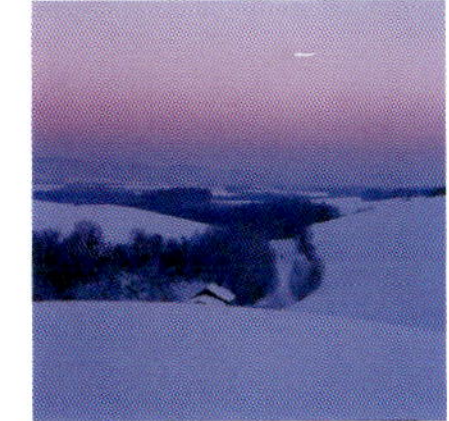
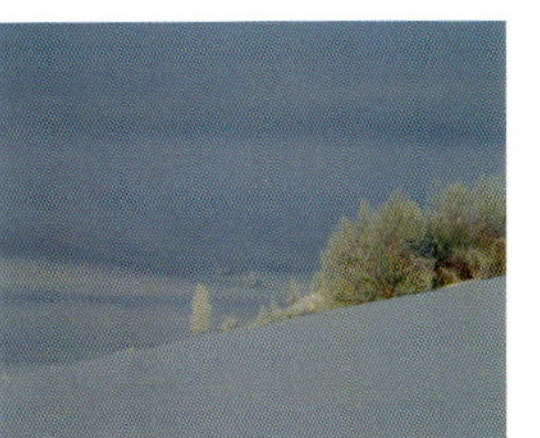
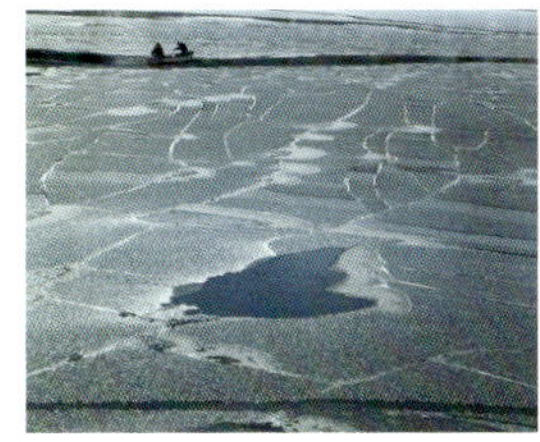
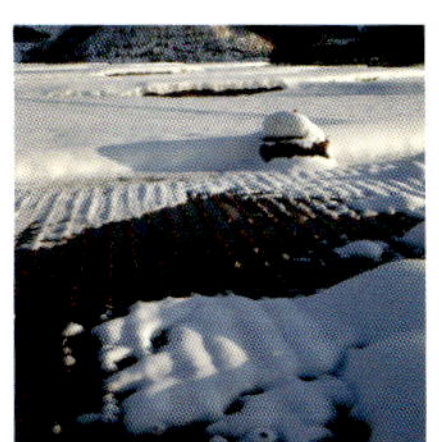
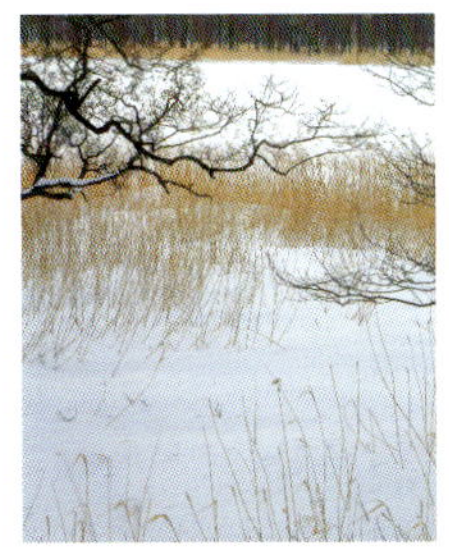
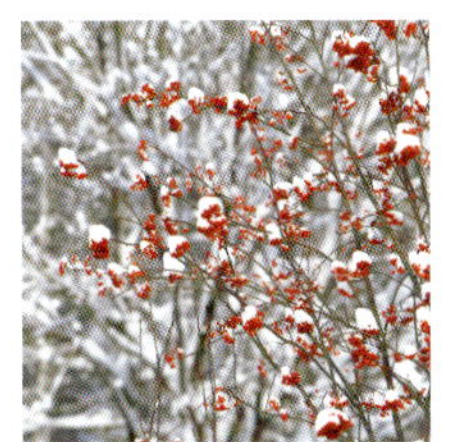
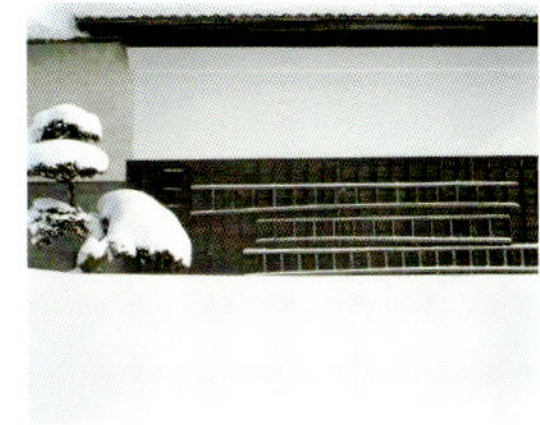
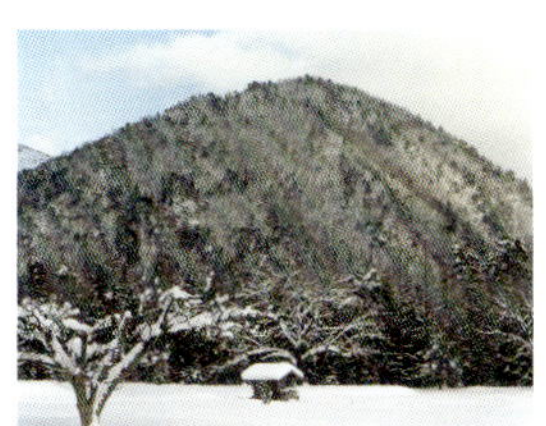
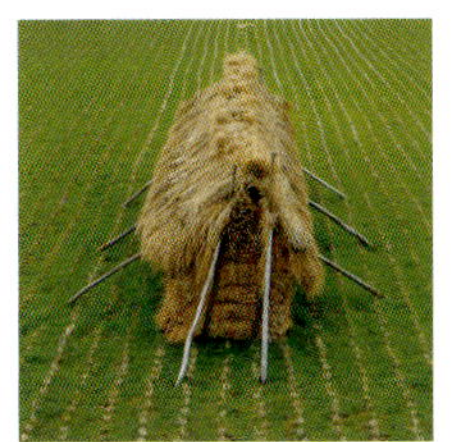
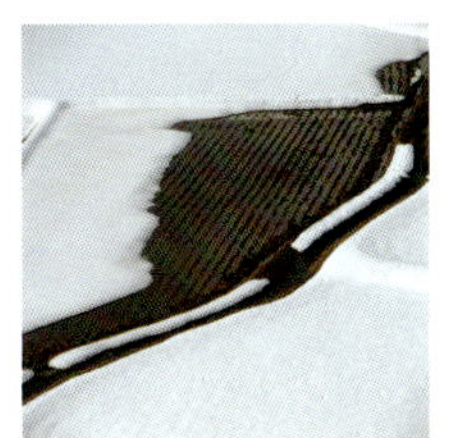
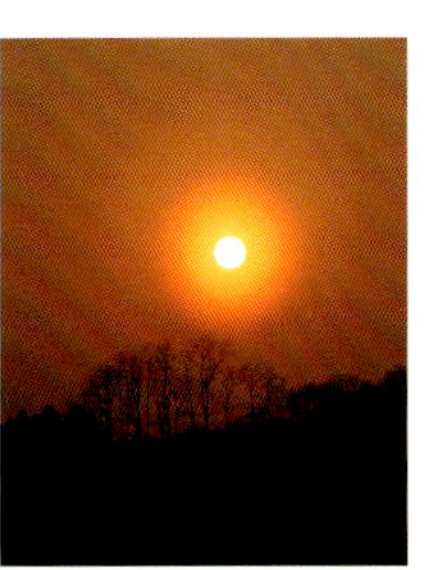

P 84–85
The austere surface of a lake in winter
Matsumotoshi, Nagano Prefecture
Shinzo Maeda 1980

P 86
Dawn in the depths of winter
Bieicho, Hokkaido
Akira Maeda 1998

P 87
Hill with diamond dust
Bieicho, Hokkaido
Akira Maeda 2001

P 88
Fishing for pond smelt
Lake Kizakiko, Nagano Prefecture
Shinzo Maeda 1980

P 89
Snowy rice field
Kofucho, Tottori Prefecture
Shinzo Maeda 1981

P 90
Lonely lakeside
Lake Abashiriko, Hokkaido
Akira Maeda 2001

P 91
Snow-covered mountain ash
Bieicho, Hokkaido
Akira Maeda 2001

P 92
Shapes by a warehouse
Toyonomachi, Nagano Prefecture
Shinzo Maeda 1977

P 93
The cold mountain sleeps
Omachishi, Nagano Prefecture
Shinzo Maeda 1977

P 94
Hayrick in winter paddy
Muromura, Nara Prefecture
Shinzo Maeda 1989

P 95
Winter watercourse
Nozawaonsenmura, Nagano Prefecture
Shinzo Maeda 1979

P 96
Setting sun in early spring
Misatomachi, Gunma Prefecture
Shinzo Maeda 1991

四季の情景
Intimate Seasons

2001年11月21日　第1刷発行
2004年3月19日　第3刷発行

写真：前田 真三、前田 晃

デザイン：白谷 敏夫［ノマド］

発行者　畑野文夫
発行所　講談社インターナショナル株式会社
〒112-8652　東京都文京区音羽1-17-14
電話：03-3944-6493（編集部）
電話：03-3944-6492（営業部・業務部）
ホームページ　www.kodansha-intl.co.jp
印刷：大日本印刷株式会社
製本：黒柳製本株式会社

定価はカバーに表示してあります。

Printed in Japan

ISBN 4-7700-2687-0